ALSO BY CLAIRE STERLING

Octopus: The Long Reach of the Sicilian Mafia
The Time of the Assassins
The Terror Network
The Masaryk Case

THIEVES' WORLD

*The Threat of the New Global
Network of Organized Crime*

CLAIRE STERLING

SIMON & SCHUSTER
NEW YORK   TORONTO   LONDON   SYDNEY   TOKYO   SINGAPORE

SIMON & SCHUSTER
Rockfeller Center
1230 Avenue of the Americas
New York, New York 10020

SIMON & SCHUSTER and colophon are registered trademarks of
Simon & Schuster Inc.
Designed by Paulette Orlando

Manufactured in the United States of America

1 3 5 7 9 10 8 6 4 2

Library of Congress Cataloging-in-Publication Data

Sterling, Claire.
Thieves' world : the threat of the new global network of organized
crime / Claire Sterling.
p. cm.
Includes bibliographical references (p. –) and index.
1. Organized crime. 2. Organized crime—Russia (Federation)
3. Organized crime—Europe. I. Title.
HV6441.S74 1994
364.1'06—dc20   94-6826 CIP
ISBN 0-671-74997-8

ACKNOWLEDGMENTS

I am grateful as always to Dr. Alessandro Pansa of the Servizio Centrale Operativo; he is one of Italy's most gifted policemen.

I am indebted once again to Maria Antonietta Calabrò of the *Corriere della Sera* for her meticulous accuracy, knowledge, and judgment.

My warm thanks to Joe Serio, who started me on my way in Russia; to Gianna in Moscow; to Rita Wallace in Bonn; and to Dan Starer in New York.

A special word of thanks to Jurgen Maurer of the Bundeskriminalamt in Wiesbaden; to Charles Saphos of the U.S. Justice Department, who was ahead of me from first to last; and to Jim Moody of the FBI for his patience and generous assistance.

I have no adequate words for my gratitude to Judith Crist, my old and dear friend.

FOR MY DEAREST VIDA AND VICTOR

CONTENTS

11

CONTENTS

PROLOGUE

When I finished writing *Thieves' World* in the autumn of 1993, a few words from a high authority in Washington provided the epilogue. "We think they have given the United States to Yaponchik," he told me.[1] "They" are the men guiding the Russian mafia in Moscow. Yaponchik is one of their three most powerful leaders.

The idea that a so-called Russian mafia could "give" the United States to a certain Yaponchik would have been laughable only a couple of years ago. Nobody in the West had heard of Yaponchik; not many had heard of a Russian mafia for that matter.

The rise of both within a few years—their ability to stake out whole blocks of the planet, half a continent here, another there—conveys all the menace of an international crime community in a phase of stunning expansion, threatening the integrity and even the survival of democratic governments in America, Europe, everywhere.

I had watched it happening from the time I began working on this book in 1990. The book was supposed to have been about a predictable surge of organized crime in Western Europe as its inner borders went down. But such simple notions were soon swept

13

aside by the uncontrollable forces set loose in the course of that momentous year.

Organized crime was transformed when the Soviet Empire crashed, and with it a world order that had kept mankind more or less in line for the previous half-century. As the old geopolitical frontiers fell away, the big crime syndicates drew together, put an end to wars over turf, and declared a *pax mafiosa*. The world has never seen a planetwide criminal consortium like the one that came into being with the end of the communist era.

Perhaps something like it would have come sooner or later anyway. Most of the big syndicates had worked with one or more of the others for years, the Sicilian Mafia with all of them. But the opportunities opening up for them in 1990 were immense—fabulous—and they responded accordingly.

International organized crime, an imaginary menace for many in 1990, was a worldwide emergency by 1993. The big syndicates of East and West were pooling services and personnel, rapidly colonizing Western Europe and the United States, running the drug traffic up to half a trillion dollars a year, laundering and reinvesting an estimated quarter of a trillion dollars a year in legitimate enterprise. Much of their phenomenal growth derived from the fact that they had the free run of a territory covering half the continent of Europe and a good part of Asia—a sixth of the earth's land mass, essentially ungoverned and unpoliced.

The whole international underworld had moved in on postcommunist Russia and the rest of the ex-Soviet bloc: raced in from the day the Berlin Wall fell. Where Western governments tended to see Russia as a basket case, the big syndicates saw it as a privileged sanctuary and bottomless source of instant wealth.

Russia had a runaway black market, a huge potential for producing and moving drugs, an enormous military arsenal, the world's richest natural resources, and an insatiable hunger for dollars of whatever provenance. Furthermore, it had a rampant mafia of its own, in need of Western partners to make the most of these prospects.

Even before the Soviet Union disintegrated altogether, the Sicilian, American, Colombian, and Asian mafias were hooking up with the Russian one, forming a borderless criminal underground that circled the globe. All have been growing prodigiously rich since then by swapping their dirty money for Russia's real estate, factories, shops, and above all weapons and raw materials, bought on the cheap and sold for up to a thousand times more abroad.

Twenty billion dollars' worth of raw materials alone were exported illegally from Russia in 1992: petroleum, timber, titanium, cesium, strontium, uranium, plutonium. Thousands of crooks and swindlers were involved, native and otherwise, many of them loners. But the big player was the Russian mafia and its foreign partners.

Though these last were making and laundering ten times as much in the rest of the world, this was the easiest, safest, and most miraculously lucrative way ever invented. Colombia's cocaine cartels are *paying* twenty cents and more on the dollar to bring their drug money home clean today. The Sicilian Mafia makes more by laundering it for them in Russia than by dealing the cocaine itself.[2]

And this is undetectable investment capital when it comes out of Russia, filtering into money markets, stock and commodity markets, business, industry, and commerce, largely in the West, helping to underwrite the most massive and insidious criminal assault in history.

Western authorities are staggered by the strength of the attacking forces and the speed of their advance, driven home by the Russian mafia's startling performance. It took just two years for Yaponchik to move from a prison camp in Siberia to the Russian mafia's top command in New York. Russia's Serious Crimes Investigator had warned me of something like this. "You people in the West don't know our mafia yet. You will, you will," he had said. He did not say how soon, however.

Yaponchik (Vyacheslav Ivankov) had barely gotten out of prison when I first went to Russia in the autumn of 1991. Sentenced to fifteen years for robbery, he had done eleven. He left Siberia in a private chartered plane and was welcomed home with a grand champagne party at Moscow's posh Metropol Hotel.[3] For Yaponchik was no ordinary Russian crook. He was one of the chosen of Russia's ancient Thieves' World, according to Russian police, an aristocrat of his profession and keeper of its code: "a thief within the code." (See Chapter 5.)

By the time I came across his name that autumn, he had already moved on to Berlin where his mafia colleagues had landed in force after the fall of the Wall. A few months later he was back in Moscow draped in gold chains and driving around in a Mercedes. Then he left for America.

He arrived exactly a year after leaving Siberia, in March 1992, on a regular business visa. Getting in was easy. The American embassy in Moscow issued 139,000 business visas to Russian citizens that year. Applicants were not checked for possible criminal records, lest that might "slow the international business process," a Washington spokesman explained.[4]

On paper, Yaponchik is in the film business in America; in fact, says the FBI, he is the supreme "thief within the code" for the United States. His fellow of that rank assigned to Berlin, Alizam Tochtachunov, recently applied for a business visa to join him, according to the FBI.

Much as Lucky Luciano did with the American mafia sixty-odd years ago, Yaponchik is turning an assortment of unruly and loosely articulated Russian gangs on American soil into a modern, nationwide crime corporation. Doubtless as Luciano would also have done in these changing times, he is "slowly building a chain from Moscow to the United States and back," declared Jim Moody, the FBI's organized crime chief.[5]

The Russian mafia can hardly be compared for size and clout to others tormenting America: the American mafia, the Sicilian one, the Chinese Triads, the Japanese Yakuza, and the Colombians. In the United States as in Europe, however, the Russians stand out among their peers because they are talented enough and frightening enough to have achieved in two or three years what the others achieved in twenty or a hundred. Nevertheless, they could not have done it before 1990. Their astonishing spurt came only when the old world order collapsed, and frontiers everywhere began to fall, and the deep but ordered corruption of the old Nomenklatura in Russia gave way to the terrible cancerous growth consuming the country now.

Inevitably, the Russian side of my story grew as I saw the drama playing out—the Russian mafia gaining an oppressive hold over the country, its lengthening reach abroad, and the arrival of world-class syndicates to share in the plunder at home.

This was how international organized crime could take a huge country captive by 1993, buying up its governing class, looting it systematically, crippling its economic capacity, and suffocating its political will.

It is not just as an object lesson that I have described these facts at length. The more urgent reason is that liberated Russia, as the underworld's new country of choice, is becoming an active danger to its Western friends. There is no way for Western law enforcement agencies to investigate, still less pursue, their own criminals drifting east. They have no lawful right to do it and until very recently did not much care. Their Eastern counterparts have practically no suitable laws of their own, no money, pitiful equipment, and hardly any properly trained personnel. There are no provisions for extradition on either side, and next to none for exchanging police and intelligence information.

In effect, then, the big syndicates have come upon a safe house the size of Western Europe and America combined where they can dodge the cops, meet, plan strategy, work out new drug routes, manage their money, settle territorial disputes, and carve up the planet undisturbed, all of which they appear to be doing.

The shift has come so swiftly that Western investigators can hardly take it in. Because the Sicilian Mafia still towers over the underworld, many still believe that the center of worldwide criminal power is Italy. In the autumn of 1993, however, the head of Italy's Parliamentary Anti-Mafia Commission made it plain that the venue had changed. "The world capital of organized crime is Russia," he said.[6]

That is the Thieves' World I have tried to describe here.

PART I

The New Underworld Order

CHAPTER ONE

Happy Families on Treasure Island

The world's first independent mafia state emerged in 1993. The sovereign Caribbean island of Aruba, sixty-nine square miles of emerald hills and golden sand, proved to belong to the Sicilian Mafia in fact if not in name. Small islands are not so hard to acquire. From this one, however, the story leads to the making of a mafia state in Russia, a hundred thousand times bigger and incomparably more crucial to our peace of mind.

Aruba was bought and paid for by the most powerful mafia family abroad: the Cuntrera brothers—Paolo and Pasquale—of Siculiana, Sicily, and Caracas, Venezuela, who had amassed a billion dollars of their own in their twenty-five years as kingpins of the mafia's North American heroin trade.

The drugging of America had provided the wherewithal for their purchase of Aruba starting in the late 1980s. From the Venezuelan mainland, just fifteen miles away, they had drawn on their seventy-odd bank accounts to buy up everything of importance on the island: hotels, casinos, tourism, building land, construction, banks, police, customs, the justice minister, the prime minister, and the governing and opposition parties.[1]

The new order has brought exceptional prosperity to the sixty-five thousand inhabitants of this former Dutch colony, which calls itself "One Happy Island." Tourists flock to its twenty-four new high-rise hotels and seven casinos, shop at its Cartier and Gucci boutiques, and drift in and out of its throbbing banks with suitcases full of dollar bills. Nobody pays taxes. Not many care to ask questions; therefore, still fewer answer any.

The Cuntreras are gone now. The Venezuelan government had always protected them from harm, and more particularly from international arrest warrants going back nearly a decade. In September 1992, however, it yielded to Italian and American pressure and deported them to Italy. The U.S. Drug Enforcement Administration had threatened to kidnap them otherwise, as it was entitled to do under a U.S. Supreme Court ruling.[2] Their work was done, however. Aruba today is just what it was meant to be when the Cuntreras' plan got under way: the headquarters of the first international joint venture in organized crime.

It was on the island of Aruba that the Sicilian Mafia and Colombia's Medellín cartel decided to join forces in October 1987. Things have moved so fast since then that the pact they sealed seems old-fashioned now. But for the late Judge Giovanni Falcone, who knew the Mafia best, it was "a shattering and terrifying portent."[3]

Judge Falcone, world famous for his valiant and resolute war on the Sicilian Mafia, did not live to see how far this pact would lead; the Mafia murdered him in Palermo in the spring of 1992. Few had understood the sweep of its imperial designs as he did.

The two giants of the underworld made a hair-raising pair. Colombia's drug traffickers are among the most vicious on earth; Sicily's, only a shade less so, are the most sophisticated and best connected. Each has a huge international army of helpers, the financial resources of a fair-sized country, and the power of a state within a state. The global turnover for the merchandise the two dealt in ran to around $300 billion a year when they came together.[4]

What frightened Judge Falcone was not so much the pact they made as his growing conviction, by the start of the 1990s, that all the great crime syndicates were coming together: the Sicilian and American mafias, the Turkish arms-drugs mafia, the Russian ma-

22

fia, the Chinese Triads, and the Japanese Yakuza.[5] Separated by thousands of miles and centuries of history, these massive criminal organizations were tending to coordinate the use of their money, men, and markets in "a kind of operational welding," Falcone said.[6]

The big syndicates had already "stipulated a sort of nonaggression pact, dividing up the world," he warned. The whole international underworld appeared to be moving toward a broader *pax mafiosa*—an agreement to avoid conflict, devise common strategy, and work the planet peaceably together. If that happened, the lawful world would be exposed to an unimaginably malignant criminal force and desperately unready to resist it.

In the space of four or five years after the 1987 Aruba summit, that did happen.

Secret conclaves like the one in Aruba rarely come to light. This one did because Giuseppe "Joe" Cuffaro, a backsliding Sicilian trafficker, was there. Picked up two years later on a drug charge in Miami, he took a plea and gave his interrogators an earful.[7]

As Cuffaro told it, the meeting had come about when the most formidable boss in Palermo, Francesco "Ciccio" Madonia, sent John Galatolo, a trusted aide, to set it up. "My godfather instructed me, but this venture is actually controlled by the four most powerful Families in the Sicilian Mafia," he informed Cuffaro: Ciccio Madonia's Family in Palermo, Giuseppe Madonia's in Gela, Nitto Santapaola's in Catania, and the Corleones, rulers of the Mafia realm.

Upon leaving Palermo, Galatolo went first to the Sicilians' enclave on Eighteenth Avenue in Brooklyn, command center of their heroin network in America for a quarter of a century. The network was an inseparable part of the triangle—from Palermo to Caracas to New York—that had created and fed what was now a heroin addict population of half a million in the United States. The men running it out of their Brooklyn headquarters were ranking members of the Mafia's inner circle in Palermo. Their advice and consent was indispensable to the deal Galatolo was about to propose.

When four or five of their top traffickers in New York agreed to come in on it,[8] Galatolo went down to Aruba, taking Joe Cuffaro with him. The Medellín cartel sent Waldo Aponte Romero, who flew in with his party from Colombia in a private Lear jet.

Photographs show Galatolo and Aponte, bronzed and smiling in shorts and flowered shirts, posing with a splendid marlin. As they sailed, fished, drank strawberry daiquiris, and sunned, they talked over a stupendous proposition.

The cocaine market was saturated in America, where consumption had shot up from thirty-one to seventy-two tons a year, forcing the price down by more than two-thirds in two years. At the time of the Aruba meet, it was selling wholesale there for $11,000 a kilo.[9] On the other hand, the rage for cocaine was just beginning to devour Europe. From "virtually nothing" in 1985, the quantity reaching the Continent was approaching forty tons in 1987 and selling for nearly five times the going price in America: $50,000 a kilo.[10]

Meanwhile, heroin was still the drug of preference in America, selling for around $200,000 a kilo. In Europe, where it was easier to procure and transport, the price was $50,000 a kilo. The Sicilians therefore proposed to swap heroin from Europe for cocaine from Colombia. That would give the Medellín cartel a chance to branch out into America's lucrative heroin market. In exchange, the Mafia wanted an exclusive franchise for the wholesale cocaine market in Europe. If not, said John Galatolo, any Colombians trying to deliver to Europe would be killed.[11]

Here was the answer to those who thought the Mafia was as good as finished. The days of its corner on the American heroin market were over. The Pizza Connection case had knocked out one of its major rings and two dozen of its best men in New York halfway through the 1980s.[12] Judge Falcone's anti-Mafia pool had closed down its refineries in Sicily during the same years and hauled the entire Mafia hierarchy into court. Chinese Triads were taking over the American supply line. Nigerians and hundreds of smaller ethnic groups were crowding into the field. Many wondered what there was left for the Sicilian Mafia to do. Cornering Europe's cocaine market appeared to be the answer.

The Colombians, who did not like being pushed around, would

have preferred to let the Mafia simply broker for them as always. It was moving "huge amounts" of their cocaine to Europe already, according to the DEA. The Cuntrera brothers alone handled nearly two-thirds of all their shipments in transit through Venezuela, and four-fifths of all the cocaine leaving Colombia passed through Venezuela.[13]

But Europe was home for the Sicilians, their prime marketplace for decades. Here they could do what the Medellín cartel could not do. "We expect the Sicilian Mafia to take over cocaine distribution in Europe. They have the network; the Colombians don't," predicted the lead prosecutor in the Pizza Connection case, Louis Freeh, now head of the FBI.[14]

So the deal was on. The Medellín cartel would ship straight to Sicily by way of Aruba, "four, five, six, seven hundred kilos at a time," explained Cuffaro. "This is one of the biggest adventures ever attempted by the Sicilian Mafia," Galatolo told him, as indeed it was. Europe would soon overtake and surpass America as the cocaine explosion took its devastating course. The forty tons reaching the Continent by 1987 would quintuple to two hundred tons annually in the next five years.[15] The Sicilian Mafia, given up for dead in some quarters, would make an enormous leap in money and criminal power.

In the space of those five years, that first deal in Aruba would lead to a second of much greater importance, elevating the Colombian-Sicilian partnership to new heights, carrying the Sicilian Mafia to rarified levels of international finance, providing a clear view of the underworld's exponentially rising interest in Russia—the *pax mafiosa* emerging.

On January 7, 1988, the *Big John* sailed from Aruba under a devil-may-care Chilean skipper, carrying over half a ton of cocaine (569 kilos). Joe Cuffaro was waiting in Palermo when it offloaded near a fishing village on Sicily's western coast. "Your shipment came in successful," he informed Waldo Aponte, waiting at a public phone in Spain.

Before the *Big John* turned to head for home, Cuffaro informed the Chilean skipper that "the Sicilian Mafia was interested to send back heroin in the same boat, send back to the United States." The skipper replied that he would be more than glad to.

The next trip was going to be "a two- to three-thousand-kilo cocaine trip. . . . So they were thinking to distribute that cocaine to other parts of Europe, Germany, France," Cuffaro told Judge Falcone, who went to New York to question him. But a hitch had set in over money.

Aside from the heroin, the four Mafia Families had agreed to pay for half of the first consignment in dollars, $12 million in all. A million-dollar down payment in cash had been sent up to Milan's wholesale produce market in a truckload of lemons and had then gone astray.

Cuffaro flew to Milan with John Galatolo to look for it, and they found it. The Colombians' Milanese money launderer had simply sent the money to the wrong place—Los Angeles instead of Aruba—a minor error that he corrected.

But Cuffaro had met him. He knew the man only as Giuseppe, a Milanese who talked incessantly of horses. Italian police, hunting for a rich Milanese who dealt in currency and loved horses, found their prey three years later. Giuseppe Lottusi, a casually elegant financier with a magnificent racing stable, was arrested in October 1991. He had been the Colombians' chief money launderer for years. After the *Big John* affair, he had become the Sicilian Mafia's as well. Lottusi was "a perfect launderer," said the head of the Italian Criminalpol's economic crime section, meaning that he was a master at bleaching the last criminal stains out of a narcodollar: through bank-to-bank transfers, loanbacks, currency swaps, stocks and bonds, real estate buys—including $100 million worth in Los Angeles—and shell companies billing other shell companies for nonexistent goods.

But Lottusi's laundry was not the only one servicing the Colombian-Sicilian joint venture. Even before it was dismantled, American and Italian police were hunting for others.

Discovering the Aruba deal underlined the urgency of finding and seizing the money. Here was the first hard evidence of a strategic merger in the international underworld, moving toward a more rationalized and cost-effective drug trade, greatly increasing its impact on Europe and America. Every effort to contain the trade on either continent had failed. Taking away the money—the sole reason for the drug cartels' existence and source of their strength—was the only thing that might work.

Some thought it might already be too late. "Colombia is *gone*. We've let them get too much money down there," said the DEA's Greg Passic. "The raw power in a billion dollars is unimaginable. . . . The Cali cartel is not afraid to put billions into research and development—not just equipment, like semi-submarines, but *experts*. They keep a videotape library on who takes bribes; they can do a file search if one gets out of hand."[16]

Whatever the difficulties, the DEA was determined to go after the money.

The biggest police money hunt on record ended in the biggest intercontinental crime bust ever made, in September 1992. An eight-country operation coordinated by the DEA, it was known as Operation Green Ice—Freeze the Green.[17] In the course of this operation, investigators came upon the second Colombian-Sicilian summit, tracked the high-powered delegations attending it, and caught them in the act.

The DEA had set out to break the Colombians' international money-laundering circuit. Forty-five DEA undercovers had passed as crooks, laundered Colombian narcodollars through a Trans-Americas Ventures Associates in San Diego, tapped phones, bugged hotel rooms, and trailed contacts throughout the Western Hemisphere and across the Atlantic. Italian undercover agents, running a similar laundry for the Colombians in Rome, were doing much the same.

When investigators were ready to move that September, they had penetrated five major Colombian cocaine cartels, nailed seven of their top financial managers, uncovered a superlative mole within the Colombian government, and learned almost everything there was to know about the second Colombian-Sicilian summit that was under way in Rome.[18]

One hundred and sixty-seven people were rounded up on a single day that September in San Diego, Los Angeles, Chicago, Miami, New York, Canada, Costa Rica, the Cayman Islands, Britain, Spain, Italy, and Colombia. A sting operation right out of the movies—an offer to invest twenty million dirty dollars—had lured the Cali cartel's financial *consigliere* to San Diego. He was Carlos Rodriguez Polonia-Camargo, inspector-general of Colombia's Central Bank, special agent of Colombia's secret anti-narcotics squad (DAS), and the Colombian government's representative to every kind of international anti-narcotics conference.

In Rome an extravagantly brilliantined gentleman dressed in dazzling white was picked up as he sipped a martini in Piazza Navona. His passport said he was José Guillermo Duran of Venezuela, but he was actually Orlando Cediel Ospina-Vargas of Colombia—the man behind Pablo Escobar's escape from a gilded Colombian prison.

"Tony" Duran headed the Colombian delegation meeting with the Mafia in Italy. This time, however, he was not merely speaking for the Medellín cartel or dealing with the Mafia's four most powerful Families. He was in Italy on behalf of all the cocaine cartels in Colombia. He had brought along their reputed top distributor for Europe, Pedro Villaquiran, also known as "Grajalas." He was negotiating not only with the Sicilian Mafia but also with all three of its Italian subalterns—the Camorra of Naples, the 'Ndrangheta of Calabria, and the younger Sacra Corona Unita of Apulia.

And he was dealing directly with the chairman of the board: Salvatore "Totò" Riina, chief of Sicily's regnant Corleone clan, the Mafia's grand *capo di tutti capi*. "Duran was going for a pact with the Cupola of Cosa Nostra," Italy's Criminalpol declared.[19]

Italian undercover agents knew all about the Colombians' proposition because they had microphones and video cameras inside Tony Duran's Rome bureau. A nest of five money-laundering offices in a modest apartment building in the middle-class district of Prati, it called itself the European Institute for the Protection of Animals. There, Duran had settled down to negotiate with a personal emissary of Totò Riina's, while Animal Protectors from all over Italy kept dropping in with cartons full of cash for the laundry.

What they agreed to, five years after Aruba, was in effect a full treaty, committing all of Italy's organized crime groups and Colombia's cocaine cartels to the kind of "operational welding" that Judge Falcone had feared. Henceforth, the two titans of the underworld would take the western half of the European continent under joint management. Evidently it was time to consolidate and restructure what had become a gigantic enterprise.

Europe was drowning in cocaine by 1992. The more than two hundred tons coming in that year—up five times since the 1987 Aruba summit—was worth $10 billion on the street. And the cocaine fever was still rising.[20]

But this was not next-door America where the Colombians could easily run in supplies by air, land, or sea, with a huge army of helpers melting into their ethnic background. Europe, four thousand miles away, was much costlier to supply and harder to oversee.

Despite their solemn covenant in Aruba, the Colombians had not given the Mafia an altogether exclusive franchise for Europe. The partnership was close, but Colombian traffickers were doing a lot of networking on their own. Many of their throwaway helpers were inexperienced, rash, slipshod, or stupid, and it showed. By 1992 the Colombians were suffering intolerable reverses on the Continent. A careless error had very nearly cost them half a ton of cocaine bound for Sicily that June. The frozen fish it was hidden in proved to be loaded with mercury. (A Mafia military commando was on the verge of mounting an attack to grab the shipment but decided to have a bogus government inspector liberate it instead.)

Earlier, in Holland, two tons of cocaine were nearly lost. Impatient to extract the packets from cans of frozen orange juice, helpers with room-temperature IQs dumped the juice into Amsterdam's canals. When the water turned orange, the police arrived.

The Colombians sent Tony Duran to Italy because they had had enough. "Tony came here to set up a point-to-point system for the most powerful cocaine and laundering network in the world," said

Criminalpol's Alessandro Pansa.[21] "The Colombians wanted stable ties with the Sicilian Mafia; they wanted efficiency, dependability, professionalism, damage control, quality control; they wanted *legality*," he explained.

Transporting the cocaine to Europe was costing them twelve times more than actually producing it ($12,000 to $1,000 a kilo).[22] They wanted the Sicilian Mafia to cut out the middlemen and cut down the risks. Under the terms of their 1992 Rome treaty, Sicilians would be stationed in Colombia to help supervise shipments to Europe. The cocaine would go directly to reliable Sicilian agents posted at strategic entry points—Amsterdam, Rotterdam, and cities in Spain, Portugal, and Germany for the new routes passing by way of Eastern Europe. Italy itself would be "the cocaine warehouse for the Continent."[23]

Communications between Palermo and Colombian cocaine depots would be strictly by radio; even cellular telephones were out. The cover for shipping the coke to Europe would have to be genuine. The product used for camouflage would have to be good, and the company receiving it legitimate and credible. If cans of orange juice were used, they would have to be imported by a firm in the business of importing and selling orange juice. If the proceeds were laundered through an insurance company, it would have to be a straight-up company selling a lot of insurance.

"Find me a company that really buys frozen fish, and we'll send them frozen fish. Open a shop that sells dried flowers, and we'll send dried flowers," the Colombians' Tony Duran told his Italian associates.

In exchange, the Sicilian Mafia and its subalterns would become part of a financial conglomerate altogether new to the underworld and more menacing to the lawful one.[24]

The Mafia had already risen above the primitive drug trafficking of the 1970s and 1980s. Moving the drugs was for its lower classes, still the best in the business. By 1992 its managerial class was engaging more and more in straight (or only slightly crooked) capitalist ventures. Half of all the Sicilian Mafia's laundered capital—*half*—was reinvested in legitimate enterprises all over the world, according to Italy's Ministry of Justice.[25]

Obviously it could provide legitimate companies to camouflage the cocaine trade, as well as the skilled professional labor to direct it in Europe. More important, however, it was ideally placed to manage the most troublesome and crucial part of the operation: the money. Colossal sums of Colombian narcodollars were backing up around the world. Getting them home clean from America alone was exhausting and endlessly complex; therefore, the Colombians asked the Mafia to take a good part of the laundry service for Europe off their hands.

In short, the Sicilians were going to launder the proceeds of the European cocaine traffic for the Colombians as well as themselves. "Corleone can wash and move any amount of money," announced Salvatore Riina's emissary proudly to Tony Duran, marking the Mafia's passage to the highest spheres of international finance.[26]

Far from the commonplace affair it may seem, laundering crime money can be an intoxicating power game. A global turnover of half a trillion narcodollars a year produces colossal amounts of converted, expendable capital that can go anywhere overnight.

A launderer converting it by reinvesting it can move faster than any company accountable to stockholders or any state agency or international body. "Look how long it takes the G-7 or the United States to get a billion dollars into Russia. The Mafia can move in liquid cash whenever it likes," observes Greg Passic. Furthermore, a good launderer today does not merely manipulate the capital of others; he acquires a healthy share.

Five hundred billion dollars of drug money means an endless torrent of cash in small bills. The ordeal of counting it is such that it is often weighed by the bale or measured by the cubic yard. (British customs found twenty cubic yards of various currencies stacked to the roof of a London safe house in Operation Green Ice.)

The Colombian cartels pay a fortune to turn this into usable money. They were offering up to 15 percent on the dollar when Tony Duran sat down with the Sicilians in Rome. The rate leaped when their money circuit was hit by Operation Green Ice. By the end of 1992 the Colombians were paying up to 25 percent to get their profits laundered—giving away twenty-five cents on the dollar.[27]

Operation Green Ice identified and destroyed seven of their major money-laundering circuits. Investigators had never cracked more than one at a time before. Nevertheless, the DEA thought there were at least another hundred, and this only in the West. It could not begin to estimate what was going on among the ruins of the formerly communist East, where the trail now led.

In 1992, in the formerly communist East, the Mafia could turn a billion dollars into four, five, even $10 billion, laundered and reinvested. It could do that for its own cut of the Colombians' drug money and for the Colombians' share without the smallest risk of detection.

The former Soviet republics had the world's largest petroleum reserves (eighty billion barrels), a quarter of the world's gold and timber reserves (twice the Amazon's), a fifth of the world's diamond reserves, and the world's second largest deposits of copper, iron ore, coal, nickel, and zinc. They also abounded in uranium, plutonium, manganese, cobalt, bauxite, chromium, lead, molybdenum, carbon, titanium, platinum, silver, tin, and a range of rare earth metals. Furthermore, they had inherited what was once the world's largest standing army, with its requisite weapons, tanks, missiles, planes, nuclear warheads, and materials.

All this was up for grabs in a prostrate and chaotic land, boiling with corruption and flat broke. All the ex-communist states were a bargain, but the Russian Republic was unique. Not only was everything for sale there at incredibly low prices, but payment could be made in local currency by a foreigner with the right connections and the wits to buy a seemingly worthless currency on the black market. A well-connected foreigner could buy a ton of crude petroleum in Russia for the equivalent of $5 in rubles in 1990 and sell it for $140 in Western Europe. This was more or less the case for all of the country's natural wealth and man-made resources.

To be well connected, a foreign crook had only to hook up with a fellow crook in the Russian mafia or a corrupt Russian politician, both readily available. The foreign crook could then obtain a Russian bank account and a license to export, buy rubles for his dirty dollars at a huge discount, and pay in rubles for his raw material exports. So he could not only launder his money but come out 400 percent or 500 percent ahead. Some were coming out 1,000 percent ahead.[28]

By the time the Colombians asked the Mafia to help launder their European profits, the entire ex-Soviet bloc had become an enormous washing machine for dirty money, rapidly replacing familiar ones elsewhere, arguably the largest, safest, and most profitable ever invented.

Naturally the Colombians were also in Russia. The Cali cartel was already selling cocaine to Moscow's new rich, working with Russian mafia traffickers to move cocaine across Western Europe, and using them to lease Russian planes—Anatov 74s fitted with two-thousand-mile tanks for high-load, low-level shipments via Mexico to the United States.[29]

The Colombians were also washing their own money in Russia. The Cali cartel in particular had hired an authentic Harvard professor named Frank Jurado in 1990 to explore the terrain. Presentable, relaxed, and urbane, Jurado had been working the whole Continent when the DEA picked him up in Luxembourg with a ticket to Moscow in his pocket. Apart from $32 million on deposit in a Luxembourg bank and $55 million in a Monte Carlo bank, he had another 115 bank accounts in sixteen other countries, including a $2 million account in Budapest, Hungary.

Nevertheless, the Sicilian Mafia had gotten there first, forming a privileged partnership with the Russian mafia just as it had with the Colombians. The Sicilian bosses who had thought up the Aruba plan in 1987 were already buying hundreds of millions of Russian rubles in 1989—the Cuntrera brothers, Ciccio Madonia, and Nitto Santapaola, among others.

The Cuntrera brothers bought only $28 million worth of rubles that year, to acquire cut-rate Soviet building materials for their new high-rise hotels in Aruba.[30] But a close fellow boss of Nitto Santapaola's bought half a billion rubles the same year. A year later the Sicilian and American mafias were part of a consortium negotiating for $8 billion worth of rubles.

Western authorities could not imagine why a Sicilian Mafia boss or any sane person would want to buy $8 billion worth of rubles at the time. Certainly they did not realize that these crooks meant to buy up all the rubles in Russia (the better to sack it) and succeeded to a great extent. The story of that monumental scam is told here for the first time. The documents confirming it are disturbing signs of the planetary criminal collusion that Judge Falcone feared. Russia is where the big crime syndicates discovered how useful they could be to one another to capture and ransack a vast and prostrate country.

Of the five thousand organized crime gangs emerging there and in the rest of the ex–Soviet Union, a thousand were working with some foreign criminal group by early 1993. This was President Boris Yeltsin's own estimate at a conference of several hundred politicians, civil servants, judges, and police chiefs summoned to discuss the spreading scourge.

"Organized crime is destroying the economy, interfering with politics, undermining public morale, threatening individual citizens and the entire Russian nation. . . . Our country is already considered a great mafia power!" he exclaimed.[31]

It was true, although no Western government appeared to notice it.

CHAPTER TWO

After the Wall

To an expectant commission of the Italian parliament, gathered in a secret location toward the end of 1992, a Sicilian Man of Honor with impressive credentials and exalted connections told an amazing story:

"One night I was in Pietraperzia, in the province of Enna, and there were lots of pairs of shoes. 'Is this a party?' I asked. 'No,' they told me. 'You should be happy because your boss was elected yesterday to be the underboss of all the criminal organizations in the world.' So they gave us all presents of expensive shoes."[1]

Leonardo Messina, descendant of a family whose Men of Honor went back seven generations, had been second in command to the boss who ranked second in power only to Salvatore "Totò" Riina, the most fearsome *capo di tutti capi* to rule Sicily's Cosa Nostra for the better part of a century.[2] In months of interrogation, Messina had provided enough credible testimony to generate two hundred arrests up and down the Italian peninsula. Much of what he said was corroborated by other mafiosi, 275 of whom collaborated with the law that year. But he alone spoke of an elected government presiding over the international underworld.

He had known since 1980 that Cosa Nostra "belonged to a worldwide structure," he declared. "There's a summit, a meeting place for everybody. We sit around a table with other organizations for consultations but also to make important decisions." Others had been in charge until November 1991, he went on. Then, at a meeting somewhere on the planet, "they gave us the *rappresentanza* for all the organizations." Totò Riina had succeeded to the top with Messina's boss at his side.

An enduring cult of disbelief where the Mafia is concerned made it particularly hard to believe this story. Even believers had trouble with the details—the table, the secret meeting place, the formal elections.

The *capo di tutti capi* supposedy elected to the supreme command seemed still more improbable when the public finally got a look at him. Captured early in 1993 after twenty-three years in hiding of a sort (he was in the Sicilian capital of Palermo all along), Totò Riina proved to be no movie godfather. Pudgy and flabby, shoulders slumped and small eyes peering out from folds of flesh, he looked and acted the part of a humble, obsequious, forelock-tugging peasant. He was nothing of the sort—his questioners found him to be astute, imperious, and indescribably frightening—which did not necessarily mean that he ruled a worldwide criminal government.

Perhaps he didn't. There is no hard proof that the elite of the international underworld—Sicilian, American, Colombian, Turkish, Russian, Chinese, Japanese—all meet at once and vote leaders in or out of office. But they have certainly arrived at some kind of *pax mafiosa*.

For all the killing on the turf of each, there are no killings where their paths cross.[3] Although more or less in the same lines of business, increasingly in the same countries where competition ought to be fierce for stakes in the billions of dollars, they may work jointly or concurrently, or withdraw from the field, but they don't fight.

"If there was competition among them, we would be turning up a lot of dead bodies. But the evidence so far is that they are looking for ways to work together," says one of Sicily's leading judicial authorities, Giuseppe Ayala.[4] Indeed, they have unmistakably reached some agreement "dividing up the world," as Judge Falcone had concluded before he died.[5]

Faced with this worldwide criminal alliance, the first in human history, lawful society continues to wage its little wars, splinter into a thousand ethnic fragments, haggle over legal jurisdiction, and perpetuate a multitude of police agencies carefully keeping secrets from one another. Sensible crooks appear to have put such futile exercises behind them.

There is room for everyone in their expanding universe. The heroin age, which they launched in the 1960s, has made them prodigiously rich; and the tremendous upheavals of the 1990s—the collapse of communism, the falling away of barriers across Europe, the mass migration of uprooted populations—are making them more so. The drug traffic alone, exceeding half a trillion dollars a year now, is the world's second biggest money-maker, after the arms traffic; and these syndicates engage in both.[6] The interest they have accumulated from investment of drug profits in the last decade is approaching a trillion dollars, according to a European Community estimate ($820 billion is the EC estimate).[7] That doesn't count customary pursuits such as theft, fraud, extortion, gambling, loan-sharking, forgery, prostitution, pornography, money laundering, and contract killing.

Wealth of such magnitude is a phenomenon altogether separate from the personal fortune of a cocaine baron who can keep a private zoo or a Palermo boss who can give somebody a solid gold bathtub for a wedding present (as one did not long ago). This is the wealth of the biggest multinational in the world, with the reach and resources to act accordingly. Using it judiciously, the big syndicates can penetrate giant corporations, manipulate the world's money markets, destabilize currencies, buy entire countries larger than Aruba, all of which they are doing or have done, as we will see. "Buying a national economy is not a criminal offense," says a state prosecutor in Russia, where it assuredly isn't.

The fact that those who own such a weapon are manifestly pooling their strength is extraordinarily menacing. All their sources of revenue have been multiplying geometrically since the Soviet empire crashed and with it a world order that had kept mankind more or less in line for the previous fifty years.

The story that follows has to do with the calamitous growth of criminal power in Europe, America, and the rest of the world since that epic happening.

At the start of the 1990s, the myth still prevailed that only Italy and the United States offered a natural habitat for the Mafia, and indeed for all organized crime. Evidence to the contrary was denied nearly everywhere else until the signs grew too alarming to ignore.

Sweden and the rest of Scandinavia, Finland and the Baltic states, Russia and the entire ex-Soviet bloc, Nigeria and the whole of West Africa, Australia and the length of the Pacific rim, most of South America and every country in Western Europe have all fallen victim by now.

Sudden recognition has come nearly everywhere at once as crime skids out of control around the globe. Seemingly overnight it has become the fastest growth industry in Britain; according to a *Manchester Guardian* survey, its turnover there hit an astonishing fourteen billion pounds ($21 billion) in 1992.[8]

Holland, an island of civility on a turbulent continent, has more crimes per capita now than twenty other countries, including Britain, France, Italy, and the United States. Australia, Belgium, and Switzerland (!) have more crime victims per capita than the United States.[9]

In the deceptive language of numbers—half a billion crimes worldwide in 1990—it is hard to distinguish between "micro" and "macro" criminality: the one largely drug-induced and poverty-driven; the other structured, efficient, and increasingly international. In the language of power, however, it is this last that has become an intolerable threat to free nations.

America, assailed by predatory gangs of staggering numbers and variety, is still the favorite of the international underworld, but Europe is where the high drama is being played out. The European Community that has just come into being is a momentous experiment in union among twelve disparate sovereign states: Britain, Ireland, France, Germany, Denmark, Holland, Belgium, Luxembourg, Spain, Portugal, Italy, and Greece.

The year 1993 was to have been a triumph, with half the Continent thrown open to a free market of fabulous promise. Sadly, there was no big bang. Hortatory rhetoric could not conceal the qualms and second thoughts, the anxiety bordering on anguish, and the hot quarrels behind closed doors when the moment came for the twelve EC states to keep their word. In the end, the barriers went down just halfway (even this partly a fiction) for goods, services, and money—not for people. People were the EC's nightmare by 1993—migrants and crooks, both in unbearable numbers.

More than any other part of the affluent First World, the EC faced an uncontrollable invasion of migrants from every direction. The noble vision of a great European space stripped of all barriers and looking outward soon receded as the poor, the oppressed, and the upwardly mobile of four continents pushed and clawed their way in. Half a million, then a million, then the imminent threat of three, five, ten million made the difference between gallant principles and reality. The image of a fortress Europe defending its wealth and privilege behind high guarded walls, once abominable to EC leaders, was no longer unthinkable.

By 1993, year of the Single Market, the military patrols by land, sea, and air, the helicopters aloft around the clock, the satellite pictures, radar and infrared night-sights, the forcible expulsions, and the boat people drowning in sight of Mediterranean shores had made the image painfully real. Every kind of criminal was riding in on this human tide, from the petty shill to the multinational troops of the big crime conglomerates. Some of the latter had been in for a quarter of a century. The rest started to come along as soon as they saw the gravy train ahead, in 1985.

When EC leaders decided that year to create a single market, the community had a combined gross national product approaching $5 trillion.[10] Its "in-house" trade ran to nearly $1.5 trillion, and it accounted for a third of the world's exports and imports. It was America's largest trading partner (a quarter of a trillion dollars both ways), largest foreign investor (over a quarter of a trillion dollars), and largest host to American investment abroad (nearing a quarter of a trillion dollars). Once its inner borders went down, a third of a billion people would be free to circulate without passport or custom controls, carry baggage and ship goods without police inspection, live where they pleased, bank or go into business anywhere. On the strength of this, the European Community stood to become the richest trading area on earth. Big-time gangsters could no more resist so intoxicating a prospect than anyone else on the make.

"The one will have a fatal attraction for the other," predicted the U.S. Justice Department's organized crime expert Charles Saphos in 1990. "The multinational crime syndicates have the largest amount of expendable wealth in the world. The Single Market will create the largest concentration of wealth in history. Criminal money will naturally gravitate toward this immense area of opportunity.

"Europe will be a great place to be a crook," he concluded.[11]

But crooks were the last item on the European Community's agenda in 1990. Engrossed in plans to make it easier to make money, EC leaders had given scarcely a thought to the opportunities for criminals to do likewise. In a warning largely disregarded, the director of the Netherlands police academy observed:

> There is no place where expertise on police in the European countries is brought together. There is no center where the problems and possibilities of internationalization of the police can be studied. There is no place to compare the different laws relevant for the police, no comparative study of police systems and their peculiarities, no comparative description and evaluation of police strategies, tactics and procedures in the different specializations, no compilation of information about training systems and equipment and facilities. There is no research on the development of police work after 1992.[12]

With the Single Market barely two years away, the twelve EC states had sacrificed few of their sovereign prerogatives. Each had its own laws on extradition, rights of asylum, hot pursuit, exchange of police and intelligence information, undercover agents, controlled drug deliveries, jail terms for drug traffickers, money laundering, phone taps and listening devices, protection of privacy in data banks.

For instance, a fugitive convicted of "association with the Mafia" in Italy could not be extradited from the other EC states, none of which had a similar law.

Belgian police could not tap anybody's phone, native or foreign, or use any electronic surveillance device, even on a truck in transit. (Drug traffickers loved to do business there.)

Dutch law forbade the release of any information to a foreign agency that might lead to the arrest of a Dutch national and forbade a Dutch citizen even to name a fellow citizen suspected of criminal activity abroad.

A German cop could not pursue a criminal into a building over the Dutch border without a formal *lettre rogatoire*, or over other inner EC borders for more than ten kilometers—six miles, a five-minute ride—and that in a plainly marked police car. (A Dutch cop could chase a criminal straight across Germany, though.)[13]

A French undercover narcotics agent could entrap a drug trafficker by putting up money, but a German narcotics agent who tried it in his country would go to jail.

A backsliding drug trafficker risked life imprisonment in Great Britain and Greece, a forty-year sentence in France, but an *optional* maximum of twelve years in Holland.[14] "The Dutch don't believe in law enforcement to fight drugs anyway," observed an aggrieved cop in France, which has the toughest drug laws in Europe.

Standardizing these regulations could take a lifetime. Indeed, hardly any have been standardized up to now. (It was hard enough to standardize a simple electrical item described by a German journalist as "the most frightful thing of all"—the SIP, the Single Integrated Plug.)[15]

In effect, Western Europe lay like a vast open city under murderous criminal bombardment. The speed and scope of the assault shocked those who had trusted to ministerial wisdom and the salutary effect of myriad ad hoc committees. Nothing in the EC's elaborate preparations brought it remotely close to catching up with the crooks. By an extraordinary twist of history, the ministers and ad hoc committees were planning to free up the western side of Europe just when communism disintegrated on the eastern side. If there was ever a chance to block a massive criminal invasion, that ended it.

Once the standoff between East and West was over, the armature keeping much of the human race in hand was gone. Boundaries started to give way everywhere; whole nations began to split up; the satellite states of Eastern Europe cracked open; the Soviet Union itself flew apart. Law enforcement broke down all across Soviet territory and in Poland, Czechoslovakia, Hungary, Romania, Bulgaria, and Albania. Border controls practically ceased to exist throughout Eastern Europe, calling the whole concept of Western Europe's defense into question.

The Single Market was supposed to be borderless inside but not outside; quite the contrary. Securing its outer border was an indispensable condition for removing internal impediments. This would have been hard enough if the EC states had only to worry about several thousand miles of ragged coastline from the Greek Islands to the Atlantic shores of Ireland. Actually, they did not worry much about the rest of their outer rim.

Stern communist patrols guarded the entire length of their eastern frontier during their planning stage. As long as the Iron Curtain was in place, the line could scarcely be breached either way. Once it fell, that border simply could not hold. Germany, which bordered nine countries, had already abolished frontier controls with six of them to the west and south (Holland, Belgium, Luxembourg, France, Austria, and Switzerland). To the east, it now shared not only five hundred kilometers of porous border with Czechoslovakia but—after annexing communist East Germany—another as long again with Poland. Through this huge gap, virtually unpoliced, a resourceful traveler with or without papers could travel more or less unhindered from Siberian Irkutsk to Paris or Brussels, and vice versa.

Practically speaking, the whole continent lay open to illicit tourists. Migrants flocked to Eastern Europe from Asia, Africa, and

South America, joining throngs of East Europeans surging west. Authentic economic refugees among them could hardly be distinguished from carpetbaggers, pimps, con men, loan sharks, black marketers, forgers, money launderers, arms runners, drug traffickers. Homeless and penniless, usually smuggled in as bonded slaves, they were the new menials of the big crime cartels.

The traffic also went the other way. As always, the crooks moved faster than governments trying to forestall them. The very day the Berlin Wall came down in 1989, they were racing east to stake out territory in ex-communist East Germany. There they met the Russian mafia coming west.

The implications of this encounter were deeply disquieting for every nation in and out of Europe, starting with the United States. The same crime syndicates meeting the Russians in Europe had plagued America for years: the Colombian cartels, the Sicilian Mafia, the Chinese Triads, and the Japanese Yakuza.

The Colombians were supplying most of America's cocaine. The Triads were bringing in three-quarters of America's heroin. The Yakuza, specializing in gunrunning, drugrunning, money laundering, and corporate blackmail, had made America "a prime investment site" over the previous decade, the Justice Department said. (See Chapter 7.)

The Sicilian Mafia, pronounced dead by certain American enthusiasts, was still rated officially with its American offspring as the country's "most serious organized crime problem." According to the FBI, it was bringing in thousands of fresh forces to rejuvenate, if not replace, the American mafia's geriatric leadership.[16]

As if arranged by some malevolent hand, the Russian mafia was also sending in thousands of fresh forces to beef up the Organizatsiya in America. Formed by older émigrés in the 1970s—simultaneously with the Sicilians and just as invisibly—the Organizatsiya was rising rapidly to mob stardom in the United States. Even in America, Russian gangsters stood out as truly gifted frighteners—clever, ferocious, and pitiless. "They make tons of money, they kill people, they are international, they are into drugs," said a harried Federal prosecutor, wondering "how the hell this Russian organized crime got so big and how we can get rid of them."[17] Possibly the most inventive swindlers alive, their multi-billion-dollar scams—at least $5 billion in America by 1992—were the envy of the Cosa Nostra. The fact that the two weren't fighting was a sign of the times: The Russians had simply agreed to pay a cut to four of New York's five Cosa Nostra Families.

Meanwhile, Russian clans stretching across eleven time zones to the Pacific were running into the Triads and the Yakuza at the other end of the map. Russian traffickers could provide new outlets to the West for Triad heroin moving through China. Georgian and Japanese gangs were hijacking used Japanese cars bound for Russia's luxuriant black market. Thus, the United States, China, and Japan were locked into a criminal underground encircling the planet. With the closing of the circle, organized crime achieved its own world without frontiers. Of all the disastrous developments since the breakup of Soviet Russia, this was among the most hidden and insidious.

For Judge Falcone, the Sicilian Mafia had no equal. "There is only one Mafia, Cosa Nostra, the most perfect and ferocious criminal organization on the face of the earth," he said. Toward the end of his life, however, he conceded that other big players could be called mafias, too, provided they were formally structured, flexible, versatile, extremely violent, capable of assuring protection at the highest levels, and very rich.[18] Organizations such as the Triads, the Yakuza, and the Russian clans "growing exponentially" were all of these things, he concluded.

These three, together with the mafias much better known in the West—Sicilian, American, and Colombian—form the worldwide criminal consortium that was taking shape in the last days of Falcone's life. Though each is distinctive to its country, they are remarkably like one another and their Western peers in their chilling blood oaths, laws of silence, codes of honor abounding in death penalties, and an unbounded capacity for larceny, ferocity, and greed.

All have granitic hierarchical commands: Interpol once described the Triad structure as a several-storied building in which the inhabitants of one floor don't know where the stairs are to the next floor. The Triads are the oldest of these crime groups, having engaged in extortion, usury, prostitution, and especially drug trafficking longer than any criminal organization extant.

Though still sworn to cast out the Manchu invaders who overthrew the Chinese Ming emperor in 1644, today's eighty thousand Triad brothers do not live on ancestral memories. They live on their cowed countrymen in Hong Kong, their home base since it became a British Crown Colony in 1842; on other fellow countrymen in Taiwan, their second home; on captive Chinese émigré colonies around the world; and, above all, on the heroin trade.

The Triads were in at the creation of the worldwide heroin trade and have held the key to the biggest source of supply ever since. Every turn of history has helped them since the mid-1880s when the British East Indies Company set out to hook the Chinese population on opium, brought in from India to pay for China's coveted tea, silk, cotton, and rice. Twenty million Chinese became addicts then. The Triads, longtime opium traders, made almost as much money as the British did.

When China, sinking under addiction, banned opium in all its forms nearly a century later, the Triads had a luxuriant black market in heroin all to themselves. When China fell to the communists after World War II, the Triads had the foresight to help a Triad brother named Generalissimo Chiang Kai-shek flee to Formosa (now Taiwan), taking along much of China's movable wealth.

As Chiang Kai-shek fled eastward, the remnants of his Kuomintang army retreated westward to the Shan states of northern Burma, heartland of the Golden Triangle in Southeast Asia. There, among the most bounteous poppy fields on earth, the Generalissimo's loyal followers forced local peasants to raise opium production from a modest 30 tons a year to 2,475 tons by latest count— well over half the world's entire supply.

No outsider could penetrate this fabulous mountain empire, defended by a formidable private army. Only the Triads have had privileged access for the past half-century. Whoever has aspired to supply the heroin addict population of the United States and Europe has been bound to apply to them ever since.

The Yakuza Man immortalized in a thousand novels and films (usually financed by the Yakuza) is a gentleman crook of knightly chivalry and suffocating virtue, seen through the mists of eighteenth-century feudal Japan. Actually, he is a villainous thug with talents that even the Sicilian Mafia might envy.

Operating through three thousand organized gangs, the Yakuza's 100,000 members control Japan's casinos, brothels, houses of pleasure, white slave trade (foreign girls "selling spring"), porno-tourism, nightclubs, theatrical agencies, movie studios, publishing houses (largely cranking out Yakuza folktales), sports, trucking, earth moving, loan-sharking, drug trafficking, gunrunning, money laundering, and corporate blackmail; these operations provide an overall income of around $18 billion a year. Much of their hold on the country has depended on Japan's excessive fear of losing face. Every human frailty, social breach, or surreptitious taste brought to light—even appearing in court or denouncing a crime—means losing face in Japan.

Thus the Yakuza has added a new dimension to *omertà* as the Sicilian Mafia uses it to hold a population hostage, compounding shame with fear. Shame has kept the Japanese government from revealing the Yakuza's true strength until very recently, or the fact that it has hooked 600,000 Japanese on "ice" (crystal methamphetamine)—a world record. Shame has kept thousands of victims from denouncing Yakuza atrocities and driven thousands of others to suicide for failing to keep up their payments to Yakuza loan sharks charging 1 percent *a day*.

Most of all, shame has put Japan's giant corporations at the Yakuza's mercy. Its professional blackmailers, known as *sokaiya*, buy a few company shares, demand a huge payoff, and, if refused, turn up at the next stockholders' meeting to spill company secrets or make a scene—shout, kick furniture, slap the chairman of the board. Thirty of Japan's largest corporations are among those who pay up.[19] (Not all are so resigned. In 1991, seventeen hundred Japanese companies tried holding all their stockholders' meetings on the same day, hoping the *sokaiya* would run out of personnel. They didn't.)[20]

World War II had taken these versatile crooks wherever the Japanese occupation army led, all over Asia. Then when Japanese businessmen hit the road after the war, the Yakuza followed. Today they are entrenched in Paris, London, Rotterdam, São Paolo, Honolulu, San Francisco, Los Angeles, and San Francisco: blackmailing Japanese corporations, trying the same tricks on big corporations in America and Europe, running drugs and arms, laundering billions of dollars, especially in the United States and Europe, for themselves and their friends.

Of all the Russian mafia's counterparts, the closest model was the Sicilian Mafia, wrote the poet and ex-thief Mikhail Dyomin after six years in Siberian prison camps in the 1960s. Its members were no ordinary thieves, Dyomin explained. They were the elite of their profession, members of a Thieves' World (*vorovskoy mir*) going back to the 1600s: a "solid corporation of underground establishments . . . embracing the full extent of the Soviet state, with one general code of ethnics prevailing from the Bay of Finalnd to the shores of the Japan Sea."[21]

Their Thieves' World had for centuries been a wholly closed society, extravagantly depraved and despairing, rejecting morality, politics, patriotism, and even social intercourse with the "outside" world. Presiding over them were men of monklike austerity who spent most of their lives in jail: Russia's incomparable "thieves within the code" (*vory v zakone*). Chosen by others for their superior intelligence and indomitable spirit, they were the strategists for all undertakings in and out of prison; the clan representatives at nationwide policy meetings; the keepers of the common kitty to finance operations, bribe officials, and support convicts' families; the mediators of internal peace and arbiters of the code.[22]

There was no greater sin in their code than dealing with any arm of the state: the police, the military, the government. Yet in the years after World War II, their once impenetrable brotherhood developed a curious affinity with the country's despotic communist rulers.

Both stole. The thieves stole the property of private citizens and the state. So did the communist Nomenklatura, through graft, expropriation, embezzlement, wholesale extortion, and "ceiling statistics" (inflated production figures dreamed up by staring at the ceiling). Indeed, the Soviet Union was a kleptocracy, said a well-known scholar.

In the course of the Brezhnev era, the two became enormously useful and profitable to each other. Thus, when the Soviet Union collapsed, its legacy to a liberated country included a mafia far more organized, worldly, and rich than the outside world could imagine, sharing power with the old Nomenklatura and, inevitably, with the one succeeding it.

As if they had all been to the same school, the Russian mafia, the Yakuza, and the Triads moving out into the world behaved much like their Western peers. They took menial jobs, sheltered among and preyed pitilessly on their own nationals abroad, invested judiciously, bribed copiously, and managed to stay out of the cops' line of vision.

CHAPTER THREE

Crime Without Frontiers

In June 1990 the prime ministers of the European Community set aside two hours at their Dublin summit to consider the Sicilian Mafia, at the insistence of German Chancellor Helmut Kohl. He feared that it would infect the entire Continent once EC frontiers went down, that what had happened to Italy would happen to Germany and all Europe.[1]

For all he knew, it was happening already, he told me in a long evening's talk that spring. Over a broad roundtable looking out on his garden in Bonn, the chancellor and his interior minister, Wolfgang Schäuble, spoke of their deepening worries for the coming Single Market: the nearly perpendicular rise in drug addiction; the drug traffickers' seemingly impenetrable cover; the banking system's permeability for money laundering; the potential for extortion, fraud, and penetration of legitimate business, corruption of the police and judiciary, and political pollution.

The Mafia was the obvious threat, he said, if only because it *belonged* in the European Community. With a home seat in Sicily, its members had all the privileges of what would come to be known as the EC's thirteenth state. They alone, among all the world's big crime syndicates, would have the legal right in the Single Market to move their men, money, and goods around the entire western half of the Continent without impediment.

Before long, Kohl thought, the Mafia—and not just the Mafia—would be using both sides of the Continent interchangeably: buying up property in the East, expanding the drug market there, laundering money, bribing bureaucrats and border guards, recruiting new talent. Among others, half a million unemployed agents of the communist security police would be for hire, he noted.

I mention this interview because it was the first indication of governmental concern in Western Europe. Nobody outside Italy was really looking at the Mafia in the spring of 1990; not many were doing so inside Italy, either, at the government level. Chancellor Kohl had forced the matter onto the agenda of the Dublin summit over stiff Italian resistance, I learned later. Italy's prime minister, Giulio Andreotti, and foreign minister, Gianni De Michelis, had not only balked at discussing it but did not even want the word *Mafia* used.

If Italian government leaders were stubbornly reluctant to talk about the Mafia, their EC partners still tended to wonder if it was real, had no idea how to detect it at work, and had certainly not done much to keep its larcenous hands off their territory. Worse, such defenses as they had counted on were caving in.

This was the stupendous year ending communist rule in Eastern Europe. Law enforcement was practically gone along the European Community's entire eastern perimeter. Men, money, and goods were beginning to move back and forth with ease where the Iron Curtain had been.

Yet, moving into the final year of preparations for the Single Market, leaders of the European Community still radiated confidence in their immunity to the ills of pathologically distressed countries—the United States, say, or their own unfortunate Mediterranean partner. When they finally began to take notice, halfway through 1990, they could not make up for five lost years. What Chancellor Kohl feared had already happened: Not only was the European Community infected but the carriers were spreading east, and a virulent new pest was coming west.

Even before the EC summit in Dublin, the familiar organizations worrying the chancellor—the Sicilian Mafia, its American off-spring, its Colombian partners—were encamped in East Germany and much of Eastern Europe. And even as the Dublin meeting convened, the Russian mafia was attending an underground counter-summit in East Berlin. Agents of the Soviet Interior Ministry had tracked ranking "thieves within the code" when they traveled out from Soviet Russia to meet with international mafia groups and leaders of the Russian mafia operating abroad, especially in Germany and the United States. (This has been confirmed by Alexander Gurov, head of the ministry's Sixth Department to combat organized crime at the time.)[2]

The Russians had been trapped behind the Iron Curtain since World War II. Only once, shortly after it ended, had they met with colleagues abroad—mostly from "the truly crook countries of Poland and Italy"—at a secret All-Thieves' Conference on the westernmost Soviet city of Lvov.[3] Now they could renew old ties and establish others. Crossing the frontiers of a crumbling Soviet empire had become "a kid's game," to quote the head of Interpol Moscow, and the great criminal clans spanning Soviet territory from the Pacific to the very center of Europe were free.

This was the summer when the last borders went down for the international underworld—well over a year ahead of the European Community's, rendering most of its strategy for defense obsolete.

The coming together of the Russian mafia and its Western counterparts coincided with an explosion of crime along the geopolitical line once dividing them. The perpetrators were a miscellaneous crowd on both sides, indigenous and foreign, reveling in the utter breakdown of law enforcement after the communist collapse. They were soon using both sides of the continent interchangeably, just as Chancellor Kohl had predicted. As if in a self-fulfilling prophecy, his own country was the frontline state.

Apart from its wealth and power, Germany had strict bank secrecy, no currency controls, unbending rules protecting privacy, a severely hobbled police force, unwary politicians, Europe's most hospitable laws of asylum, and a commanding geographical position astride the Continent. Its borders were already down by mutual agreement with most of Western Europe; and after annexing ex-communist East Germany, its new border with Poland became a freeway to and from all Eastern Europe. Thus, before any other country in the West—and more intensely, continuously, and disastrously—Germany felt the full shock waves of organized crime from the East.

The 431-kilometer Oder-Niesse line is not much in the way of a frontier. The Niesse River is only ten meters wide, and the Oder is often shallow enough to wade across. Frankfurt an der Oder, chief checkpoint on the German side, was manned in 1990 by a demoralized and virtually decapitated Bundesgrenschutz (border guard). The checkpoint on the Polish side was scarcely manned at all.

This was where the huge hole began, known in Eurospeak as the EC security deficit. After seventy years of communism, it could not be sealed. The whole eastern frontier of Germany, formerly a rigid communist police state, was virtually unpoliced. Stasi's 100,000 agents were gone; the Vopos (Volkspolizei) were gone; customs officers, courts, and magistrates serving the old regime were gone—and could not be replaced for years.

Germany wanted and needed to keep the border open anyway. Poland, the first satellite state to fight free of the Kremlin, had strong moral claims on all its western neighbors. A prime victim of Hitler's occupation army, it had a particular claim on the German conscience. "Never again barbed wire, an army, a wall—never again!" exclaimed a captain at Bundesgrenschutz headquarters in Berlin.[4]

Perhaps more to the point, Poland was the gateway through which Germany now hoped to gain economic ascendancy over Central Europe. Therefore, Chancellor Kohl's government could not and would not put up a high fence against it. Nothing short of that was likely to avert onrushing disaster. Poland's new democratic order, destitute and exceedingly fragile, could not even begin to deal with the policing of its frontiers in any direction.

Like Czechoslovakia, lower down on Germany's eastern flank, post-communist Poland offered marvelous opportunities for crime. The collapse of the most efficient, brutal, and oppressive police system ever created had left a terrible void. Policing under the communist regime had consisted largely of suppressing political dissidents. Those who had been good at it were opting for hasty retirement. Few breathing the bracing air of freedom cared to take their place.

"Not only do we have no computers, no faxes, no cars, and no money, but we have no training and no manpower," said Commander Marcinkowicz, Warsaw's deputy police chief. "We have 30 percent vacancies in the police force. People can't forget the secret police. Even though our civilian police were never political under the communists, that's the image. The spirit of liberty rules. Nobody wants to be a cop."[5]

Apart from a severe shortage of personnel, Poland had no visa requirements for the rest of Eastern Europe and no hope of plugging the leaks in a thousand-kilometer frontier with Russia. Here was Europe's swinging door, the sole Soviet bloc country offering practically free passage from the rest of the bloc to the West and vice versa. "We cannot control our borders; in effect, we *have* no borders," said an Interior Ministry spokesman. Desperate migrant populations from everywhere were already forming a critical mass in the country, soon to burst upon Western Europe. A sizable criminal contingent moved among them.

By 1990, two million itinerant Soviet traders were quartering Polish territory, destined to become seven million in barely another year. With "personal invitations" bought or forged, they were crossing over at Brest-Terespol, Mosciska-Medyko, Grodno-Kuznico, by car, train, bus, or truck.

Bivouacked around the Palace of Culture in the capital and pushing out to the remotest provinces, they were hawking shoddy Soviet goods for the Polish zloty—the sole Soviet bloc currency convertible to dollars. "For Russians, even Poland is a paradise," a saddened Polish reporter observed.

The Russian mafia was collecting payoffs from all of them, said Poland's former prosecutor-general, Alexander Herzog.

> We've known for many months that the Russian mafia
> is operating here. We know these traders have to pay

the mafias in Moscow, Leningrad, and Minsk, through their bases in Warsaw.

Even in everyday life we see that this flow of traders is not spontaneous. In a small village in the south, where I would not imagine it could happen, I saw busloads of Soviet citizens arriving from Lithuania, Belorus, Russia, Georgia, and Mongolia—two or three buses a day. They knew exactly where to peddle, where to sleep. They were organized.

This mafia is bringing violence we've never seen here before. Shootouts with machine guns, gas guns, bodies dumped from cars, car bombs. . . . We never catch the killers; their own people are afraid to testify, just like in the movies. We expect that to grow because our police are not prepared to fight such crimes—not here or anywhere in Eastern Europe. And Europe's borders are loosening: This Russian mafia is ready to move on.[6]

In the course of 1990, the Russian mafia moved on to Berlin. It was descending on Germany in force. Criminal bands erupting in all the ex-satellite states were drawn inevitably into its orbit: Romanians, Hungarians, Czechs, Bulgarians, Yugoslavs, and, especially, Poland's own expert crooks. As if cloned by the Nomenklatura of Brezhnev's day, the Russians were quickly gaining dominion over organized crime throughout Eastern Europe. Berlin, where their "thieves within the code" gathered that summer, was their natural destination. A sizable Russian émigré colony there offered what captive émigré colonies everywhere offer predatory countrymen: excellent camouflage and a steady income.

This particular colony also contained many fugitive crooks from the old country who had their own protection racket going and controlled 85 percent of Berlin's gambling halls. The new Russian mafia was soon blackmailing the old Russian mafia fugitives and selling protection to Russians already paying the old fugitives for protection.[7]

In addition, Germany had inherited a quarter of a million Red Army troops in the eastern provinces, due to remain for another four years. No sooner were these regions annexed to Federal Germany than the Red Army's camps became a grand bazaar. Sixty thousand Kalashnikov rifles disappeared from its armories within a few weeks; antiair missiles were selling for $450.[8]

A Russian "business mafia" began to collect state tax refunds on nonexistent imported goods for the troops, to bring pinball machines into the officers' mess, to trade in black market alcohol and cigarettes, and to strip the barracks of anything not welded to the floor.

Meanwhile, a Russian-Polish "car mafia" appeared, stealing only the biggest and best. Twenty-four thousand Mercedes Benzes, Audis, and BMWs went east that year—ten hours to Warsaw and another ten to Moscow.[9] Drivers ordered to stop at the Polish border simply crashed through the barrier and drove on.[10] In those early days, German authorities were no more aware of the Russian mafia's presence *as a mafia* than of a whole submerged community of foreign crime groups in place for years.

Germany had nearly five million guest workers in dozens of émigré colonies. Apart from the Russian one, there was a small but fast-growing Chinese one, notable for its proliferating Chinese restaurants with few customers and visibly affluent proprietors.

Much larger communities of Italians and Turks had settled in over the years, along with Yugoslavs, Romanians, Kurds, Afghanis, Sikhs, Tamils, Palestinians, Iranians. They all had wolves among the sheep; Yugoslavia's were particularly ferocious. Defeated by a babel of strange tongues and the usual wall of silence, however, German police had neither the fortitude nor the will to try singling these out. Few believed in the bogeyman of organized crime up to then. The very phrase, *Ok-Organizierte Kriminalitat*, was alien and frightening in a country convinced that it had none.

Though Germany had been the main Western outpost of the Turkish arms-drugs mafia since the 1970s, the BKA (Bundeskriminalamt, Germany's FBI) did not recognize the existence of a Turkish mafia (to the considerable irritation of Turkey's government). Though the Turkish mafia had been the Sicilian Mafia's main partner in Germany and all Europe for just as long, the BKA saw no criminal conspiracy there, either. Indeed, its inability to perceive the extraordinary configuration of Italian criminals on German soil almost surpassed belief. If the Sicilian Mafia existed at all—BKA agents weren't sure that it did—it was Italy's problem. The odd Sicilian crook in Frankfurt or Düsseldorf was to be expected. The names called to their attention now and then by the Italian police rang no bells, tending to run together in a blur of Italianate vowels.

Actually, Germany had been the Sicilian Mafia's second home in Europe since the 1960s. The same bosses running the Sicilians' heroin network in America had used German territory all along to hide out from the law (and each other, when they fought), expedite drug shipments, launder money, and park their hit squads or sleepers. (A Sicilian drug trafficker caught in Germany in 1992, resident in the country since 1970, had been photographed by the FBI at a Mafia meeting in New York in 1946.)

Exactly as they did in Brooklyn, they took cover among seventy thousand Italian workers in the country, worked hard, and opened chains of pizza parlors wherever they went. It was exceptionally difficult to mistake the distinctively felonious spoor of the pizza parlor. From the early 1960s onward, nearly all Sicilian mafiosi slipping into America had gone into the pizza business, sheltered behind it, laundered their drug money through it, skimmed the cash take, worked it to extort payoffs by arson, acid, bombing, and murder, and shifted dope from one of its kitchen doors to another.[11] They were doing the same in Germany for a quarter of a century before anyone caught on.

The Mafia's footprints were all over the country—in small towns such as Sankt Ingbert or Dormagen, in big industrial cities such as Frankfurt, in Baltic beach resorts and southern health spas such as Baden-Baden.

Agostino Flenda, the Sicilian Mafia's point man for heroin in Northwest Europe, had operated out of a dingy Munich pizzeria since the early 1970s.[12] Roberto Palazzolo was living in Munich when he was arrested for massive money laundering in the Pizza Connection case, reportedly as much as $5 billion.[13]

Agostino Badalamenti, whose uncle Gaetano had headed the

Mafia's governing Cupola in Palermo, was shot and chopped to pieces in Solingen in 1984. (Gaetano, among the biggest international drug traffickers alive, was "revered as a god on earth" by his Mafia subjects, said the famous defector Tommaso Buscetta.)[14]

Giovanni Caruana, whose family was intermarried with the unforgettable Cuntrera brothers, was shot and nearly killed in Sankt Ingbert in 1975; four of his nieces and nephews had pizzerias in Germany. One, Alfonso Caruana, began laundering narcodollars there in 1978. (He arrived that year with $600,000 in a suitcase, after paying a fine in Switzerland for failing to declare the money.)[15] Alfonso's brother Pasquale was picked up in Weil Am Rhine a decade later on an Italian warrant for drug trafficking. His traveling partner, Giuseppe Cuffaro (not the Aruba Cuffaro), was caught soon afterward in Baden-Baden overseeing heavy heroin shipments in transit from Thailand to America.[16]

Directing the Mafia's heroin traffic to the West since 1970, the Cuntreras had strategic forces positioned wherever necessary: Montreal, Miami, London, Brussels, Geneva, Malta, and Germany, of course. They had actually *invented* their money-laundering system in Germany and so had an obvious interest in it when Pasquale Caruana was arrested there in 1988. He had been cruising the German countryside for six weeks at the time. His partner had spent 220 days in Baden-Baden, clocking thirty-three thousand kilometers for side trips in a rented Mercedes. (Between jaunts, Cuffaro had flown four times to Thailand, once to Venezuela, and again to Canada, and made phone calls to Thailand, Canada, the United States, Venezuela, Belgium, Spain, Luxembourg, and Italy.)[17]

Interrogated by an Italian magistrate, Pasquale Caruana said he intended to establish residence in Germany, which the judge took to mean that he intended to "create operative bases for the Mafia's drug traffic and money laundering" there. All of Italy's crime groups were paying serious attention to Germany by then. Totò Riina often visited in person on "fact-finding missions." Lorenzo Nuvoletta, a top Camorra boss and a made member of the Mafia as well, had an official residence in Karlsruhe, near Baden-Baden. The Camorra's superboss, Carmine Alfieri, maintained a home in Nuremberg.[18]

They had wonderful facilities in Germany by the late 1980s: a point-to-point circuit of pizza parlors, several thousand resident Sicilian mafiosi, and Neapolitan camorristi without rap sheets; straw men to buy real estate or rent warehouses; and plenty of throwaway Italian helpers—*kanonenfutter*, cannon fodder, Germans call them.

The BKA had nearly all the pieces of this picture but could not see the whole. Its director, Hans-Ludwig Zachert, a trim, closely barbered and faultlessly tailored executive, is competent, conscientious, and generally on top of his job. Until the autumn of 1990, however, he lacked the indispensable key to detecting the Mafia's presence. Alessandro Pansa, one of Italy's most gifted cops, called it "a reciprocal knowledge of reality": an instant perception beyond Italy's perimeters of how mafiosi think, infiltrate, camouflage their operations, and deploy their forces abroad.

For instance, said Pansa: "Early in 1990 we informed the BKA that a suspected Sicilian mafioso had bought three hotels near Frankfurt. They checked him out and said he was clean. We advised them to watch out for arson in the neighborhood. A couple of months later, six nearby hotels were burned down."[19]

Arson, as Pansa knew but his German comrades did not, was standard Mafia practice for frightening businessmen into making the monthly payoff—the *pizzo*, which means "wetting a small bird's beak"—that had provided its basic income for nearly a century. When, during the following year, 142 pizzerias and hotels were burned down in just two regions—Lower Saxony and Rhine-Westphalia—the BKA was not so easily gulled. "We're 100 percent sure the Mafia was behind them," director Zachert told me then.[20]

The BKA's long voyage of discovery did not begin until the autumn of 1990. That September, two Sicilian waiters working in a pizzeria called *Ai Trulli* in Leverkusen flew to Sicily, shot a judge dead, and flew back to wait on tables the same night. A witness actually saw them ambush Judge Rosario Livatino along the road to Agrigento on the southern Sicilian coast, chase him through a field, and shoot him in the mouth when he tripped.

The Ai Trulli pizzeria had been on German police blotters since 1986 when a group of Sicilian mafiosi gathered there for a "dinner of reconciliation." The dinner had ended with a car trip to a nearby forest where one of the reconciled diners was tied to a tree and burned alive.[21] Four years after what had seemed like an isolated episode, this finally registered as part of an ongoing sinister design. Two of Judge Livatino's killers, swiftly caught and arrested, proved to belong to a whole team of Mafia hit men nesting in Germany—one of many.

Their hometown was Palma di Montechiaro in the province of Agrigento, centerpiece of Giuseppe di Lampedusa's classic work, *The Leopard*, and famous even in Sicily as an area of high Mafia density. A thousand Sicilians from Palma di Montechiaro lived in Mannheim, among fifteen thousand Italian guest workers. Dozens were thought to be commuting from Germany as "groups of fire" in Palma's endless Mafia feuds.

Giuliano Guazzelli, a sergeant in the Carabinieri (Italy's elite paramilitary police), stationed in Palma since 1960, could guess the identities of Judge Livatino's killers merely from a meager description of "two tall young men who didn't even look like Sicilians." He was killed for that a year later. Some weeks after Livatino's death, the BKA invited Judge Falcone to Wiesbaden. Chancellor Kohl had been pressing for more information on the Mafia since the Dublin summit the previous June, Dr. Zachert told me. Falcone brought "a burst of light," he said.

The Mafia was not an association of independent Families, Falcone explained; it was "one and indivisible" with "extremely rational and functional rules." The threat it posed, therefore, was not so much in its numbers as in its "structure and capacity to put a unified strategy into place."[22]

"He gave us a picture of what Italian investigators were learning about the Mafia's network in Germany—much worse than we dreamed," Zachert said. "He warned that we should expect a still bigger invasion because the Mafia was looking for new markets in Eastern Europe. He turned over names of people in seventy-six Mafia Families. We set up a computer network to check this with our own criminal files. The computer threw up 480 of these Sicilians in files, some going back a quarter of a century. Now we're checking 4,000 more."[23]

Eventually the BKA's list of suspected mafiosi on German soil ran to twenty-seven typed pages. Sixty-eight Italian crime cells were detected across the country—around Munich and Frankfurt, along the Rhine, in Cologne, Hannover, Stuttgart, Berlin, Leipzig, and the outlying eastern region.[24] New settlers kept arriving, sent up from Sicily with seed money to expand operations, as Italian investigators were told by the endlessly informative Mafia defector Leonardo Messina.

Looking back, the BKA realized what all this meant. The Sicilian Mafia had "chosen Germany as its operative base in Europe for the years to come," declared BKA's director Zachert.

These were the years starting January 1, 1993, for which the Mafia had been preparing from the start. "They're going to open the frontiers. If Italy is big, Mr. President, imagine how big Europe is. That's why we had to think ahead," explained a major defector, Antonino Calderone, to Italy's Parliamentary Anti-Mafia Commission.

Thinking further ahead, Men of Honor were staking out territory in Germany's new eastern provinces well before 1993. Only hours after the Berlin Wall came down late in 1989, a mafioso positioned in West Berlin received his orders to cross over. Italian police were listening in as Giovanni Tagliamento, reputed member of the powerful Morabito Family of Catania in southeastern Sicily, called with the instructions:

"Go in there and start buying."

"What should I buy?"

"Everything—restaurants, discos, pizzerias—everything!"[25]

Chancellor Helmut Kohl knew next to nothing of these matters when we talked in Bonn just months after the Wall fell. The awakening came afterward when a horde of newcomers from every corner of the globe—racketeers, con men, contract killers, gamblers, pimps, car thieves, burglars, swindlers, counterfeiters, money launderers, arms runners, and drug traffickers—swept into Germany like an army of omnivorous ants. A rolling criminal tide hit the country, stirring a diffuse sense of uncertainty and unease.

The crime rate doubled in Berlin in barely six months. Car thefts shot up to forty-six thousand over the next year and eighty-seven thousand the year after, nearly one in every five stolen all over Western Europe. Prospective buyers took to crossing over from Poland and photographing the car of their dreams in some East German driveway, for delivery to Warsaw the next morning.[26] Fraud, forgery, arson, smuggling, prostitution, gambling, and daytime burglary spread like a monstrous inkblot. A million stolen car radios were shipped out of the country in containers, bound for Poland, Russia, Hungary, and Czechoslovakia. One hundred and twenty-five thousand credit cards were filched.[27]

The *pizzo* or rakeoff—*schutzgeld* in German—was replicated in a dozen languages. Four out of five Italian businessmen in Frankfurt were paying it, as were similar proportions of Yugoslavs, Turks, Russians, and Chinese.

Violence erupted: bodies in cement coffins, murder on the steps of a courthouse, muggings, break-ins, shootouts in broad daylight.

An estimated two billion deutsche marks' worth of narcodollars washed through German banks within the year. (An American Mafia courier was picked up with $1.2 million at Los Angeles airport, heading for Frankfurt.) A torrent of counterfeit dollars poured in.

Seizures of heroin quadrupled in 1990, the bulk coming from Czechoslovakia and Poland. Overdose deaths rose by 50 percent in a single year (from 989 to 1,500). By year's end Germany was said by Interpol to have become "the main point of transit for the entire European heroin market."[28]

An incredible two and a half tons of cocaine were confiscated that year. "Certainly more than our German market could stand, *so they are creating demand*," said the BKA's man for narcotics.[29]

This was not just the work of lawless foreigners, although these became the pretext for ugly racist violence. Germany's own criminals, many and tough, actually accounted for nearly two-thirds of all the crimes on the books in 1990.[30] Increasingly in partnership with the big foreign syndicates, they were up to their eyes in some of the biggest operations across the country. In a single two-ton shipment of cocaine, German traffickers were entangled with those of eight other nationalities: Yugoslav, Dutch, Austrian, Chinese, French, Venezuelan, Uruguayan, and Sicilian. (The Sicilians were giving the orders, though, BKA agents said.)[31]

For all the pickings in Federal Germany, the big crime groups were unmistakably focusing on the new eastern region. Barely a year after the communists' fall, intelligence analysts in the BND (Bundesnachrichtendienst) sent a disturbing position paper to Chancellor Kohl. The international drug cartels were "setting aside as much as half of their income to develop new markets in the European Community," the BND said.

In particular, the Mafia, the Yakuza, the Colombians, and the Turks were investing in government bonds, real estate, building societies, hotels and casinos, finance and leasing companies, banks and insurance companies. They were buying up airlines and trucking concerns to handle their own distribution, acquiring shares in newspapers and radio and TV stations, and donating to political parties.

Though all twelve EC states were targeted, the "heaviest concentration" was in Eastern Germany, the BND found. The Italian Mafia alone had invested fifty billion deutsche marks there, it maintained.[32] Some of this appeared to be guesswork. Investigators in those early days were just picking up the first stray signs of an unknown animal, moving through dense undergrowth and exquisitely gun-shy.

Regular police in the BKA could not find proof of anything like a fifty-billion-deutsche-mark Mafia investment, for instance, but they did find "clear structures of organized criminality" emerging in the eastern regions:

> Criminals from organized crime strongholds have been buying fixed assets, founding firms, and buying into existing companies on former East Germany territory. Dummy enterprises are used to get licenses, especially for sex shops, videotape libraries, restaurants, amusement arcades. . . . The goal is not merely to invest laundered profits but to use legitimate enterprises for criminal operations.[33]

The BKA did not know then that the Mafia was penetrating major legitimate enterprises in the west of Germany as well as the east.

In the summer of 1990, Italy's Guardia di Finanza had uncovered a disturbing Mafia deal with Philip Holzmann AG of Frankfurt, a colossus of the German construction industry. Holzmann, beating out a Fiat subsidiary, had won a $6 million contract to build a dam in Corleone, Sicily, home of Totò Riina and Luciano Leggio, the notorious *capo di tutti capi* preceding him. The contract, awarded in 1988, had been hailed as marking Sicily's entrance into the Common Market. But, according to the Parliamentary Commission, the Mafia had procured it for Holzmann in exchange for getting all the subcontracts.

Italy's Parliamentary Anti-Mafia Commission found a number of things wrong with the whole project: the absence of inert materials anywhere in the area, for example, and excessive delays in expropriating the land. Despite the German firm's known efficiency, construction costs kept rising. The dam was nowhere near completion two years later.[34]

Mafia salesmen had been making similar offers all over Western Europe, the Guardia di Finanza discovered. Over six hundred charges were brought against a Mafia holding company that was distributing the subcontracts throughout Italy. Nobody knew how far the Mafia infection was spreading. Before much longer, however, its powers of corruption would appear to bear out Chancellor Kohl's blackest premonitions.

Germany had its share of homegrown corruption. By authoritative estimate, four out of five public works contracts in Frankfurt, the quintessence of free enterprise, were "decided in advance."[35] As Kohl had told me, however, he *knew* that kind of graft. It was some unknown foreign kind that he feared. In fact, Germany in 1990 was like a flower bed ready for Mafia planting. Twenty or thirty years of patient cultivation were paying off for the Sicilians' underground crime colony. Mafiosi laundering and reinvesting billions of dollars there could not conceivably be doing so without help from politicians, businessmen, and forces of the law. They "probably had relations and connections" with the German establishment, admitted director Zachert two years later. "We have suspicions, not proofs, that our institutions are compromised," he told a conference in Rome.[36]

There was no longer any doubt, then, that Germany's police were beginning to succumb. In heavily populated North Rhine-Westphalia, beset by Yugoslav, Turkish, Polish, Russian, and Italian as well as German hoods, one in every five organized crime cases reaching court involved corrupt cops.[37]

Within a remarkably short time all of Chancellor Kohl's presentiments were coming true. Germany was "the face of a criminal Europe without frontiers," warned an association of Italian businessmen in a chilling survey of the Continent's underworld scene.[38] More perilously exposed than any of the EC twelve save Italy, it embodied their paralyzing state of unreadiness to meet the enemy.

Apart from reasons of self-interest common to all, it was a victim of its admirable intentions. Repelled by memories of Hitler's brutal police state, German lawmakers had gone as far as they could in the opposite direction.

"Why did your people choose Germany?" director Zachert would ask Tommaso Buscetta, the Sicilian Mafia's most celebrated defector, after discovering its shocking strength there. Because of Germany's "excessively punctilious legislation" and "total lack of regulations for money laundering" was Buscetta's reply.[39]

Indeed, Germany's legal code was an iron defense of the individual's right to be safe from government intrusion.

Datenschutz, the basic law protecting privacy, was sweeping, rigid, and seemingly unalterable. German police could not use phone taps except in life-threatening or serious property damage situations. They were flatly forbidden to put a bug in a wall. They could not wear body mikes except in self-defense, or present such tapes in court even then. They could not effect surreptitious entry under court order. They could not infiltrate an undercover agent without risking his likely death since he could do nothing illegal such as trespassing or betting in a poker game with the mob.

They were obliged to report a crime on sight—"to strike before the iron is hot," as a sympathetic American colleague put it. They could not make a move without convincing evidence that a crime was about to be committed. They could not check a suspect's bank records. They could not investigate tips on money laundering, which was not a criminal offense.

Such strictures meant that the BKA, though forewarned, could not listen in when delegates from the American mafia's Patriarca Family of Boston met with German counterparts in a Wiesbaden hotel to talk about gambling casinos.[40] Nor could it open a file on the Sicilian mafioso with orders from Palermo to buy up everything in East Berlin. Nor, despite urgent signals from the Italian police, could it go after a lengthening list of others investing dirty money in the East; the source of the money could not be questioned.[41]

An American judge's request to freeze $20 million of suspected drug money in a German bank account could not be granted.

Two Turkish drug traffickers caught by border guards with $700,000 in cash could keep the cash and run. (They did not even lose their social welfare checks as registered political refugees since cross-information among German agencies was not permitted.)[42]

These laws, sacrosanct in a resolutely free society, were being used to beat the law and savage the society. With exemplary intentions, Germany had become a privileged sanctuary for every kind of international crook.

The fact that many of the crooks invading Germany answered to one or another of the big international syndicates—Sicilian, Turkish, Colombian, Chinese, Russian—was just beginning to register, but not the fact that the syndicates were joining forces. Secret criminal brotherhoods in planetary communion might have been a script for a bad movie. Most Western investigators would have taken the idea for fiction in 1990. A handful, mainly Italian, had reason to know better.

Early that year Italy's Parliamentary Anti-Mafia Commission had sent an urgent message to the U.N. Assembly. Organized crime was "taking on the characteristics of an extremely dangerous world calamity," the commission said:

> International criminal organizations have reached agreements and understandings to divide up geographical areas, develop new market strategies, work out forms of mutual assistance and the settlement of conflicts . . . and this on a planetary level.
>
> We are faced with a genuine criminal counter-power, capable of imposing its will on legitimate states, of undermining institutions and forces of law and order, of upsetting delicate economic and financial equilibrium and destroying democratic life.[43]

The report dropped like a lead balloon at the time. Later, when the signs grew more insistent, the press took to speaking of a "Euromafia," presumably under the Sicilian Mafia's command. This was unfair to the Mafia's big-league colleagues. Obviously, the criminal legions advancing on Europe were not solely under Sicilian command. But they *deferred* to the Sicilians, as all law enforcement agencies on the Continent agreed. The Mafia's structure, sophistication, and connections in the outside world, its lines of command binding Europe to America, the subtlety of its hold on men and its extraordinary staying power came closer than any to meeting the needs of the times. It was organized crime's "role model for the year 2000," Italy's interior minister said.

PART II

A Meeting of Like Minds

CHAPTER FOUR

The Sicilian Mafia Looks East

"If you want to know if I worry about dying, I began to worry as soon as I joined. Everybody worries about dying in Sicily. Once the bosses used to die in their beds, now nobody dies in his bed anymore." This was Leonardo Messina, the Man of Honor with impressive credentials and exalted connections, describing the Sicilian Mafia's long slide into manic distrust and coarse butchery.[1]

He was testifying at a time of intense drama, in the months following the terrible murders of Judges Giovanni Falcone and Paolo Borsellino in the spring of 1992.[2] Not in more than a hundred years of killing had the Mafia killed with such satanic ferocity: a hundred pounds of explosive to blow up Judge Falcone, his wife, and three bodyguards; a bomb for Judge Borsellino blasting the walls of four apartment buildings up to the tenth floor.

Two hundred and eighty mafiosi had broken their blood oath of *omertà* since then, and crossed over to the side of the law. Some were sickened by the Mafia's growing savagery; others were simply running for their lives. They described a criminal fraternity in the grip of a tyrant bent on destroying all that preceded his rule—a whole generation of Mafia bosses and soldiers, a timeless Family structure, a fruitful partnership with Italy's governing class going back half a century—indeed, the very survival of what Messina called "historical memory" in the ranks of Cosa Nostra.

The tyrant was Salvatore "Totò" Riina, nicknamed "the Beast," soon to fall into the hands of the state he had plundered, manipulated, and humiliated for twenty years. Chosen heir of the notorious Luciano Leggio, imprisoned since 1974, Riina had presided over the longest era of ferocious bloodletting in Mafia history. The Great Mafia War of 1981–83, which he won, had left over a thousand of his enemies dead: shot, strangled, burned, beaten, tortured, dismembered, beheaded, trussed like a goat, hacked with an axe, dissolved in acid, barbecued on a grill, thrown to the pigs.

The Mafia's parallel war against the Italian state in those years, which he led, had featured the murders of five judges, a prosecutor-general, a state prosecutor, two police chiefs, a colonel, and a captain of the Carabinieri, a crusading journalist, the Christian Democratic Party's provincial secretary, the Communist Party's regional secretary, the president of Sicily's regional government, and the prefect of Sicily, General Carlo Alberto Dalla Chiesa, the state's highest representative on the island.[3]

Neither war ever ended. Other judges, prosecutors, journalists, and policemen were murdered periodically before Falcone and Borsellino went down; and after finishing off his enemies within Mafia ranks, Riina took to killing off his allies.

Nobody was safe from his corroding suspicion after the earliest defectors appeared. The death sentence for them was extended not only to their close relatives but to their friends and mere acquaintances. Agents of Riina's personal intelligence service were planted secretly among Sicily's 150 Mafia Families from then on.[4] Riina's Mafia was more frightening and mysterious than anything in Italy's experience when the new defectors appeared. Exposed briefly to the light after the Great Mafia War, it had quickly snapped shut again.

Earlier defectors in the 1980s, known as *pentiti*, had had their day in court. The Pizza Connection case had knocked out top leaders of their heroin network in the United States. Judge Falcone and his small pool of investigators had sent 474 Mafia defendants to trial in

Palermo; 323 had been convicted in 1987 and sentenced to some twenty-six centuries in jail. Yet barely a year after Palermo's historic maxi-trial, it might never have happened. Judge Falcone's anti-Mafia pool was dismantled, investigation was at a standstill, and the Mafia was going from strength to strength.

In a grotesque parody of justice, Italy's Corte di Cassazione, the highest court of appeal, had overturned 480 Mafia convictions since 1986. Only 60 of the 342 mafiosi found guilty were still in custody (down to ten by 1992). The others had either gotten out provisionally and vanished, or gotten out, period. (In January 1992 a member of the Cupola, sentenced to life imprisonment for ninety-nine murders, strolled out of a Palermo hospital in his pajamas, leaving his cellular phone on the bed.)[5]

The fact that these criminals could walk free was not just a joke on Italian justice. The entire structure of Mafia power depended on this freedom. One reason was its need to project an image beyond human reach: a disembodied, malevolent power dealing death and destruction, impervious to the law. But its more pressing need was to protect its own men. Sicily's Men of Honor had to be sure they would not go to prison, or if they did, would not stay long. Their methods of assuring this had worked smoothly since the midnineteenth century (except for a brief interlude under Mussolini).

Today we know the secret of their seemingly miraculous recovery from every legal affliction. The fix was in. The new *pentiti* have explained exactly how it was done.

The trials were "adjusted," Messina said:

> Why didn't Cosa Nostra give a damn when the maxi-trial began? Because we knew it would end in a soap bubble; that was the word passing around to tranquilize our men.
>
> The word was out that this trial, like all the others, would go a certain way in the lower court. . . . But everybody knew it would have to go well in the Corte di Cassazione. . . .
>
> Why did we kill Judge Scopelliti, who was going to be

the prosecutor in the Corte di Cassazione? Because he was talked to, and he wouldn't promise to take the right line.

When a Man of Honor has to go on trial, everybody on the bench and on the jury is "talked to." We talk directly to the judge. There are judges who've been contacted by Cosa Nostra, who wouldn't promise to let us off. They were killed on the street. . . .

When they can't control judges, they kill them. Look how many have been killed—count them.[6]

So while a handful of judges and cops laid their lives on the line to fight the Mafia, its men could feel free to kill them off with impunity. "If I'm a mafioso killer and I know the trial can be *adjusted*, I'll get more arrogant, no? That's why we're so arrogant, because we always knew the trials could be adjusted," Gaspare Mutolo, another important defector, testified.[7]

In January 1992, however, this time-tested arrangement broke down. The Corte di Cassazione upheld the verdict in Palermo's maxi-trial.[8] Men of Honor convicted but out of jail were hauled back in. The politician serving as the Mafia's main liaison with Rome had failed to deliver.

The Mafia's first response to this electrifying event was to kill the politician who had failed to deliver. Salvo Lima, Sicily's top Christian Democrat and longtime spokesman for Prime Minister Giulio Andreotti, was gunned down on the streets of Palermo. His death was an arrow in the heart of the Italian establishment. Many believed it was a direct message to Andreotti, the most powerful politician in the country since World War II. It was primarily because of his enduring relations with Lima that Andreotti came under judicial investigation afterward for an allegedly "positive contribution," neither "episodic nor marginal," to the Mafia's "interests and aims."[9] Lima was a made member of the Mafia, a secret revealed months after his murder. Guarantor of Andreotti's electoral base in Sicily for a quarter of a century, he was described by several important defectors in 1992 as "our best guarantee that everything could be settled in Rome."[10]

The verdict in Palermo's maxi-trial was by far the most urgent matter to be settled in many years. When the Corte di Cassazione upheld the verdict instead of reversing it as expected, the Cupola decided that Lima "was no longer any use to us," Messina said. "We had to show that anyone who doesn't keep his word must die. Cosa Nostra is like that."

Salvo Lima could not keep his word because the Palazzo, the faceless command of the Italian establishment, could not keep its end of the bargain anymore. With the collapse of communism in Eastern Europe, the whole structure of political power in Italy was coming undone. Fear of communism had held the governing parties together and kept them in office since the start of the Cold War. Once the fear was gone, voters might feel free to toss them out of office.

For fifty years they had preferred to coexist rather than collide with the Mafia. Some politicians might have hated the thought, but they managed to live with it. Those who ran the Palazzo were active accomplices, providing political and judicial cover in exchange for votes, power, and a share in Mafia payoffs.

By court estimate, the Mafia had upward of half a million captive votes in Sicily alone: one in every five or so on the island, one in every two polled by Christian Democrats, the swing vote for a tenth of the national electorate. With its allies on the southern Italian mainland, it controlled or conditioned around three and a half million votes altogether—a third of southern Italy's.[11] Regularly, at election time, the top Mafia brass decided how to hand the votes out, as dozens of *pentiti* have explained.[12]

Since the Mafia always collects, it was paid off in a thousand ways, with rigged public contracts, giveaway state credits, pork-barrel jobs, plummy government posts, golden gifts of silence, and "adjusted" trials guaranteeing its perpetual immunity.

Nobody suspected until 1993 how much help the Mafia may have had in such matters from a singularly potent deviate wing of the Masons—how smoothly the two had meshed in penetrating to the innermost circles of the Italian establishment.

Defectors now claim that in 1977 a covered Masonic lodge formally invited the Mafia to enroll two members from each of its provinces in Sicily, guaranteeing secrecy. (A covered Masonic lodge is a secret one whose membership is not revealed to anyone, even within the Masonic community.) The invitation was debated at a regional Mafia conference and finally accepted, on condition that the Mafia would learn the Masons' secrets but not the other way around. Nearly all the top bosses joined, defectors said.[13]

"Men of Honor who get to be bosses belong to the Masonry. This must not escape you," Messina told the Anti-Mafia Commission. "Because it is in the Masonry that we can have total contact with businessmen, with the institutions, with the men who administer power." Indeed, Messina added, this secret Masonic connection is "an obligatory passage for the Mafia on a world level."[14]

Through any of Palermo's fourteen covered Masonic lodges, among others, the Mafia could in fact reach up to Licio Gelli's now defunct Propaganda Due, the P2, and so to the topmost levels of the Palazzo.[15] (A stupefying list of P2 members found in 1981 included seventeen army generals, four air force generals, nine Carabinieri generals, eight admirals, the heads of all three secret services, thirty-eight deputies and senators, fourteen magistrates, three cabinet ministers, and five prefects.)[16]

No amount of rumor and speculation over the years could match the reality, as the new *pentiti* provided a lengthening list of politicians, judges, policemen, and intelligence agents forming an intricate web of complicity enmeshing the Mafia with Italy's governing class. This was why, despite Totò Riina's unrelenting assault on the state, the Italian establishment was compliant throughout his long reign.

But even a governing class so deeply compromised could no longer resist the pressure for change by January 1992, and not just from its own electorate. Chancellor Kohl knew by then that the Sicilian Mafia was using Germany as its operational base for Europe. He was not the only one leaning hard on Andreotti's government to bear down on it; the whole European Community was doing so. The community's inner borders would be coming down in just another year. Italy's foreign minister, Gianni De Michelis, confronted by blunt-spoken colleagues in a swing around EC capitals, came back shaken in 1991. Italy, "cradle of organized crime in Europe," was "the biggest single risk to the community's security in an open market," declared a majority of the European Parliament's deputies that year.[17]

Starting in the winter of 1992, therefore, the government moved to close some legislative loopholes, coordinate police work, protect defectors turning state's witness, close down dubiously elected city councils in the south, and bar Mafia-prone politicians from office. Somebody also saw to the Corte di Cassazione when the maxi-trial came up on appeal. The court's incorrigible sentence-basher, Corrado Carnevale—the untouchable judge who had thrown out 480 Mafia convictions since 1986—was taken off the case.[18] Carnevale had been "Cosa Nostra's guarantee" in Italy's highest court, the *pentiti* said later. "When we were told, 'Carnevale's there,' we'd say, 'Jesus be praised!' " Mutolo declared. "This defeat was like a poison to us. We had to overturn everything—the judiciary, the political world."[19]

Upon Carnevale's removal and the subsequent court ruling, the Mafia broke off relations with its old political partners. The Cupola's choice of strategy was an ultimate declaration of war, the supreme expression of Totò Riina's preference for military force over other forms of persuasion. The Mafia was dismissing the politicians and parties it had used for half a century and setting out to find new ones who would get the point—come to terms, give up all thoughts of resistance, back off.

The strategy was worked out at a conclave of top bosses lasting some three months in the Sicilian province of Enna.[20] The death of Salvo Lima immediately afterward was a warning. The real message came when the highest symbols of resistance to the Mafia, Judges Falcone and Borsellino, were literally blown away in a deliberately terrifying show of strength.

Totò Riina, all modesty in his wilted shirt and crumpled pants, rising to his feet deferentially to answer a judge's questions, looked as if he needed help to read and write. Yet during his reign the Mafia had grown into an impenetrably complicated corporate monster.

Contrary to the school of wishful thinkers, the Mafia has not been crowded out of the heroin trade. Although its dominion over the world market is gone, it still has "the central role in controlling the internal market and traditional traffic with the United States," said Italy's Interior Ministry.[21] Heroin and cocaine are still "its principal source of income at home and abroad," but the Mafia has diversified. Its strength can no longer be measured by conventional crime statistics in a single country—certainly not in Italy alone. It operates in dozens of countries and spreads its wealth among them in a thousand undetectable ways.

The days are gone when its finances were entrusted to a couple of identifiable crooked bankers such as Michele Sindona and Roberto Calvi, both of whom died for failing to deliver. (See Chapter 12.) Today the Mafia not only uses hundreds of bankers, it buys banks.[22] Its members take along financial advisers in their travels abroad and live in good part on the income from a mountain of accumulated capital.

"Drugs have made us immensely rich," testified Leonardo Messina. "When a heroin deal is on, the Families are asked if they want to chip in. There are some who chipped in two hundred million lire long ago, and in three years they had twenty-five billion. The fathers die and leave it to their sons."

By now, therefore, the Mafia has reached a "third level" in its financial affairs, say Italian authorities. It no longer depends wholly on crime for a livelihood. Half of its revenue comes from laundered capital reinvested in legitimate enterprises around the globe: financial and leasing companies, real estate, commerce, industry, agro-industry, gold mines.[23] Not that the Mafia is going straight. As Judge Falcone said shortly before he died, "A mafioso never ceases to be a mafioso." Legitimate enterprise is used to cover the illegitimate kind, as always.

Since such foreign revenues are largely untraceable, the only estimates available are those of its gross *domestic* product in Italy: $20 billion to $25 billion a year. Drugs account for only a fifth of that. Extortion, public works contracts, bank robberies, and theft account roughly for another fifth each, and fraud, gambling, prostitution, and smuggling for most of the rest.[24] The fraud has included swindling the EC out of a quarter of a billion dollars just for grain in 1992.[25] The Mafia's worldwide money laundries and arms traffic are not included in these figures.

The figures are supposed to take in four Italian organized crime groups, but the four are really one, defectors say. Messina declared,

> There is only Cosa Nostra; the others are simply a manner of speaking. You can call it Camorra or 'Ndrangheta or Sacra Corona Unita [the younger United Sacred Crown, C.S.], but those are just expressions. The structure is always Cosa Nostra. . . .
>
> The people you call camorristi belong to Cosa Nostra. The summit of the Camorra is Cosa Nostra; the summit of the 'Ndrangheta is Cosa Nostra.
>
> The Mafia *invented* the Sacra Corona Unita. The 'Ndrangheta is only a name; the Sacra Corona is a nickname.[26]

Together, the Mafia and its wards have about fifteen thousand members and perhaps ten times as many helpers, occupying the contiguous regions of Sicily, Calabria, Apulia, and Campania, surrounding Naples. These are called the "regions at risk" in that the Mafia controls the territory there—the entire southern third of the country—in which the government cannot enforce the law.[27] Controlling the territory means "knowing and preventing the maneuvers of an adversary, exercising dominion over the population, practicing extortion, imposing recognition as the authority that knows everything and can do everything," said the Parliamentary Anti-Mafia Commission.[28]

In this third of Italy, three of every four businessmen pay the monthly *pizzo*. They have even been assured officially that it is legal. In a ruling that scandalized the press and public, a Sicilian magistrate has held that owners of a business have a right to avoid "conflictuality," by which he meant being burned down, bombed out, or shot.

"Whoever doesn't pay should know what happens sooner or later. Somebody in the Rinascente Department Store group refused to pay, and forty billion lire went up in smoke. If everybody did that, all Sicily would go up in smoke," the magistrate said (whereupon Palermo's Chamber of Commerce proposed to make protection payments tax deductible).[29]

This is no longer the old-fashioned shakedown; it is the way in for a commercial kill. "First they ask you for money . . . maybe 400, 600, or 800 million lire ($700,000), then they offer you loans at low interest or none, they tell you what suppliers to use, they make you hire their friends. Finally they tell you they're joining your company, then they take everything," said the president of Catania's Association of Industrialists.[30] Or else they buy up all the company's outstanding debts and then come around with their enforcer-bailiffs to collect or take over. (Perhaps they learned this trick from the Yakuza, who have done this for years.)

Nobody in the Italian south gets a public works contract unless the Mafia says so—at least up to now. Until its exposure in 1993, Sicily's entire multi-billion-dollar public works program was controlled directly by the Mafia through a regularly constituted company called Sirap. Founded a decade earlier in the office of Salvo Lima, who headed it, Sirap awarded the contracts, collected the rakeoffs, and parcelled them out in fixed percentages.

The contracts were allocated in Lima's office and rubber-stamped by city councils or Sicily's Regional Assembly. Consenting politicians received their cut, but a Mafia "ambassador" dispensed it, answering directly to Totò Riina.[31] There were no competing bids. "If somebody gets in the way, he dies," explained Leonardo Messina. Northern companies coming south had to "adjust to Cosa Nostra's ways," Messina added, and they did. Fiat, building a $6 billion car plant in San Nicola di Melfi, reportedly paid a 7 percent commission at every stage of construction. The Roman earthmoving company laying the plant's sewer network allegedly shelled out $200,000 up front and $16,000 monthly thereafter.[32]

*　　*　　*

The Mafia was able to get away with this for fifty years because many northern Italians saw it as a peculiarly Sicilian phenomenon; it was dangerous, violent, grasping, stifling, arrogant, but workable in the poor, backward, derelict south. Once it became a national incubus—the source of a nationwide narcotics epidemic, an arbiter of the nation's finance, a direct menace to the nation's governing class and threat to its credibility in Europe—opinions changed.

As all Italy knows now, the Mafia has been implanted in every major city north of Naples for a long time. In the course of 1992, police uncovered a cell in wealthy Bologna led by Totò Riina's eighty-four-year-old uncle, in command of all Mafia cells in the region for two decades. Another cell, near civilized Florence, managed a weapons supermarket. A third, in the prosperous Tuscan town of Prato, operated a busy money-laundering machine.

A joint police survey throughout affluent Tuscany found Mafia investments in factories (Prato), hotels (Versilia, Montecatini, Terme di Chianciano), fisheries (Viareggio), marble (Carrara), and the splendid vineyards around Siena.[33] A consortium of all four crime groups was found to be running drugs and arms for the entire north out of a Milanese car park that autumn; a ton of cocaine was on the way there when police arrived.[34]

Milan has always been the big attraction. Capital of the wealthiest region on the Continent, this is the most sophisticated and European of Italian cities—the nerve center of industry and banking, the nation's window on the financial world, the natural channel to the money markets of Frankfurt, London, Tokyo, and New York.

By the 1980s, Milan had become a crossroads for Europe's drug traffic and the epicenter of its arms trade, racked by violent crime and awash in dirty money. Some twenty-five thousand *picciotti*—helpers, peons—are working the region for the Mafia and its affiliates today, the Parliamentary Anti-Mafia Commission says.

Narcodollars are flooding through Milan's banking system, stock market, and legitimate business—"rivers of it," according to Confindustria, the Italian manufacturers' association.[35] "If not a single dirty lira remained in the stock market, trading would drop 15 percent," an authoritative source told the Anti-Mafia Commission.[36] Huge amounts are invested in anonymous government bonds, which finance Italy's enormous national debt. Buying and selling these in great blocks, the Mafia can condition the value of the lira, says Italy's Interior Ministry.[37] "There are operations here forcing the money market up and down to recycle dubious capital," says Milan's prosecutor-general, Francesco Saverio Borelli.[38]

The Mafia is "taking over the market, taking over commerce, taking over real estate, taking control of the territory," says FIPE, the Italian federation of bar and restaurant owners.[39] Half of FIPE's 210,000 members are paying the *pizzo*—more than half. Their stories have a dreary sameness: threats of an "accident," then the broken windows or burned cars, the loans at low or no interest, the demand for shares in the company, the takeover—just as in the south.

Many victims are driven to the edge of bankruptcy, FIPE reports. "They're taking 30 percent of everything out of my pocket," a Milanese restaurateur testified. "When I tried to say it was ruining me, they left a pack of bloody syringes at my door with a note saying, 'Be good or next time we'll put AIDS under your skin.' "[40]

No judge seemed able to lay a finger on them until 1992. (Among other things, they had encouraged the destruction of incriminating records in Milan's courthouse by leaving bits of cheese among the pages for resident rats; so we are told by the president of the Chamber of Commerce.)[41]

In 1992, however, a spectacular court case known as the Duomo Connection exposed the workings of just one crime ring in Milan. Its leaders were ranking members of Cosa Nostra and the 'Ndrangheta, connected to the Cupola in Palermo and the powerful clan of Santo Pasquale Morabito in Calabria.

With kidnap ransom money from Calabria, they were paying for cocaine imported from Argentina, laundering the proceeds in Switzerland, and reinvesting the money in Milanese real estate. At the same time they were bringing in heroin by truck from Turkey and importing weapons—Kalashnikovs, Uzis, Walthers, and carbines—from Switzerland for distribution to the Camorra in Naples.

Meanwhile, they had set up thirty finance and real estate companies, running at a generous profit from no apparent source. With part of the proceeds they had built an entire residence complex in a Milanese suburb, after bribing officials to falsify papers, speed up their permits, and alter the city's whole urban development plan. In violation of the city plan, furthermore, they acquired permits to build thirty hotels for the expected throng of viewers for the World Soccer Cup, only one of which was open in time for the games.[42]

To be fair, they were not the only ones. Milan, known now as Tangentopoli for its generous political *tangenti*, or payoffs, has turned out to be one of the world's leading payola capitals. Exposed in 1992, it touched off the most thunderous judicial investigation in Italian history.

"Operation Clean Hands," led by three unflappable young magistrates, showed that a huge percentage of Milan's officials were on the take. Eventually the same pattern emerged throughout the country.[43]

In or out of office, politicians on the mainland were doing exactly as the Mafia did. For at least a decade they had exacted a percentage on all public works contracts, based on a sliding scale, the money divided with mathematical equity among governing and opposition parties.

Spreading from Milan to Venice, Turin, Rome, Naples, and Reggio Calabria, Tangentopoli has become legitimate Italy's own monster. Five former prime ministers, a host of former cabinet members, and nearly three thousand other politicians and businessmen were accused, indicted, or jailed for corruption by mid-1993; the nation's entire governing class has been devastated.[44] In the south, from Naples down, the graft proved to be under joint management by politicians and the Mafia, Camorra, or 'Ndrangheta. In Milan, however, only a tenuous if intriguing connection has come to light. Both the city's crooked politicians and the Mafia were using the same Swiss office, Li-Mo, to launder their money.[45]

If nothing else, though, the Mafia could turn the pandemonium in Milan to good use.

Major industries engaged in public works were paralyzed when the Tangentopoli story broke; hundreds of large and small companies came to a standstill. As a first batch of company directors and politicians were led off to jail, the president of Milan's Chamber of Commerce set alarm bells ringing.

"The banks are cutting off credit to the companies in trouble, but the Mafia has the money to buy them out. It is happening in these days, in these hours," he warned.[46]

Italy became too small for the Mafia long ago, but no government anywhere knew how far it was spreading abroad until the 1990s. Even then, most were inclined to say it was all Italy's fault. Actually, the Mafia's men have found sanctuary, complicity, and safety from the law wherever they have gone, in Europe especially.

Europe's guilt, going back decades, should have shamed its leaders in 1992, in a case provoking some hilarity instead. That winter, Italy's finance minister took an outraged but futile swipe at the Camorra by banning the sale of Philip Morris cigarettes. Since World War II, the Camorra has had a black market monopoly on Philip Morris tobacco in Italy, more or less the size of the state's monopoly and growing.[47] Several million Italian smokers are pleased to dodge a 65 percent tax on their favorite Marlboros by buying them on the black market; nearly half a million earn a living by selling them; twenty-five thousand smugglers bring them in by speedboat and truck.

Consequently, popular fury erupted when Marlboros disappeared from state tobacco shops, and the Camorra's street corner stands came under astounding police scrutiny. The foreign press jeered. The Philip Morris Company appealed to the European Commission in Brussels. The commission, at its bureaucratic worst, pronounced the ban in contravention of free trade.[48] Forced to back down, Finance Minister Rino Formica made one last try: He offered a government job to any tobacco smuggler willing to go straight. Just one took him up; not enough money, the others said.

Colossal stakes were riding on this seemingly comic exercise: a billion-dollar-a-year profit on black market tobacco, another billion in lost taxes for the state. On top of that, the black market cigarette trade is closely linked to an international narcotics trade worth far more and to an exceptional international chain of money laundries.[49]

The Camorra's contraband tobacco moves through an elaborate circuit from Switzerland, Belgium, and Holland (manufacturing states) to Hungary, Romania, Bulgaria, and Turkey (storage depots) to Yugoslavia and Albania (staging areas for the final run across the Adriatic into Italy). This circuit in reverse constitutes the famous Balkan route. The biggest two-way trade in arms and drugs ever uncovered has depended on it since the 1960s. Three-quarters of the heroin reaching Western Europe and a substantial portion of America's travels along it.

It was the Balkan route and the money in Marlboros that brought the Sicilian Mafia into partnership with the Camorra in 1974. The capital was needed to bankroll the Mafia's grand entrance into the worldwide heroin market. The smuggling circuit was tested, manned, and demonstrably safe from surveillance across nine national frontiers. A year later the Sicilians sealed their pact with the Turkish arms-drugs Mafia in a village near the Yugoslav-Italian border, whereupon morphine base and heroin started to roll back over the same frontiers.[50]

In the two decades since then, smuggled tobacco has kept moving more or less freely over these nine frontiers. Police and customs agents look for the heroin; the tobacco usually passes. The billion-dollar cash flow finances an army of drug couriers, heavy investments on the French Riviera, and the extravagant plans of the Camorra's tobacco kingpin, Don Michele Zaza, a wonder at staying out of jail.

Known as Michele 'U Pazzu—Crazy Michael—the not so crazy Camorra boss is also a ranking member of the Sicilian Mafia, sworn in by the Cupola's "Pope" himself in 1974. Indeed, defectors have fingered Zaza as the Mafia's liaison with the Camorra for their shared traffic in heroin and cocaine. Falsely humble, illiterate, shifty, and garrulous, Zaza managed to befuddle and elude the police of his three favorite countries—Italy, France, and the United States—for three decades.

The best years of his life began in 1984 when, after a short stay in an Italian prison, he got himself transferred to a Rome clinic, walked out casually, and moved to France. He had always run a good part of his tobacco and drug trades from the French Riviera; the Camorra and the Mafia had been firmly planted there since the 1960s. By the late 1980s he had a mammoth operation going along the Côte d'Azur from Nice to Marseilles. From there, reported a special commission of the French parliament in 1993, Zaza "led an organization grouping some thirty companies in Europe, the United States, South America, Panama, and the island of Saint Martin, with perfect logistics for transport over a good part of the planet."[51]

The Caribbean island of Saint Martin is also known as Sint Maarten. Formerly under French and Dutch colonial rule, the island is divided into two sovereign states under the respective wings of their former rulers. Each has privileged access to the European Community, meaning free entry with no police checks or customs clearance. Both states have fallen into Mafia hands since the conquest of nearby Aruba, which also enjoys free access to the EC. Sint Maarten is largely used to move drugs; Saint Martin, to launder the proceeds.[52]

Sint Maarten was a key port of call in Don Michele Zaza's new itinerary for shipping dope. His containers of cigarettes traveled in trucks as far as Marseilles, where the cigarettes were offloaded and replaced with heroin. Then the containers were shipped to Sint Maarten, for relay to Aruba with easy access to the American mainland. Calling at Panama and Venezuela on the return trip, the same vessels were taking on cocaine bound for Spain and Italy.[53]

Zaza had five companies in the port of Marseilles for this purpose, the French parliamentary commission found: "one for transport, one for customs clearance, one for maintenance of the containers, one for transporting the containers, and one for the organization's own trade"—heroin going out and cocaine coming in. There was "good reason to believe that the organization also controlled several shipping companies, such as the Dutch-owned Nordana Lines," the commission said.

To launder their profits, Zaza's Camorra-Mafia crowd in France used to operate through luxurious private clinics around Marseilles until American DEA agents came snooping around. In the autumn of 1989, therefore, bosses of the Camorra, the Mafia, and the Corsican Milieu (the Mob) gathered in Marseilles to plan a switch to casinos.[54] Using a front company called Sofextour based in Monte Carlo, they were going after eight major casinos along the French coast, the Commission said, starting with the famous one at Menton, to be flanked by new luxury hotels. Even without fixing the games, they would have netted close to a billion dollars a year and laundered as much or more through the most elegant set of laundries on the Continent.

Everything was lined up by the spring of 1991—real estate, banks, notaries, accommodating police inspectors, croupiers— when a thousand land, sea, and airborne troops of the French and Italian police made dawn raids on Paris, Marseilles, Nice, Cannes, Menton, and Naples. Fifty men were arrested, not including Don Michele. He was in a French jail already, at last, for running a truckload of Marlboros (471,000 packs) from Holland to France. With thirteen previous convictions in Italy for drug trafficking, multiple homicide, and so on—only one of which had landed him briefly in jail—Michele 'U Pazzu had been a fugitive, in a manner of speaking, since 1984.[55] From then until 1989 he had traveled around undisturbed in his bulletproof Rolls-Royce and lived in a sumptuous villa on the French Riviera. (His million-dollar mansion in Beverly Hills had been rented out to the French consulate in California since the early 1980s when he had fled the United States a step ahead of the DEA.)[56]

Repeated Italian requests for his extradition after he had settled on the Riviera failed to move French authorities, who showed no particular interest in his Marseilles drug business, either. He was given just three years in France for running tobacco and was out in two for "certified heart trouble." During his short stay in prison, he continued to collect rent from the French consulate in California for his million-dollar Beverly Hills mansion.[57]

Back in his sumptuous villa on the Riviera, Zaza took up just where he had left off. For the next two years he ran a $2 billion Camorra-Mafia money laundry through a huge network of legitimate French and Italian companies.[58]

The French sent Zaza back to jail in the spring of 1993, an apparently sincere if belated act of penance. It was no longer possible to ignore the dangerous presence of the Mafia and Camorra in France or anywhere in Europe.

Starting that spring, they lost their lifelong immunity in Italy itself. Up to then, Mafia bosses supposedly in hiding were visiting colleagues in Palermo's Ucciardone prison, walking freely around the island's capital, dining in deluxe restaurants, and living within blocks—yards—of their family homes.

In 1993 they were picked off one by one. Totò Riina was the most spectacular catch, but police also caught up with Riina's number two: the vicious Nitto Santapaola of Catania, who once had four kids strangled for snatching his mother's purse. Riina's number three, Giuseppe Madonia of Gela, was intercepted as he was slipping off to Germany with a suitcase full of deutsche marks.

The boss who had walked out of a clinic in his pajamas, Pietro Vernengo, was recaptured within a few months. Gaetano Fidanzati, a fixture in the intercontinental dope trade for forty years, was tracked down in Argentina. The Cuntrera brothers were flown back from Caracas in handcuffs.

Francesco "Ciccio" Madonia, whose emissary had set up the Colombian deal in Aruba, was not only captured but stripped of his worldly goods: 250 bank accounts, 202 buildings, 62 commercial companies, 262 cars including a Ferrari, a Maserati, and a Rolls-Royce, 43 valuable real estate plots, and 6 yachts anchored in the Gulf of Palermo.[59]

The Camorra lost not only Zaza in France but its reigning prince in Naples, Carmine Alfieri. A self-made billionaire who read Dante and collected Impressionist paintings, Alfieri complimented the police for finding him in a hiding place under the floor of his villa. His own number two, Pasquale Galasso, was captured soon afterward and talked, ending the careers of nearly all the politicians who mattered in the city. For the first time since the Sicilian Mafia was born nearly a century and a half before, Men of Honor who went to jail realized that they were going to stay there.

In the first half of 1993 the crime rate in Italy fell 20 percent below the previous year's rate. The drop in Italy's southern "regions at risk" was 38 percent.[60] These seemingly miraculous achievements were all the more extraordinary for coming at the worst moment in Italy's postwar history. The economy was in deep crisis, the lira was in a free fall, the Tangentopoli scandal was at its height, and the parties governing Italy for forty years were hitting bottom.

Whether because or in spite of its approaching demise, the old order in the Palazzo surrendered. Unseen but insurmountable obstacles to a resolute war on the Mafia fell away: The police and judiciary were free to do what they then proceeded to do superbly well. They were spurred by a popular revolt such as Italy has rarely seen. When Judges Falcone and Borsellino were killed, not only grief but cold anger swept over the country—everywhere, but especially in Sicily. Sicilian students, schoolchildren, housewives, and tradesmen marched in the streets, hung out sheets in mourning, and spoke out on television. Many started to help the police, defying Sicily's ageless law of *omertà*.

Having brought this on itself, the Mafia appeared finally to have gone too far. But it is not an impulsive organization. As if defining the terms of his own death, Falcone had once explained that "Mafia violence must not be considered as a manifestation of gratuitous or unmediated cruelty, even in its most shocking forms. The Mafia always obeys a rigorous logic, or else it wouldn't be the formidable organization it is." Therefore, it must have calculated the odds.

The Mafia was "moving on a worldwide chessboard" in 1992, said Italy's Interior Ministry. This is where it stood when it killed Judge Falcone, the ministry reported:

It was taking on major new commitments in the drug trade; modernizing its "circuits of investment in legal enterprises"; expanding its extortion rackets; investing "hundreds of billions of lire" in government bearer bonds, bought through foreign banks. It was strengthening ties with other mafias abroad for drug trafficking and money washing, "especially on the American continent"; using Germany and Austria as "bridgeheads" to the east; "expanding massively" in Eastern Europe and Russia; reaching agreements with the Russian mafia and American Cosa Nostra for economic fraud there; bringing "colossal sums of dirty money" into Russia; trading narcodollars for rubles; going into "multiple ventures" in real estate throughout the former U.S.S.R.[61]

By the end of 1992 the Sicilian Mafia had in fact reached a secret agreement with the Russian mafia in Prague, confirmed by a high authority in Russia's Academy of Science. The pact was designed "to protect their new illicit trade throughout Central Europe, establish a global network for the drug trade and marketing of nuclear components, and create a lethal squad of killers" made up of ex-KGB agents, he said.[62]

In short, the Mafia was in a phase of intensive growth at home and imperialist expansion abroad; therefore, it could not afford to be *seen* to be on the defensive. Its first, imperative priority was to put on a show of overpowering strength. The point, then, was not merely to kill the Mafia's two strongest adversaries in Italy but to do so with maximum theatrical effect. The deaths of Giovanni Falcone and Paolo Borsellino were meant to impress a worldwide audience—and did.

Italy's response may have surprised, perhaps stunned, those who planned the attacks. The wave of defections and secrets betrayed, the rejection symptoms in their own Sicilian hinterland, the national army sent in to patrol Sicilian streets, the drastic new government decrees, incredible arrests, and what they considered the appalling confiscation of their wealth ($3 billion seized that year)—these things had to mean that the Mafia was hurting. Some defectors even thought it could be destroyed at last. "You must give them no room. You must give them no time. You have to crowd them. If you want to, you can win right now!" testified Leonardo Messina.

But the Mafia is not beaten yet, nor has it shown a sign of retreat. Men of Honor and their *picciotti* are still doing nearly everything they were doing before, says Criminalpol's Alessandro Pansa. Experts believe they are already finding new political partners in Rome. Judging from their military preparations, they have plainly set out to frighten the judiciary, the police, the governing class, and the public into surrender.

In sixty-nine raids on their various arms caches during the last four months of 1992, police found 377 machine guns, 291 pistols, 195 bombs and rocket launchers, and a ground-to-air missile, all made in Russia or elsewhere in Eastern Europe, along with over a ton of explosives and a half mile of fuse.[63]

Mysterious bombings, anonymous threats, planted rumors spreading fear and confusion, all point to a new strategy of terror—possibly this time with the help of what Italian authorities call "occult international forces," meaning the Mafia's powerful criminal confederates around the globe.

CHAPTER FIVE

The Russian Mafia Looks West

There are fifty ways of saying "to steal" in Russian, and the Russian mafia uses them all. Frustrated citizens claim it is the only institution that works in post-communist Russia. In any event, it is the world's largest, busiest, and possibly meanest collection of organized hoods. By last count it consisted of five thousand gangs and some three million helpers, controlling the territory in all fifteen of the former Soviet republics, covering eleven time zones and a sixth of the earth's land mass, now foraging far beyond as worldwide barriers fall.[1]

Its alarming proportions affect the whole tormented question of what the West should do about or for Russia and the rest of the former U.S.S.R. The mafia intrudes in every field of Western concern: the nascent free market, privatization, disarmament, conversion of the military-industrial complex, foreign humanitarian relief and financial aid, even state reserves of currency and gold. Furthermore, it has begun to intrude directly on the rest of Europe and the United States: "looking at the West as a wolf looks at sheep," an analyst observes.

This mafia is not the old nebula of common criminals, familiar since tsarist times, or even the more accomplished crooks of Brezhnev's day. It is a union of racketeers without equal. Unlike the true Mafia in Sicily, it has no home seat or central command, no hierarchical structure, ancestral memories, common bloodlines, sworn members. Yet its proliferating clans are invading every sphere of life, usurping political power, taking over state enterprises, fleecing the nation of its natural resources, engaged in extortion, theft, forgery, armed assault, contract killing, swindling, drug-running, arms smuggling, prostitution, gambling, loan-sharking, embezzling, money laundering, and black marketing—all this on a monumental and increasingly international scale.

Rising from the ruins of the Soviet empire, the new mafia has far outclassed the one flourishing under communist rule. That one, the Brezhnev solution for a stifling centralized economy, had provided illicit goods and services—primarily but not only for the Nomenklatura—by stealing from the state, buying protection, smuggling, cheating, bullying, and bribing its way straight into the Kremlin.

A team of a hundred investigators uncovered it, set loose by the KGB just before Brezhnev died, probing for the next five years. "We have run into a mafia," announced the team leader, Telman Gdlyan, finally to *Izvestia* in 1988. There followed the trial of the U.S.S.R.'s interior minister and his deputy, Yuri Churbanov, Brezhnev's son-in-law. Putting him in the dock caused a sensation, but Churbanov, greedy and foolish, was merely a political collector's item. His loot came from the mafia of Uzbekistan in Central Asia, three thousand kilometers from Moscow. Every party apparatus from the district *oblast* to the Central Committee of the Soviet Union was hooked in to the Uzbek mafia. Among the first to be caught was a member of the Soviet Interior Ministry's Anti-Corruption Squad in the Bukhara region; stashed at his home were diamonds, rubies, blue jeans, thousands of Swiss watches, a million rubles in pocket money, and a full mile's length of gold brocade.[2] His mafia boss, chairman of the presidium of Uzbekistan's Supreme Soviet, had squirreled away over two hundred pounds of gold bullion, five thousand gold coins of imperial mint, twelve thousand precious jewels, five cars, eleven TV sets, and hundreds of expensive furs.

The Uzbek mafia used to provide, for a fee, everything from military medals, decorations, dachas, and cemetery plots to Party membership cards, government posts, and seats on the presidium. Through faked "ceiling statistics" it extracted a quarter of a billion rubles from the state for a million tons of nonexistent cotton.[3]

Competing for pride of place with the Uzbek mafia was another in Azerbaijan on the Caspian Sea, this one headed by the Soviet Union's first deputy prime minister, Geidar Aliev. A full member of the Soviet Politburo, restored to power in Azerbaijan in 1993, he presided over a "petroleum mafia," a "fishing mafia," a "fruit and vegetable mafia," a "caviar mafia," a "railroad mafia," an "export mafia," a "customs mafia," and a "militia mafia" operating inside the Interior Ministry's Division for Fighting Violators of Socialist Property and Speculation.[4] Through these various branches the Azerbaijan mafia earned a king's ransom by poaching sturgeon, packing and exporting clandestine caviar, running underground factories with stolen state materials, and shipping its black market goods all over the Soviet Union.

All the regional mafias of Transcaucasia ran such illicit factories—often inside the state's own factories but free of taxes, overhead costs, and impossible production norms. "In my time I estimate that about a third of the clothing and shoes in the Caucasus were made underground," said the former head of the Prommontazh Trust order department. "During my career I bribed sixteen hundred people, of whom two-thirds were party, Soviet, and state enterprise officials. Criminals keep track of such things."[5]

Nobody was happier with the system than Brezhnev, comforted by a miraculous supply of consumer goods, glowing production figures, and due tribute for a ruler of his mold. Among the gifts showered on him by Azerbaijan's mafia boss was an outsized diamond ring encircled by smaller diamonds for each of the fifteen Soviet Republics, symbolizing "Brezhnev the Sun King." The boss of Uzbekistan gave him a solid gold bust four feet high.[6]

These revelations in 1988 were followed by a purge of over 100,000 police officers, 15 percent of the entire Soviet police force.[7]

This was *korruptsiya* communist style, a shared monopoly of power between politicians and crooks. Liberated Russia deserved better. But yesterday's politicians are still largely in place, yesterday's crooks are today's free entrepreneurs, and *korruptsiya*, spreading uncontrollably as things fall apart, has become the curse of a stricken nation. "Corruption is devouring the state from top to bottom," exclaimed Boris Yeltsin after watching it grow for a year.[8]

Everything about the former U.S.S.R. seems so much larger than life—its geography and ethnic diversity, its gifts from nature and man-made calamities, the dramatic sweep of its history, the magnitude of its misery—that facts and figures strain credibility. Some may think there are three too many zeroes or a misplaced decimal point in what follows. The numbers in this story of crime and corruption are bound to look unreal.

In 1991, the year of the communists' fall, the All-Union Research Institute of the Soviet Interior Ministry estimated that half the income of an average government functionary was coming from bribes, compared to "only 30 percent" before 1985.[9]

Some time before, the Soviet prosecutor-general informed the Second Congress of People's Deputies that "a third to a half of all heads of cooperatives" in most regions of the U.S.S.R. were probably embezzling funds. (These were state cooperatives with extremely limited autonomy, not the free-enterprise kind.) His office had indicted 225,000 officials on this charge, the prosecutor-general said. Of seventy found guilty in a single case, eighteen worked for the Department to Combat Embezzlement.[10]

Some twenty thousand police officers were being fired yearly for collusion with the mafia by 1991, double the rate under Brezhnev.[11] A Moscow Policeman of the Year was convicted of bribery.[12] Four out of five agents in the Soviet Interior Ministry's militia were thought to be on the take—this according to the head of the ministry's Sixth Department to Combat Organized Crime, Alexander Gurov. "There's no doubt that a third of the mafia's profits go to militiamen and our functionaries," he said.[13]

These were merely symptoms of a malignant growth pervading the economy, the banking system, and the body politic. Millions of ordinary citizens have succumbed, making off with state property, black marketing, swindling, and buying or selling protection. Obviously they aren't all tied to the mafia. Russia is so chaotic and broke that hardly anybody can stay honest and survive.

"You westerners may call this corruption, but we say *nishinstvo* in Russian, a term describing a poverty so desperate that one loses one's shame and moral compass," said Moscow's police chief in that first tremendous year of freedom.[14]

If not every lawbreaker is a mafioso, however, the mafia swims among them like a great predatory shark, recruiting some, exacting payoffs from others, frightening away any rival eyeing its prey. Insatiable and seemingly invulnerable, it is swallowing up factories, coops, privatized enterprises, real estate, raw materials, currency, gold—a quarter of Russia's economy in 1991, between a third and a half by 1992, according to Russian authorities, 40,000 privatized firms by 1993, according to Russia's Interior Ministry. By the end of 1992, "nearly two-thirds of Russia's commercial structure had ties to the growing criminal world"—this according to President Boris Yeltsin himself.[15]

Between 1989 and 1991, the last years of communist disintegration, the mafia's turnover shot up from less than a billion rubles to 130 billion—the size of the national deficit—reported the Interior Ministry's Alexander Gurov. "In the next few years its turnover will reach 200 billion rubles; organized crime will then control approximately 30 percent to 40 percent of the country's GNP," he warned at the time.[16]

The accompanying kill rate has climbed to a world record. Once, Soviet leaders had taunted America for its sixty-odd murders a day, a mark of capitalist depravity. By 1993 murders in the Russian Republic alone were running to over eighty a day—this not counting the other fourteen ex–Soviet republics.[17] Russia was getting to be such a dangerous place that its own prosecutor-general, Valentin Stepankov, advised every citizen "to defend himself by every means, and we won't ask if he's exceeding the limits of legitimate self-defense.

"It is very difficult to do work like mine in a country which has the most profound lack of respect for the law," he observed.[18]

Many of the dead were victims of drunken brawls, racket enforcers, armed robbery, or gang warfare, but murder by contract was coming into use simply as a way of climbing the free enterprise ladder. Fifteen hundred contract killings were racked up in 1992. The following summer, the president of Russia's Young Bankers' Association sent an anguished appeal for help to President Yeltsin. Ten directors of the country's largest commercial banks had been murdered in the previous weeks, presumably for failing to extend still more outrageous loans than those they had granted already.[19]

A disturbing number of other victims were policemen. Lost amid all the rest of the doom-ridden news from Russia is the fact that its mafia has become the world's leading cop killer. Neither in Sicily nor in Colombia have so many policemen fallen under criminal fire: 186 in 1989; 193 the next year; 300 the year after; and as many again the year after that. Another 719 were attacked by gunmen in St. Petersburg alone in 1991.[20]

This was the year the Soviet Union's outer borders opened up while inner borders closed around fifteen newly sovereign ex-Soviet republics. All nationwide Soviet institutions were gone by the start of the following year, including those for law enforcement. The Soviet-wide Sixth Department, created by Gorbachev barely three years earlier for a concerted assault on organized crime, was dismantled. No central authority remained to coordinate police intelligence, order arrests, control thirty-six thousand miles of Soviet land and sea frontiers, or movements of men, money, and goods from one to another of the new independent states. No laws governed passage from one to another. The only organization fully operative across the length and breadth of the former U.S.S.R. was the mafia.

In two or three years it had doubled in size (from twenty-five hundred to five thousand clans) and increased its business activities more than a hundredfold. Its leaders had established contact with their Western counterparts, and thousands of its members had expanded operations in the United States and Western Europe. It was moving heavily into the international drug trade and had mastered the complexities of shady international finance. By all odds it was the fastest-growing crime consortium on the planet. And it was still a shared monopoly of power between politicians and crooks.

There are elaborate theories to explain how so commanding an organization can seemingly have neither head nor tail and yet manage to be everywhere and nowhere. Indeed, the Soviet mafia is a hybrid monster hard to describe. "Brigades" emerge and disappear, leaders come and go, bands migrate from the Caucasus to Moscow or to Vladivostok on the Sea of Japan. Some are known by nationality: Chechen, Armenian, Azerbaijani, Georgian, Russian, Ukrainian, Uzbek, Ingushy. Others are known by occupation: the drug mafia, the gambling mafia, the taxi mafia, the gold mafia, the currency mafia, the stolen car mafia, and so on.

Territories may be staked out by a tribe, a region, an urban neighborhood, or simply a marauding and charismatic boss. A single gang raided in 1992 was found to embrace five hundred members of smaller gangs equipped with "firearms and knives, ammunition, modern means of radio communication, foreign cars, and half a billion rubles in cash."[21] A "Big Urals" gang absorbing six smaller ones works the entire ex-Soviet territory from Moscow to the Baltic states to the Far East.

Myriad organized gangs may be mistaken for the real thing, from Asiatic bandits to a Russian version of Hell's Angels. Lines are indistinct between mafiosi and ordinary swindlers or black marketers. Often there is no discernible line at all between mafiosi and their political confederates. Nevertheless, there really is an authentic criminal organization known as the Russian mafia, richer by far than forces of the law and much better equipped in weapons, communication systems, and transport. It admires and copies the Sicilian Mafia as the highest standard of excellence. "Now, my dear friends, we are living the most solemn moment here in Diomga, our little big Palermo," said the flamboyant "Dzhem," boss of Komsomolsk-na-Amure in the Soviet Far East, toasting his mafia's "immortal ties" to the Sicilian confraternity at a grand wedding. Five hundred mafia heavyweights, gathered there from Siberia, the Caucasus, Chechenya, Tatarstan, and Uzbekistan, cheered him on. (Police have a secretly filmed video of this memorable event.)[22]

Members of this mafia are admitted only with a mafia sponsor and only after proving their valor by killing somebody on order, preferably a friend or relative—exactly like their admired Sicilian colleagues.[23] Once in, they still live largely by the code of the old Thieves' World, risk its abundant death penalties, communicate in their private jargon, and flaunt the tattoos marking their eternal membership: a spider web for drug traffickers, an eight-point star for robbers, a broken heart for district bosses.

Loosely articulated, they form something like the classic criminal pyramid. Common thugs make up the base at street level, under gang leaders running their territory like military boot camps. Above are a "supply group" and a "security group," the one largely a conduit for communication with the other.[24] The security group forms an umbrella of respectable citizens—journalists, bankers, artists, athletes, politicians of the old and new Nomenklatura—providing intelligence information, legal aid, social prestige, and political cover.[25] Above them are the godfathers, the indomitable *vory v zakone*, "thieves within the code" who still command the heights of the Thieves' World, preserving its "thieves' ideology," administering justice, plotting strategy.

There are seven hundred known "thieves within the code" by now, at large or in prison.[26] Guiding rather than governing, they provide most of the brains for their subalterns. Although far from being absolute rulers over violently unruly and fiercely competitive gangs—there is no Totò Riina among them—they are "the mafia's Politburo," to quote a captain in the Sixth Department, the arbiters of the criminal world.

"Our 'thieves within the code' are vital to the mafia's internal order," said I. Pavlovich, deputy chief of the Russian Republic's Sixth Department. "Each sphere of influence is under their control. They meet periodically, settle territorial disputes, decide on operations, make policy."[27]

The power emanating from these mafia conclaves inevitably surpasses a fragile Russian government's in that their edicts are instantly transmitted, unmistakably enforceable, and almost universally obeyed. In January 1991, for instance, the most authoritative "thieves within the code" gathered from all over the country to discuss a financial emergency—so we are told by Alexander Gurov, head of the Sixth Department at the time. Soviet Premier Valentin Pavlov had suddenly withdrawn all fifty- and one-hundred-ruble notes from circulation. (See Chapter 9.) Everybody in the mafia kept illicit cash reserves in these notes, the largest denomination issued up to then.

"My operational report showed that these 'thieves within the code'—the supermen, the big-time mafiosi—got together to discuss ways of selling off or exchanging the banknotes for new ones or getting them out of the country," Gurov said later on national TV. "The 'thieves within the code' decided where the rubles had to be exchanged or smuggled out. Then they gave permission to set aside a quarter of the entire sum for bribing the administration."[28]

The underworld mobilized overnight. "Black market currency sharks vanished from Moscow," Gurov declared. The ruble notes were rushed to corruptible state factories and banks in remote regions to be exchanged under the counter. The Konkuret coop, with only 1,000 rubles in its account, handed in 190,000 rubles in fifties and hundreds for exchange into smaller denominations at the local bank. A shop in Novosibirsk taking in 10,000 rubles a day "contrived to hand in" 240,000. Hundreds of millions of rubles were laundered with little trouble. Unlike the poor, who lost lifetime savings they had been hiding under a mattress, the mafia came out very well.

The godfathers met again in the winter of 1991 to consider Gorbachev's five-hundred-day program for transition to a free market. They liked it. A free market in the U.S.S.R. meant not only mobility, relaxed borders, and dollars from abroad but a chance to mount the most colossal criminal buyout in history. For all the wreckage of Russia's economy, it still had the world's richest natural resources. And once privatization got under way, the whole country would be up for sale.[29]

Though few realized it then, the Russian mafia was about to make a big strategic leap—from merely feeding off the economy to owning it. To prepare for privatization, however, the godfathers needed time. Accordingly, they decided to stall the entire government program until they were ready. In the event, they stalled it for a year.[30]

Late in January 1992, the Tass section of *Krim Press* reported that the godfathers had reconvened at a dacha near Moscow. "Therefore, privatization of the capital's trade and service sectors, delayed because various mafia clans were resolving the distribution of enterprises among themselves, is likely to go ahead soon," the Russian news agency said.[31]

First the godfathers had to impose a new peace among Moscow's eternally warring clans. The truce they had worked out in 1988, at Dagomys on the Black Sea, had ended in an orgy of bloodshed after barely a year. But the first stage of privatization was, in effect, an imperative call to order.

"The Yeltsin government is selling state enterprises amounting to ninety-two billion rubles this year. Organized crime is putting fifty billion rubles through the banking system. So the mafia can buy up more than half," said the Russian Interior Ministry's top social economist Tatjana Korjagina, leader of the first Parliamentary Anti-Mafia Commission in Soviet or Russian history.[32]

The logic of peace was unarguable. Once inner harmony was restored, the godfathers divided zones of influence and went after the six thousand properties coming up for auction in Moscow. The rules for privatization were fluid, corrupt officials were easily come by, and most Russians had no money to speak of. In a matter of weeks the mafia had the city sewn up.

"According to sources who spoke on condition they were not identified, the mafia has already privatized between 50 percent and 80 percent of all shops, storehouses, depots, hotels, and services in Moscow—the biggest enterprises providing for the city's vital activities," reported Tass *Krim Press*.[33]

Where standard bribery failed in the course of the takeover, the mafia had only to apply a little force. To acquire a popular Gastronom delicatessen in the capital, it simply prevented employees from bidding by locking them up for an entire afternoon.[34] (In another year it would be grabbing enterprises by killing off its own more successful businessmen instead: the young director-general of a prosperous real estate agency, the director of a metal factory, the director of a brokerage, the vice-president of Tekhno-bank. "They were dressed by Valentino and Calvin Klein, but underneath they had tattoos on their chests [the Russian symbols of a gangster]," wrote *Komsomolskaya Pravda*.)[35]

In the end the Moscow properties were sold off for only 200 million rubles, whereas the city had been expecting 1.6 billion.[36] Asked how he felt about the whole larcenous affair, the head of the City Council's Privatization Committee replied: "Why not? If the mafia guarantees law and order, food in the shops, and washed floors, then I'm for the mafia."[37]

There was no protest from Moscow's mayor, Gavril Popov, who, if anything, had outdone the mafia. In November 1991 the mayor had actually signed over an entire district of the capital to a French-Russian joint venture called UKOSO in which he and his minister for the municipal economy were accused of holding 40 percent of the shares. The "October" district covered four million square meters of choice real estate from the splendid Gorky Park to Gagarinsk Square, occupied by academies, monasteries, a hospital, and 220,000 residents including Mikhail Gorbachev. It was worth about $30 billion, but UKOSO received a ninety-nine-year lease at $10 a year.

I was among the incredulous readers of this improbable news story. Later, however, it was confirmed to me by an impeccable source. Tatjana Korjagina lives in the "October" district and pays her rent to UKOSO.[38]

To suggest that the mayor was a bigger crook than the crooks is to draw too fine a distinction. Popov, who eventually resigned but kept his loot, was "selling the city's best real estate and historic landmarks to foreigners, censoring all criticism of the criminal activities of the city's leadership, and mixing executive power with criminal elements, creating a unique mafia network that controls the life of the city," as a top Russian manager put it.[39]

* * *

Gavril Popov was never taken to court because, like two and a half million government officeholders in the former U.S.S.R., he had official and unconditional immunity. Russia had no law to punish corruption anyway. It had no law permitting access to Popov's or any bank accounts, no mechanism for controlling private banks, no sanctions for money laundering, no screening for civil service applicants, no inspectors to check the source of foreign capital, no tax audits, no legal provisions against organized crime, and no protection for government witnesses (whose names *and addresses* had to be listed in indictments).

Under a High Court ruling, furthermore—rigged in 1986 to protect the Uzbek mafia, and modified later only in part—a defendant in a criminal case could not be convicted unless he pleaded guilty. "This is a disaster from which we cannot recover," says the prosecutor-general's chief investigator for serious crimes, Boris Uvarov.[40]

The lack of a legal framework to fit a wholly new political structure, a desperately urgent problem, was one of too many to be dealt with by a frail and uncertain government. On top of it, the KGB was in a state of penury and purge; and the militia, facing an army of dedicated cop killers, struggled with ancient telephones, aging patrol cars, no gas, no computers, and no money. Earning about $10 a month, they made sporadic raids that were understandably halfhearted.

On one occasion, twenty-four thousand militiamen rounded up 7,709 presumably dangerous criminals in the capital, of whom 479 were charged for petty hooliganism, 1,520 for lacking residence permits, 147 for drunken driving, 519 for drunkenness, 165 for vagrancy, and 14 for brewing illegal vodka. "The inhabitants of Moscow can sleep more soundly now," said the militia's crime prevention chief without a shade of irony.[41]

So, singularly free from harassment, the political-criminal force called the mafia has in fact come to control the life of Moscow and of all Russia and the other commonwealth states.[42] Its terrible strength emerged in the desperate winter of 1990–91 when, with a free market on the way, food vanished from Soviet shelves. The food was there, but not in the shops.

An Italian TV crew filmed twenty heavily loaded trucks leaving Moscow's wholesale produce market, not one of which unloaded at a retail outlet. Hidden in the basement of shop number nineteen in the October district police found 700 kilos of chicken drumsticks, 400 kilos of butter, and nearly 2 tons of meat. At the Nizhnedevitsk slaughterhouse in the Voronezh region, 1,707 kilos of meat and 50 sheep carcasses were dumped and covered with earth. One hundred and ten tons of rotted vegetables were discovered at a storage facility in the Odessa region. Similar reports came from Syktyvkar, Chernovtsy, Perm, Vladimir, and Suzdal.[43]

Foreign food aid approaching $13 billion over the next winter ran into inexplicable delays. Trainloads from Western Europe were shunted to sidings in Moscow and left there. Britain's 120-ton shipment of frozen meat was rejected altogether at Moscow's Sheremetyevo Airport, allegedly for being infected with "mad cow" disease. (It wasn't.)

A "consistent part" of European Community shipments were "systematically stolen by organized bands," said Larissa Pikhacheva, directing foreign aid for Moscow. Red Cross offices in Moscow's Perovsky and Proletarsky quarters found aid cartons "systematically opened and stripped of coffee, biscuits, and chocolate." (Two hundred grams of this coffee were selling on the black market for three hundred rubles, an average month's salary.)

Fifty-four planeloads sent in America's spectacular airlift, Operation Hope, had to be escorted by Red Army troops and kept under armed guard around the clock. Of eighty thousand packages sent to St. Petersburg by the German Arbeiter Samariterbund, only ten thousand reached the population; another thirty thousand were blocked in the harbor. A caravan of German aid trucks was forced to turn back at the border after failing to find a customs agent to clear them; others passing through were stoned. "An adventure in peace looked more like a mission of war," said a young Russian interpreter in the caravan.[44]

The strangling of the nation's food supply was a gargantuan

operation to force up prices and expand the black market in food-stuffs. Millions of citizens had a hand in it, but Boris Yeltsin himself spoke out angrily against "the mafia that controls the markets."[45]

Not all the black marketing is so closely held. Much of it is really a free market for anything sold off the books, from a used can-opener or Red Air Force uniform to computers or dented samovars.

Russians travel for six days to Peking on the Trans-Siberian Rail-way to trade Russian watches, cameras, and exotic puppies for Chinese clothing and bicycles; Vietnamese buy Russian bicycles and teakettles to sell in Hanoi; Mongolians pick up cheap Russian food blenders and fake Johnny Walker whiskey to peddle from a fruit crate in Warsaw.

The mafia's five thousand gangs don't necessarily run this vast itinerant army, but they rarely fail to collect their cut.[46] Moscow is smothered by them. Twenty criminal "brigades" hold the city with more than six thousand armed thugs. Everybody in some kind of business—restaurants, food markets, gas stations, flower stalls, newsstands, casinos, beggars' corners at the Kremlin—is "under somebody" who collects a monthly payoff.

The Dolgoprudnaya, who drive around in Volvos with heated seats, have a corner on the best protection rackets. The Lyubertsy run prostitution; the Solntsevo control slot machines; the Ingushy smuggle contraband leather and skins to northern Italy; the Azer-baijani keep a corner on the drug trade by turning their rivals in to the cops; and so on.[47]

Then there are the Chechen, with their own army of six hundred killers in Moscow. Natives of a self-proclaimed sovereign enclave in the northern Caucasus (population 700,000), they are the most notorious and versatile of all Russia's mafiosi at home and abroad. There are many Chechen gangs, not necessarily friendly to one another but uniformly vicious and assured of perfect sanctuary in their tiny mountain republic. Upon declaring its independence in 1991, its president, General Dzahkar Dudaeyev, opened its prison gates, let everybody out, and closed the prisons down.[48]

The Chechen are hated and feared in Moscow but cannot be dislodged. Their swaggering toughs are also taking over the streets in Berlin, Warsaw, and Prague; stealing cars in Germany, Austria, and Sweden; running drugs into Western Europe; working fraud and currency scams in the United States.[49] Wild, cruel, and impenetrably secretive, they are singularly frightening villains.

Chechen gangs do almost anything imaginable that is illegal, starting with "protection," the Russian equivalent of the *pizzo.* Protection is the racketeer's "main function and service," explained a Chechen entrepreneur to the *Chicago Tribune*'s Thom Shenker:

> No businessman wants the militia interfering in his affairs. Nor does he want riots with one hundred people from opposing groups brawling over his restaurant or enterprise. Our function is to control the criminal situation, prevent unrest and acts of vandalism. We provide favorable conditions for development of business and the prosperity of businessmen in Moscow.[50]

I ran into Chechen controlling the criminal situation on another beat when two agents of the Sixth Department took me on a crook's tour of Moscow. The place was Uzhny Port on the river, a terminal for stolen cars from all over Western Europe. Here, among humbler models on a vast, icy used-car lot, stood rows of Audis, BMWs, and Mercedes-Benzes—the cars mourned by so many of the eighty-five thousand Germans who lost theirs in 1991.[51] (Another mafia ring, from Georgia, was pirating used cars shipped from Japan to Russia's Pacific coast, attacking caravans with razors, knives, and machine guns.)[52] We received no welcoming salesman's smiles from the stone-faced, heavy-browed Chechen in greasy leather coats, watching us as we watched half-frozen militiamen lift car hoods, peer inside, and move on. The Chechen were paying $1,000 a month for that blind policeman's eye, my guides said.

Every kind of scam awaited the unwary customer: a Mercedes refitted with an East German Trabant motor or a cash payment vanishing with a uniformed "cashier." A Moscovite rummaging for spare parts in a mountain of junk would not leave his own car unguarded, the agents said, for fear of its being not only stolen but *sold* behind his back.

The tour led from Uzhny Port to the Polayana Dom in front of

Moscow's planetarium for the electronic goods mafia; a jewelry shop on Sirenevy Boulevard for the gold mafia; the Hippodrome, built by Tsar Nicholas I and transformed into the glittering Cafe Royale Casino, for the betting and gambling mafia; a billiard parlor next to gracious Ostanskinsky Park reserved for "the intelligentsia of the underworld" ("because gambling needs brains"). Then came the Foreign Trade Bank for the hard currency mafia; the Intourist Hotel in sight of the Kremlin for the prostitution mafia and a dozen others; the Danilovsky market for the Azerbaijani drug mafia.

The Danilovsky market, although a beacon for addicts, can hardly convey the magnitude of the drug mafia operating across Russia and all the commonwealth states.

Nature, more generous than man to this Soviet land, has endowed it with a prodigal source of narcotics. The ex-U.S.S.R. produces twenty-five times more hashish than all the rest of the world. Cannabis grows wild on seven and a half million acres of its territory, in Kazakhstan, Siberia, the Far Eastern republics, the lower Volga River Basin, the northern Caucasus, and southern Ukraine. (Truck drivers cut it to dry on an outward journey and gather it to smoke on the return run.)[53]

Opium poppies flourish anywhere in Kazakhstan's Chu Valley, sixty thousand kilometers square. Luxuriant poppy fields sprawl over Uzbekistan, Turkmenistan, and Tadzhikistan.[54]

The latter three Islamic republics have the same soil and growing conditions as contiguous Afghanistan and Iran, with whom they are inevitably in league. Afghanistan has just overtaken Burma as the world's largest opium-producing country. With Iran, it forms the Golden Crescent, the world's second largest source of supply.

In the old days, Tadzhikis would set out pots and pans at nightfall and pick them up filled with Afghan dope in the morning. Trained driverless donkeys with one-hundred-pound loads would cross over from Iran to Tadzhikistan.[55] Even these precautions are no longer needed; the borders among these Moslem states have been abolished altogether.

For once, organized crime was late in spotting a potential bonanza—the chance to create and feed a huge addict population and export for dollars. The possibilities were overlooked, perhaps deliberately so; Soviet controls were severe. Opium and hash, used for centuries in the harsh mountains and deserts of Central Asia, were largely consumed where they grew. When Soviet controls fell apart, things changed. By 1992 family-sized poppy fields yielding two crops a year were rationalized and under heavy armed guard.

New plantations in Uzbekistan increased by a thousand percent. Around 200,000 acres were planted with poppies in Kyrgyzstan. The number of opium growers tripled in Kazakhstan's Chu Valley. Plantations were springing up in Tajikistan. Others were spreading over a thousand square kilometers of empty radioactive terrain around Chernobyl. Altogether, the 1992 crop was expected to be worth $5 billion.[56]

There was no proof up to then that the opium was being converted into refined heroin for export. But that was bound to come and was "probably happening" already, said the U.N.'s anti-drug chief in Vienna.[57]

Meanwhile, an ant army of heroin couriers was moving up from the Golden Crescent through Tajikistan, Uzbekistan, and Turkmenistan with forged papers, radio telephones, and paramilitary protection, crossing the breadth of Soviet territory bound for Odessa on the Black Sea, or Finland, the Baltic states, Poland, Western Europe, America.[58] Similar movement was under way from the Golden Triangle in Southeast Asia, the heroin traveling across Southern China into Kazakhstan and Kyrgyzstan.[59]

The drug mafia was taking over horizontally and vertically, from production and processing to transport, distribution, and marketing.[60] Free of centralized surveillance, it moved largely unhindered across the crazy quilt of internal commonwealth borders, ignoring ethnic tensions.

"Our 'thieves within the code' have ruled that nationality conflicts should not be allowed to interfere in the work of the professional criminal core," said Alexander Gurov when the Union of Soviet Socialist Republics came crashing down.[61]

Apart from heroin and hash, underground laboratories started to produce synthetic drugs such as Krokodil and Chert (Devil), a thousand times stronger than heroin. The most lethal, methyl-fentanyl—diluted in proportions of one to twenty thousand—was made exclusively in Russia. These were cheaper than homegrown natural drugs, themselves two hundred times cheaper in Russia than in the West.

Soviet cities had always been a market of sorts, expanding as soldiers got hooked on heroin in the Afghanistan War. But galloping addiction set in only after traffickers mounted their assault around 1985. From then on, the addict population doubled yearly.[62] By 1992, Russia had one and a half million *registered* addicts and occasional drug users, according to General Alexander Sergeev, the Russian Interior Ministry's anti-narcotics chief. The figure was all the more startling for the carefully preserved fiction that socialist Russia had no addicts whatever. In fact, some Russian experts thought the "real" figure was "at least three to four times higher." St. Petersburg's anti-narcotics chief thought it was ten times higher.[63]

In that one year the drug mafia's profits increased fourfold, from four billion to fifteen billion rubles—this even before its first harvest of modernized, commercialized crops. Thus, Russia had the rare distinction of being at once a user country, a transit country, and a producer country, all three on its customarily extravagant scale.

Russian traffickers were known to have been working heroin with Western counterparts, the Sicilian Mafia especially, since 1985.[64] By 1992 they were delivering heroin to Sicilian mafiosi in New York, selling amphetamines on the American market, moving cocaine in Vienna, Budapest, and Frankfurt, and were said by Interpol Poland to have reached "precise agreements in Warsaw with big German and Dutch cocaine traffickers, and Colombia's Cali cartel."[65] That year, in fact, a shipment of pure Colombian cocaine, shaped into thirty-four thousand pairs of Peruvian-made plastic sandals, was sighted in Moscow, heading for Warsaw.[66]

Even then the U.S. State Department did not list Russia among forty-eight producer or transit countries in its International Narcotics Control Strategy Report for 1992. No Western government publication did. In another year or so they would. "Russia may well become the bridgehead for all European traffic in drugs. Be warned!" said the head of the Russian prosecutor-general's research institute, Vitaly Karpetz.[67]

Of all the Russian mafia's occupations, the biggest by far had to do with plundering the economy through multifarious, unbelievably lucrative fraud. This is where a prostrate country lay open to the international underworld. A gluttonous horde of foreign carpetbaggers, speculators, and assorted felons showed up as soon as Russia began to look west. "It's like the old Texas oil-boom towns, a constant parade of con men, promoters, and shady customers . . . the greatest collection of sleazebags in the world," remarked U.S. ambassador to Moscow Robert Strauss.[68]

The foreign invaders might be skinned by Russian partners or walk off with the store; one American skipped with nine billion rubles—around $60 million at the time—while his Chechen partners awaited him in Moscow with axes and hatchets.[69] Nevertheless, there was money for all in a partnership joining Western dollars with Russian expertise.

Russian criminals are unrivaled in the art of turning a dishonest dollar after seventy years of communist rule. Nothing is too small or too big, from selling unpaired shoes to clearing 100 billion rubles with fake Visa credit cards. The latter was just one of their more glittering operations in 1992.[70]

That spring the Chechen mafia stole 30 billion rubles outright from the Russian state—roughly $200 million in mid-1992.[71] A straw bank in the minuscule Republic of Chechenya sent bogus "credit advisories" for that amount to Russia's Central Bank—statements saying it had the sums on deposit. On the strength of this, the straw bank asked for a credit line in Moscow to import computers. The money didn't exist, nor did the bank in Chechenya, but Russia's Central Bank "had no time" to ask questions, observed serious crimes investigator Boris Uvarov, for whom this was the most serious crime yet. The Central Bank sent the money to a dozen commercial banks in Moscow—"the real money," Uvarov explained. Then, informed that the computer deal had fallen through, the commercial banks obligingly allowed the cash to be withdrawn and sent back to Chechenya, minus their cut.

Soon afterward another fake credit advisory from Chechenya cost the Central Bank another 1.5 billion rubles. The money, invented again, was meant to pay for five hundred imported Chrysler Jeeps. This time an American apparently made off with the money. He was associated with American Grain Company and a Russian-based joint venture called BOL-CO, and he was supposed to buy the Jeeps in the United States. Instead, he used the rubles in the Russian account as security to get a line of credit in dollars in his own American account and vanished.[72]

Over the next months the Central Bank was swamped with phony credit advisories from St. Petersburg, Novgorod, Volgograd, Chelyabinsk, Daghestan, Perm, the Tatar Republic, the Chuvash Republic, and elsewhere. Altogether, the Russian Interior Ministry announced, the Central Bank converted 270 billion rubles from fake paper to cash in the course of 1992—around $1.8 billion snatched from an exhausted treasury, nearly twice the total foreign investment in all joint ventures up to then.[73]

During the same year Russia's Foreign Trade Ministry "lost" $2 billion, Boris Yeltsin told a special conference on crime and corruption; the funds had simply disappeared from the ministry's balance sheet.[74] Officials of the Defense Ministry were "stealing entire ammunition depots without fear of being caught," Yeltsin said. Criminals were bribing heavily to get export licenses, buying petroleum and precious metals with rubles, and selling these resources abroad for hard currency "at a huge profit," he added.[75]

Petroleum, in the country with the world's biggest reserves, was among the hotter items in what had become one big bargain basement of Russian resources. Almost anybody properly connected could loot the store, but the unique Soviet version of the joint venture was the best way in. Conceived as a magical bridge to capitalism, the joint venture was supposed to transform the Soviet economy with model factories using Western money and expertise. Dismayed by the unsteady Russian scene, however, serious Western investors held back. Shady investors had fewer qualms, especially with a smart mafioso for a partner.

Despite the ancient stricture of the Thieves' World—a death sentence for working in the "outside" world—half the mafia's "thieves within the code" were going directly into some new joint venture upon getting out of jail. (The other half were unemployable invalids.)[76] With them were the stars of the old Nomenklatura, unfailingly summoned as "consultants." Even hard-lining ex-Premier Valentin Pavlov, jailed after the failed putsch of August 1991, was offered such a job once "certain legal and physical aspects" of his situation were resolved.[77]

Under these auspices, the magical bridge to capitalism quickly became "a crooked world of rampant bribery and financial manipulation, aimed mainly at finagling permission to export cheap Soviet raw materials for enormous profit," wrote investigative journalist Elmar Guseinov in a major exposé in *Izvestiya*. "The joint ventures we have now are contemptible and must die—will die," he concluded in 1990.[78]

Instead, they grew so pervasive and prosperous that even those under unmistakable mafia management—especially those, because of their energy and resourcefulness—were seen by many as the only way to effect Russia's transition to capitalism. Some said without blinking that the mafia should actually be legalized to speed up the process. ("These people are insane," said Boris Uvarov.)

Capitalism generally starts out with a generation or two of piratical robber barons who build railroads or drill oil wells and end up as the backbone of the nation, the argument went. They create wealth first and then pick up acceptable ethics to go with it, as John D. Rockefeller did with Standard Oil in America. Such reasoning implied that people who fought America's robber barons a century ago were not only wasting their breath and often their lives but actually getting in the way of progress. Put baldly, it suggested that a democratic society is not necessarily menaced and may indeed be strengthened by a rising class of businessmen-hoods.

If any new democracy offered monumental proof to the contrary, it was Russia. While its cleaner joint ventures contributed marginally to the economy, those under criminal management contributed nothing, produced nothing, risked nothing, and created no wealth save for the country's 100,000 new millionaires, who simply robbed what was there.

Robbing Russia's wealth needn't mean breaking the law. In the prevailing state of judicial chaos, there were few laws to break.

The case of Artjom Tarasov, free Russia's first accredited ruble millionaire, showed what a sharp businessman could do with a joint venture and sheer brass as free enterprise got under way in Moscow. Tarasov, a young, dapper, and fast-talking deputy in the Russian parliament, formed an independent joint venture called Istok in 1989. Founded by the Moscow Innovation Commercial Bank, it was authorized by the state to conduct various export-import transactions in raw materials and "provide assistance in organizing barter deals with foreign partners."[79] As Tarasov has said himself, he could only carry out such transactions "by using *untraditional methods*" (his italics). He explained:

> Untraditional methods entailed very difficult work, which Istok did. To explain the essence of this work, let me propose shipping a small amount of fuel oil. No one will let you have the oil; the money for the purchase must be borrowed on interest from a commercial bank; no one will provide transportation; and if you find it, carloads are lost mandatorily on the way. The port does not even want to talk because it is overloaded with planned shipments; you find a tanker yourself, and, finally, no one will let you export fuel oil on a Russian license, and no one on the foreign market wants to buy it since its quality is low-grade. We solved all these "little" intermediary problems, and that is why we were untraditional.

Tarasov has never disclosed how he solved the little problems, leaving the Russian press to draw its own conclusions. This is *Izvestiya*'s version, among others:[80]

Soon after forming Istok, *Izvestiya* said, Tarasov went after Russia's petroleum. On behalf of an American associate wanted by the FBI—Marc-David Rich, the biggest tax swindler in American history, about whose Russian swindles more later—he got four mil-

lion tons of crude out of Russia on a legal export license; he bought
at 50 rubles a ton ($5 on the black market then) and sold at $140 a
ton abroad.[81]

In the summer of 1990, Tarasov asked the premier of the Russian
Republic, Ivan Silaev, for a license to export 500,000 tons of heating
oil on the grounds that Russia had too much of it and lacked
storage facilities. (Actually, Russia had a cruel shortage of heating
oil the following winter.) The license granted, Tarasov received
government credits to pay for the heating oil. The head of customs
was directed to accelerate shipment, while the Ministry of Transport provided the necessary railroad tankers. By the time the presumably unsalable low-grade heating oil reached the port of
Odessa bound for the West, it was found to be "a higher quality
than indicated in the export contract—almost high-quality gasoline!—raising its sales price by a factor of two," Tarasov conceded.

Then Tarasov asked Premier Silaev for permission to put the
proceeds of his heating oil/gasoline sales into an Istok account in a
Western bank; this would dodge a 40 percent tax on hard currency
imposed by the central Soviet government—the enemy for the Russian Republic's government in 1990. With the Russian premier's
permission, he opened an account in the Monaco branch of the
French bank Paribas, sold the oil in Western Europe at a record
price—$176 a ton, because of the Gulf War, he says—turned over
$9 million of the proceeds to the Soviet government, put the rest
into his Paribas account, and left Russia.

How much stayed in the Paribas account has never been estab-
lished. According to Tarasov, "Eleven million dollars remained in
Monaco"; *Izvestiya* spoke of $46 million; Tarasov's successor at
Istok referred to a "shortfall" of $27 million.[82]

Whatever the sum—and it must have been substantial—the bal-
ance did not go back to Russia, nor did Tarasov. Although it might
be argued that no law had been broken, he nevertheless told *Izvestiya*, "I assure you, I am ready to fly back tomorrow, but I am
not sure that I would not be arrested right in the airport."[83]

*   *   *

Such room for maneuver inevitably brought Russia's talented crooks and their political accomplices into burgeoning partnerships with Western counterparts: manipulating the country's currency, destabilizing its fragile economy, and stripping it of its oil, gold, timber, copper, cobalt, aluminum, titanium, steel, uranium, plutonium, and rare-earth metals.

Describing the scene in the summer of 1992, Deputy Chief Anatoly Terechov of Moscow's Interpol declared:

> Less than half of our joint ventures work. Only a quarter deal with their declared activities. Two or three out of five are financed with money of dubious origin.
>
> Many joint ventures are fictitious. Often they're one-man operations to swing hard currency deals. Four thousand of them have right of access to the foreign market.
>
> At least five hundred of our Mafia groups use them to link up with international crime—in the United States, Italy, Germany, Austria, France, Canada, Poland.[84]

Six months later Boris Yeltsin himself adjusted this last estimate upward. "At least a thousand mafia groups have contacts with international organized crime," he said.[85]

The American and Sicilian mafias were the first in, by way of what was arguably the biggest black market currency swap ever perpetrated. (See Chapter 9.) As they and others moved in deeper, their Russian confederates moved out farther.

In the opinion of Serious Crimes Investigator Uvarov, Western authorities still didn't realize what was going to hit them. "Naturally it's wonderful that the Iron Curtain is gone, but it was a shield for the West," Uvarov said. "Now we've opened the gates, and this is very dangerous for the rest of the world. America is getting Russian criminals; Europe is getting Russian criminals. They'll steal everything. They'll *occupy* Europe. Nobody will have the resources to stop them. You people in the West don't know our mafia yet. You will, you will."[86]

PART III

The Pax Mafiosa

CHAPTER SIX

In Europe

The map of the underworld in 1993 was full of surprises. The Russian mafia turned up in Sweden, Belgium, Holland, Luxembourg, Britain, and several new American cities. The American mafia appeared in Russia. The Sicilian Mafia was also in Russia, working with both the Russians and the Americans.

American and Sicilian mafiosi operated a "South Russian International Bank" in Sverdlovsk, heart of Russia's military-industrial complex; this according to Russian intelligence.[1] Russian and American mafiosi ran a bank called Himbank in Rochester, New York; this according to Italian intelligence.[2] An 'Ndrangheta clan in Calabria was buying $2 billion worth of rubles from a German bank to buy a bank of its own in St. Petersburg, along with a Russian steel mill and an oil refinery.[3] The Russian mafia's Chechen were setting up a financial base in the City of London.[4] The Colombian gangs had an "office of representation" in Warsaw,[5] and a spectacular cocaine deal with the Russian mafia in St. Petersburg.

Sicilian Mafia Families were suddenly found to have a considerable presence not just in Germany but in France, Belgium, and Holland. Other Sicilians appeared to be taking over at least two American mafia Families (in Philadelphia and Boston).

Yakuza leaders came out from Tokyo to confer with their Western counterparts in Milan, Venice, Geneva, and London.[6] The Triads were bringing massive reinforcements from Hong Kong to
America, Britain, and Holland, and filtering into nearly every state
of Western Europe.

These were visible signs of the planetary attack force forming
among the most powerful crime syndicates in the third year of the
post-communist New World Order—a phenomenon the world has
never known. Free nations, slow to perceive it, had nothing like
the strength needed to resist it—not in Europe, not in America, not
anywhere.

Germany was the critical battleground. Criminals of seventy-nine
nationalities were now operating on its territory. More than half
were in mixed international groups with triangular connections:
from Berlin to Russia and America, from Frankfurt to Italy and
America, from Munich to Thailand and America.[7] Distinctions between Europe and the United States were meaningless in this kind
of criminal warfare. The BKA, much wiser since the fall of the
Berlin Wall, could prove it in a hundred ways.

Proof was hardly needed for the Sicilian Mafia, commuting between Germany and the United States since the 1960s. The startling performers were the Chechen, the Georgians, the
Ukrainians—the whole villainous crew invading Germany from
the former U.S.S.R.

The Russian mafia was doing just what investigators in Moscow
had been predicting since Soviet frontiers gave way. Barely three
years after reaching Berlin, it had transferred $7 billion illicitly to
Germany and was reportedly notching up almost a third of the
organized crimes there. Three hundred gangs were installed in the
country, dealing in drugs, weapons, radioactive materials, antiq-
uities, stolen cars, money laundering, and blackmail, with hooks
out in every direction.[8]

The BKA had watched the pattern unfolding since the summer
of 1991. The Chechen and Georgian clans, working their rackets

inside the Russian émigré colony, were hardly noticed until they started to fight over turf. That June the Chechen shot the Georgians' leader, Tengis Marianashvili, in Berlin; he didn't die, and shot back. The following April the Chechen killed him in Amsterdam. Three months later a Georgian avenger killed one of the Chechen shooters in New Jersey, U.S.A. Half a year afterward the Chechen killed an aide of the dead Georgian leader in Luxembourg. What were the Chechen doing in Luxembourg, Amsterdam, and New Jersey? They were *traveling*, said the BKA. Everybody in the Russian mafia traveled.

One of their interests came to light in February 1993 when over a ton of cocaine was intercepted in St. Petersburg. The largest shipment ever seized in Russia and the second largest in Europe, it marked the Russian mafia's maiden appearance on the big-time drug scene.

The Cali cartel had made the arrangements with Israeli traffickers in Colombia, who worked with a Russian mafia gang in Belgium, who worked with other Russian hoods in Amsterdam, who sent their people to pick up the cargo in St. Petersburg and ship it to Germany.[9]

Not everybody would see the logic of shipping dope from the Western Hemisphere to Western Europe by way of Eastern Europe. In fact, any entry point in Western Europe from the East was wonderfully restful for traffickers compared to western entry points teeming with narcotics agents.

Five or six of the Russians in the St. Petersburg shipment were involved in much deeper matters. The same men were among the Russians watched by a special BKA team for over a year. As soon as Germany's eastern borders went down, Russian crooks settling into Berlin began to set up an intricate web of interlocking joint ventures with Moscow, the BKA team found.

Parent "export-import" companies were always located in Berlin; "daughter companies" began to appear in Belgium, Holland, Luxembourg, Hungary, South Korea, New York, Los Angeles, and Miami. By the winter of 1993 new "daughter companies" were spreading to all three Baltic states.

"The same owners and managers appear over and over again,"

the head of the BKA team, Wolfram Bieling, told me. "Five or six run the show abroad, and they are very, very busy. They have ties with diamond dealers in Antwerp and with the Russian mafia in Brooklyn. They have contacts all over eastern Europe. They go back and forth to Russia. We know they're in permanent and close contact with the biggest mafia bosses in Moscow and St. Petersburg."[10]

The BKA could not break through their cover. Since the main characters involved were Chechen, it was assumed that they were swindling, which Chechen crooks did everywhere, and were bound to be laundering, which they were now going into in a serious way. (Two fellow Chechen had settled in London in March 1993 with a million pounds sterling in cash to establish a base in the city. Both were murdered in their opulent and atrociously furnished London flats on the same day.)[11]

The Chechen were believed to be moving heroin. Their companies were shipping regularly by airfreight from Southeast Asia to the United States, ostensibly in transit for Berlin; but what usually reached Berlin was a cheap leather jacket or coat in an otherwise empty container.

While the BKA couldn't prove the heroin, it did find proof that they were manufacturing amphetamines. Two of their companies, American Eagle and MS International, were importing the basic materials from Eastern Europe and using chemists from Stasi, the former communist secret police. The refining was done inside Red Army barracks in Germany.[12]

Stranded when the Soviet empire fell apart, the Red Army's 280,000 troops in Germany's eastern provinces were patsies for the Russian mafia. A good number were actually part of it. Four hundred and twenty Red Army gangs in Germany were working for mafia dons in Moscow by 1991, according to Soviet military intelligence. Some of their highest ranking officers, reportedly including the commander-in-chief of the Russian forces in Germany, were involved in "economic irregularities."[13] They were an inexhaustible source of every material item that a quarter of a million troops might possess. "The Russian barracks are wide open. Anybody can load up with booze, cigarettes, furniture, weapons, ordnance. . . . It's a nightmare," said an American customs agent back from a visit.

Newly established in-house companies such as Russobalt West and Nevikon Share Holding were selling off weapons in bulk: Kalashnikovs, rockets, mines, antitank missiles. Fragmentation hand grenades were on sale for five deutsche marks apiece ($3). Safe from government intrusion, the troops had duty-free clearance for these and all army supplies, and their own private border crossing into Poland, at Katnin-Swinemünde, solely under Russian military control.[14]

Many Russian crimes did not show up in official German crime statistics. Although the fact seemed contrary to their nature, the Russians looked better on paper than most. The bodies they wrapped in concrete were fellow Russians; the people they terrorized were Russian émigrés. They weren't laying a finger on German citizens or killing rival foreign crooks. Their main source of revenue was defrauding the German government, with little need for violence and practically no risk.

They used the Red Army to smuggle alcohol, cigarettes, videos, TVs, computers, and weapons in and out of the country free of inspection and customs duties. They faked army commissary receipts and demanded tax refunds on enormous nonexistent consignments. They stole consignments actually sent and collected the tax refund. (Two hundred tons of pure alcohol shipped to the troops in Germany ended up on the Polish black market.) Above all, they claimed hard currency from the German central bank for fictitious trade with the ex-Soviet bloc—the transfer ruble scam, their master stroke.

The transfer ruble was not currency but an artificial paper price agreed upon for trade within Comecon, the Soviet bloc's soft-currency common market. It made no economic sense in a free market where it spread havoc for two years after the Soviet bloc collapsed. As East Europe's communist regimes began to go under in 1989, their central banks were obliged to honor the transfer ruble, and they continued to honor it until it was formally abolished in January 1992. This window of opportunity allowed the Russian mafia and the KGB, among others, to rob the banks blind.

In Poland, whose zloty was convertible, 158 phony export-import companies appeared out of the blue, presenting bills to the Central Bank for 2.5 billion rubles' worth of fake shipments to Russia. Several turned out to be KGB fronts; the Polish Interior Ministry thought the rest were either KGB or Russian mafia or both.[15] Whoever they were, they collected $3 billion in U.S. dollars from Warsaw's Banku Handlowego in 1991, forty times the rubles' worth by then.

Germany was hit much harder. After forming a monetary union with communist East Germany, the German central bank had to pay double for the transfer ruble since it was paying in Federal deutsche marks that were worth twice East Germany's deutsche mark.[16] Here the Russian mafia and the KGB were joined by the former East Germany's Stasi. Three ex-Stasi agents alone were accused of faking transfer rubles to milk the Bundesbank for anywhere from a third of a billion to two billion dollars.[17]

Nevertheless, Russian crooks stood out as always. "They *romped* through this scam," said Jurgen Maurer, the BKA's organized crime expert. "They worked through the Deutsche Augsenhandelsbank in East Berlin using forged contracts with Russia, forged documents for goods 'made in the German Democratic Republic,' forged bills of lading, and so forth. The bank accepted any piece of paper. There were Russian murders here for the transfer rubles."[18]

Thousands of fraud charges started to back up in the Berlin prosecutor's office. Russian crooks were still forging back-dated documents to file new claims in 1993. Sixty prosecutors expected to be working on such cases for the next ten years.

Altogether the bill for scams in this category amounted to four or five times more than all the damage inflicted by domestic and foreign organized crime in Germany by 1993. ZERV, the special German commission investigating unification frauds, put the estimated loss at seven billion deutsche marks just for transfer rubles and twenty billion deutsche marks for all the scams combined—about $13 billion.[19]

*　　*　　*

The damage could not be reckoned merely in money. The Russians and criminals of seventy-eight other nationalities were inflicting severe psychological injury on the country. Although these represented only a fraction of Germany's five million resident foreigners, they were now committing half the nation's crimes.[20] Highly visible and dangerously provocative, they provided the excuse for an eruption of vicious racism such as Germany had not seen since Hitler's fall.

Crime was becoming an obsessive German concern. Six million incidents of criminal violence in 1992, a "dramatic deterioration" of law and order, and "an enormous increase in aggression," every third family with a crime victim, 232,000 emergency calls to the Berlin police alone, SWAT teams going in against killers with Kalashnikovs and pit bulls, 140,000 actual criminal acts, 623 organized crime cases before the courts, 130,000 stolen cars, a steady rise in new heroin users, 2,091 overdose deaths, three murders a day—this, for an orderly population of eighty-five million, was "getting close to an American level," observed an indignant newspaper editor.[21]

The big players were growing bigger and more efficient. The Turkish mafia was bringing in three or four hundred kilos of heroin at a time, nearly all on the new Balkan route through Eastern Europe. Kurds in the communist PKK (a terrorist organization), financing their terrorist assault on the Turkish government, were bringing in a ton a year.[22]

Powerful Triad structures were forming in Hamburg, Hannover, Mannheim, Frankfurt, and Stuttgart, with connections to Amsterdam, London, Hong Kong, and Macao. Triad gamblers, arsonists, and killers, drifting into the country with forged British passports, were passing counterfeit currency, stealing credit cards, bringing in Asian prostitutes, and dipping into the fragrant oil in Germany's small Chinese colony. Within barely a year they had smuggled in at least ten thousand illegal immigrants from Hong Kong, Macao, and the Chinese mainland. Nearly a thousand a month were being *caught* at the East German border by 1993.[23]

Some were used as enforcers or drug couriers, others as indentured servants paid one dollar an hour in Chinese restaurants, the

Triads' version of the Sicilian Mafia's pizza parlor. Germany had three thousand Chinese restaurants by 1992, up from nine hundred the year before.

Mixed teams of various nationalities with a hundred members or more were emerging across the country. They did heroin and cocaine, burglary, theft, prostitution, and so on, and they didn't fight. "The killings are always within each of the big groups, not across lines. Italians kill Italians, Russians kill Russians, but they don't kill each other," says the BKA's Jurgen Maurer.

Maurer and his colleagues had learned a lot since the shock of exposure in 1990, especially about the Italians. The more they discovered, the larger the Sicilian Mafia loomed as the most dangerous threat of all. The Sicilians and their associates on the Italian mainland were increasingly present and known to be present, yet maddeningly elusive.

Four out of five Italian businessmen in Germany were paying the *pizzo,* now spreading for the first time to German citizens in Frankfurt. Killer commandos answering to Palermo or Catania or Palma di Montechiaro were parked in a dozen German cities or small towns. Nearly every important drug bust revealed a shadowy Sicilian figure somewhere in the background. A major Sicilian-German drug ring was moving cocaine directly from Colombia to Frankfurt to Milan. The Russo brothers of Gela, wanted in Sicily for extortion and multiple murder, reportedly had an arms-drugs gang of a hundred members in Dortmund, seat of a ring linking Germany to Italy and Belgium.[24] Counterfeit currency, stolen credit cards, burglary, gambling, loan-sharking, sex shops and porno, passing stolen checks and bonds, running stolen cars into the country and weapons out of it—all these were in their range.

And Italian mafiosi were swarming over Eastern Germany. Two thousand camorristi were working the eastern provinces, according to Naples Police Chief Umberto Vecchione. These were the *magliari* (sweater peddlers, a term of contempt), using the same cover here as everywhere; they ran cheap leather and textile shops, and hawked tatty clothes with big labels.[25]

The Mafia was sending new men up from Sicily, with 150,000

deutsche marks in seed money to open discos, casinos, and pizzerias. "After a short while they set up chains of pizzerias that hardly make a profit. But they drive around in big cars, and they're big spenders. So they're laundering money," a BKA agent explained.

Leipzig and Dresden, the two key cities of Eastern Germany, were practically sewn up already. The Mafia's Morabito Family of Catania, run by the same Santo Pasquale Morabito who controlled the 'Ndrangheta's Morabito clan in Calabria, was said by German intelligence to have bought $100 million worth of real estate in Leipzig—not just any real estate but the choice part in the city's historic old quarter.[26] Dresden was falling or had fallen to the Family of Gaetano Fidanzati, the Mafia's onetime ambassador to the Camorra in Naples and one of the most assiduous drug traffickers.

From their bases in Eastern Germany the Italians were spreading eastward over an open border to Poland and Czechoslovakia. The Camorra's Licciardi clan had built up a heavy trade with Warsaw and Moscow, and had particularly close ties to the Chechen.[27] Germany had no laws to stop them. Rumors had the Mafia buying real estate up and down the Rhine Valley and along Frankfurt's "noble mile," laundering a fortune in narcodollars through German banks and investing it in East German land, buildings, and factories privatized by Treuhand, the national agency in charge.

Almost none of these rumors could be proved, however. The BKA was still too hobbled to go after dirty money. A new law in September 1992 made laundering a criminal offense but hardly improved the chances of detecting it. No investigation was permissible without convincing evidence that the money to be laundered came from a specific crime or that the crime of laundering itself was about to happen. In effect, this meant no investigation.

BKA agents could not check out a Sicilian suspect on a police tip from Italy; they could only work from police records. They could not begin to investigate one known Sicilian mafioso, convicted in Italy, without strong evidence that he was on the verge of committing a crime. "He's just a guy who lives in Germany," responded a prosecutor who refused to open the case.

Agents could not use any instrument of surveillance, even binoculars, unless its use was specified by law; anything else was an invasion of privacy. They could not hire non-German agents to deal with crooks who spoke no German. They could not bug a hotel room under any circumstances or even make practical use of an undercover agent. Undercovers were still forbidden to commit any criminal act such as trespassing or playing a hand of poker with the mob. The new law made a single exception: It allowed them to use false papers. Thus, in order to entice a real launderer, the agent could set up an undercover company that seemed *ready* to launder drug money, but he could not *actually* launder it without being guilty of laundering himself.

A lot of money was being laundered safely in Germany, therefore. The BKA, too severely restrained to investigate in depth, could only guess how much. Though intelligence analysts spoke of fifty billion deutsche marks invested by the Italian Mafia, they couldn't prove it. "We tried for a year to check this out, and we couldn't find any sources to confirm it," Jurgen Maurer reported.

That didn't necessarily mean there were no big investments, he added; quite the contrary. In the newly annexed Eastern Germany, normal capital was holding back, put off by administrative confusion and uncertain property rights. But illicit capital didn't mind. In the view of authorities such as Maurer, the big crime cartels had "very big possibilities" for investment in the East German provinces.

The fact that Germany couldn't find the dirty money was not just a matter of permissive laws for criminals and restrictions for cops. Most western states had tougher laws by 1993 and couldn't find the money, either. Yet it was there, more than $120 billion a year of criminal capital moving around the world according to the Group of Seven's financial task force, GAFI (Groupe d'Action Financière Internationale). Four-fifths of this staggering sum was invested in the West, festering in free societies like a wasting disease with few outward symptoms. "We can't say where it is; we think nobody can," said Jurgen Maurer. "No agency knows how much is invested in Germany or in Europe or in America."[28]

THE YAKUZA

Europe's Single Market was barely a few months away when a Japanese passenger of evident means and sober bearing was picked up at Charles de Gaulle Airport in Paris and shipped home. He was Masaru Takumi, underboss of the Yamaguchi-Gumi, the Yakuza group with thirty thousand members, by far the strongest in Japan.

Takumi had just gotten out of jail in Osaka, where he had been detained for five days on a charge of illegal currency dealings in Canada. Free to travel despite his brush with the law, he had taken off for France to keep an appointment there with two other members of the Yamaguchi-Gumi hierarchy and its all-powerful top boss, Yoshinori Watanabe. From Paris they were planning a swing around Europe—London, Geneva, Venice, and Milan. After Takumi's run-in with the French police, the trip was called off.

That was just one trip, however. Five hundred members of the Yakuza traveled west in the course of 1992, according to Tokyo's deputy police commissioner, Akinori Tsuruya. "They were going to visit their mafia colleagues for the first time," he said.[29] But it was not the first time. A similar delegation had made almost exactly the same swing around Europe in 1984—Paris, London, Geneva, and Rome. Indeed, the Yakuza had been working the West for years.[30]

The United States, their prime target since the 1970s, was a long while spotting them, but European authorities took still longer. Aside from one seemingly minor episode, not a single Yakuza operation had caught police attention on the Continent for a decade. The apparently minor episode happened in Paris, in April 1992, shortly before the Yamaguchi-Gumi's aborted visit. A hundred and fifty Asians laundering for the Yakuza were rounded up at one time. They were "worker ants," shopping daily at Hermès and Louis Vuitton boutiques for expensive items to be resold at a discount in Japan. Four Japanese and two Chinese money launderers had recruited them through newspaper ads and supplied them with the necessary cash. The money was arriving in France by way of the Channel Islands, Luxembourg, and Switzerland.[31]

The trick looked very nearly harmless, particularly since nobody knew where or how the money had been made in the first place. If the Yakuza were running true to form, however, the money was likely to have come from trafficking in guns or amphetamines, loan-sharking, high-stakes gambling, the sex trade, or multinational corporate blackmail. (The Yamaguchi-Gumi also had an overseas department that rented out killers.)

Such activities had been impressed upon the minds of American authorities since 1984 when an *oyabun* (top boss) of the Yamaguchi-Gumi described its spreading subterranean operations in the United States to the President's Commission on Organized Crime.[32] Two years before that, Japan's police commissioner had accidentally bumped into a number of gunrunning Yamaguchi-Gumi members in Paris. That year a member of the Yakuza's Kyosei-kai was picked up in Japan for smuggling three hundred Garesi handguns from Milan.

During the previous year, one of the Yakuza's most polished *sokaiya*, Seiji Hamamoto, had set up a "foreign correspondent office" in London to blackmail the big Japanese companies there.[33] By 1984 another *sokaiya* group, Rondan Doyukai, was storming the heights of European finance. Departing from custom, they took on three non-Japanese firms, all powerful and immensely rich: Rotterdamsch Beleggings Consortium, Compagnie Française des Petroles, and Compagnie Financière de Paris et des Pays Bas, better known as Paribas.

Not all of the *sokaiya's* traditional methods were workable here. Shouting, throwing furniture around, or slapping the chairman of the board was less likely to cause shame than shocked outrage in these boardrooms followed by a rude journey to jail. But other classic methods might work: a threat to circulate rumors of company malfeasance or raise incandescent questions at stockholders' meetings or publish falsified statements of corporate earnings in several thousand copies. The *sokaiya* have tried these tactics on some of the biggest corporations in America.

Doubtless it was with something of this sort in mind that the Rondan Doyukai *sokaiya* bought thousands of dollars worth of shares of the three companies in their sights. They were moving in for the kill when somebody in Paris spotted them.

These details, published in the fine book *Yakuza* in 1986, were practically unknown to European authorities until five years later when a European parliament report mentioned the Paribas affair. "The attempt to take over Groupe Paribas was only just avoided," the report noted.[34]

Soon afterward Germany's intelligence agency, the BND, warned that the Yakuza was investing heavily in all the EC states. Two senior Japanese police officers confirmed that it was "laundering money everywhere, in every kind of financial institution or industry, legitimate or illicit"—just like the Sicilian Mafia, they agreed on a visit to Italy.[35]

Alas, the two mafias had much in common, observed Palermo's police chief. In fact, they were working together on at least one project by then—in a Yakuza-backed construction company, building the Sydney Harbor Tunnel in Australia.[36]

The Yakuza's silent invasion of Europe has continued undisturbed nonetheless. No agency on the Continent keeps a close eye on it even now. The FBI does, convinced that syndicates like the Yamaguchi-Gumi are riding on the backs of Japan's giant corporations to build a singularly seditious power base in America. (See Chapter 7.) Yet the true relationship between Japan's crooks and capitalists abroad is hardly much clearer to the FBI than to its opposite numbers in Europe. Nobody knows which of Japan's corporations in the outside world may be secretly at the Yakuza's mercy, how much money it may be extracting from them or investing through them, or what hidden pressures may be at work behind politely closed doors.

THE TRIADS

In the summer of 1992, a Chinese girl living in Rome named Lyao Zing Yang was kidnapped in Paris. Her Triad captors demanded a ransom of 400 million lire, about $350,000. But Lyao Zing Yang jumped out of a bathroom window and escaped, whereupon the kidnappers were arrested instead. This might be a humdrum story if not for the Triads' whereabouts. Most people thought they were just in New York, Amsterdam, and London, where they had been implanted for a hundred years. In fact, they had snatched the girl in Paris to avoid drawing police attention to Rome where a flourishing Triad group calling itself Red Sun worked in tandem with others in Florence, Milan, Padua, and Turin, linked to still others in Paris, Marseilles, and Barcelona.[37]

Red Sun's supreme leader in Rome, arrested some months later, turned out to have been the president of a small but swiftly expanding Chinese émigré colony there. The Triads had smuggled eight thousand illegal Chinese immigrants into Italy in just two years, nearly half again the size of the country's entire Chinese community. Around eight hundred more a month were arriving in Milan, authorities thought.[38] The same passports were used over and over again to sneak them in. Some were blanks sent out in bulk from China in cartons of ginseng and Kung Fu slippers. Most were stolen from Japanese tourists by light-fingered South Americans who sold them to the Triads. Replacing the photographs was no problem: Chinese often look alike to Western eyes (and vice versa).

Those "in search of the full moon" were charged up to $25,000 just to get out of China—to Moscow by train (six days), to Budapest by bus, to Yugoslavia by taxi (for an extra $5,000), or straight to the Italian border by train again. Whoever couldn't pay was put to work as a bonded slave in Italy's proliferating Chinese restaurants or in Florentine sweatshops stitching expensive handbags. Two thousand Chinese illegals worked eighteen hours a day in eighty cramped shops like these along the Via Pistoiese, in the Florence suburb of Dannino. Taken over from Italian owners for considerably more cash than they were worth, these shops were now under Chinese management. Surprising amounts of capital were also going into new Chinese restaurants with empty tables. Police were particularly intrigued by one in Rome's historic center that cost $17 million.[39]

What worried Italian authorities more were the better-heeled young Chinese in snappy suits and dark glasses, arriving in the hundreds. These were the *cho-hai*, the sharks—killers, enforcers, pimps, those who beat up recalcitrant Chinese businessmen with chains or kidnapped their wives and daughters.

The *cho-hai* were mostly coming down from a booming Chinatown in Paris where affluent newcomers from Hong Kong were buying up shops around the Place d'Italie for well above the market price, paying cash. Others were putting cash into more ambitious projects such as a shopping center and two luxury hotels on a three-hundred-acre plot along the River Seine, one hundred kilometers from Paris.[40] Several were found to be working with the Medellín cartel's men in a ring that laundered a third of a billion dollars (1.5 billion francs) in 1991 through exchange bureaus in the Basque provinces of southern France.[41] (Police had learned about these bureaus because clients came at midnight with suitcases full of cash.)

France and Italy appeared to be the Triads' new countries of choice; so the police of both agreed at a crisis meeting in Lyon. But the *cho-hai* were fanning out across all the rest of the Continent. Like the Yakuza, their closest friends, the Triads were flocking to the honeypots of Europe. This was no reflection on America. No country compared to America where the Triads were now the Justice Department's "number two priority after La Cosa Nostra." They were on a roll everywhere, but Europe figured large in their plans.

The tens of thousands of Chinese illegals smuggled by Triad "snakeheads" were not only more profitable than heroin, they were a practical necessity. Hong Kong, the Triads' window on the world for over a century, would revert to communist China in 1997. The Triads might go back to the mainland they had fled after the communist takeover—many were in fact going back—but it would never be home.

They were still relatively free in the British Crown Colony, despite being outlawed. The law provided only a six-month mandatory sentence for Triad membership, a one-time offense. "Once you get convicted, you can't be charged again. It's fashionable to get convicted; you just do your time," said Paul Nesbitt, a Hong Kong police officer on loan to Interpol.[42] Here, for all the efforts of a frustrated police force, they refined and shipped dope, worked gambling, usury, extortion, and vice, laundered and invested ten-digit sums, and made the most of awakening China's insatiable hunger for the baubles of an affluent society. For instance, they were averaging a million dollars a night smuggling stolen luxury cars to the Chinese mainland—Mercedes-Benzes, BMWs, and Toyota Crowns, ferried across in super speedboats.[43]

Although unlikely to find such working conditions elsewhere, they had to move their money out, organize new refineries, relocate terminals for their underground communications and banking system, and build up more and bigger Chinese colonies to insulate their bases abroad. This was an immense undertaking for one of the six biggest crime cartels on earth—the only one soon to be without a country of its own.

The Triads had grown beyond recognition since the start of the heroin age. Once they had merely preyed on their countrymen in the Chinatowns of Amsterdam, London, San Francisco, and New York. By the 1990s they had outposts on three continents. A hundred thousand members were spread out in loosely associated gangs across the Chinese mainland, Southeast Asia, Western Europe, and North America.

Great umbrella groups held smaller gangs together. The Sun Yee On had forty thousand members positioned all over the map from Australia, Thailand, and Vietnam to the United States. The United Bamboo Gang had fifteen thousand reaching from Taiwan to Saudi Arabia to Los Angeles. The 14K had twenty-four thousand strung out from China, Taiwan, Macao, and the Philippines to the United States, Canada, Australia, New Zealand, Germany, Britain, Holland, Italy, and France.

Like the Sicilian Mafia before them, they were rising to the heights of the underworld on heroin. Despite their privileged access to the poppy fields of Burma, the Triads had yielded to the Mafia for twenty years. While the Triads had a handle on two-thirds of the world's heroin supply, the Sicilians controlled the market. Since they were not good at operating outside the Chinese community, the Triads left it like that.

The two brotherhoods had always gotten along. In New York, where Little Italy and Chinatown are back to back, one or the other "only had to cross the road from Mott Street to Mulberry Street and make contacts with people interested in the narcotics business," a DEA agent once observed. "Maybe the Chinese had two, three, four, five Italians that they trusted, and the Italians trusted *them*. You would never, never hear of a Chinese guy being arrested and giving up an Italian. You would never hear of an Italian giving up a Chinese, never."[44] (See Chapter 7.)

So for two decades the Triads let the Mafia buy all the Southeast Asian heroin it wanted in Thailand—China White, the addicts' favorite—and the Mafia let the Triads bring in about a fifth of America's. By 1983, Thailand swarmed with Sicilian traffickers whose Chinese suppliers were selling to them by the ton. One alone, Koh Bak Kin, consigned 3,750 kilos of morphine base on his first delivery to Palermo from Bangkok—enough to produce nearly four tons of the six tons of heroin consumed yearly in America. He was filling orders for another ton or so when he was arrested.[45]

Halfway through the 1980s, however, Italian and American authorities cracked down on the Sicilians' network. Though far from wrecked, it was disrupted, whereupon the Triads set up their own refineries in Thailand and elsewhere and filled the breach. In the space of just a few years, the roles were reversed. The Triads came to provide nearly four-fifths of the heroin reaching New York and about a fifth of Europe's on top of that.

Europe was obviously next. Its heroin market was going through the roof—the EC's addict population hit a million in 1992—and the Triads were going after it. Their conduits were London and Amsterdam, which had the largest and oldest Chinatowns in Europe. London was getting tough for them, but Amsterdam was now the center of the entire Continent's heroin trade.

Nearly everybody dealing dope passed through its Schiphol Airport, a notorious pushover, or the docks of Rotterdam or along the

Balkan route, which ended in Holland. From there the junk went one way, to New York, or the other way, to Germany, Belgium, Italy, or France.

Competition was especially fierce from Turkish traffickers, whose countrymen in Holland outnumbered the Chinese 400,000 to 100,000, of which nearly half were illegals. The Triads couldn't hope to overtake the Turkish mafia in Europe anyway. Nevertheless, they had an airlift going from the Far East to Schiphol Airport, new refineries and shipping routes on the Chinese mainland, and thousands of captive Chinese helpers arriving on the Continent.[46]

East Europe was opening out to them or their potential captives. "More and more Chinese" were going to Poland, reported the head of Interpol in Warsaw. Trainloads of Chinese illegals were crossing the Ukraine into Hungary, now offering residence permits to any Chinese citizen of Hong Kong for $100,000. (The Hungarian airline Malev carried the ad.)[47] Others were slipping into Austria, Scandinavia, and Spain. Doubtless the Triads weren't winning, but they were gaining.

The Sicilian Mafia did not fight them in America, nor was it fighting them in Europe; it was brokering for them. Partnered with Turkish traffickers for twenty years, it was brokering for the Turks, too.

THE SICILIAN MAFIA

Like their opposite numbers in Russia, Sicilian mafiosi *traveled*. Who would expect them to turn up in Sverdlovsk, deep in the Ural Mountains, a thousand kilometers from Moscow? Yet Russian intelligence agents came upon a Sicilian mafioso in February 1993 when he and an American mafia colleague turned up connected to the South Russian International Bank there.[48]

What the pair had in mind can only be guessed. The city of Sverdlovsk, in the region of the same name, is at the center of the famous military-industrial complex that once drove the Soviet economy and equipped the Red Army. Its factories are still turning out tanks and sophisticated weaponry that the Red Army can no longer afford to buy. Others can buy the weaponry *freely and le-*

gally, however, provided the transactions are not for direct export.[49] Quantities are exported indirectly and illegally, reaching world markets through front companies in northern Italy by way of a KGB agent's network in Vienna. (See Chapter 11.)

Sverdlovsk is also the region embracing Tyumen, which has more petroleum reserves than the entire Middle East. Furthermore, Sverdlovsk is the home base for the Big Urals, the consolidated Russian mafia gang now operating across ex-Soviet territory from the Baltic to the Pacific.

Perhaps the operations of these mafiosi in Sverdlovsk will have come to light by the time this book is published; perhaps not. Detecting the crimes of a crooked bank in today's Russia is extremely difficult, and nailing the crooks is even more so. Other mafiosi, Sicilian and American, were certainly operating in the ex–Soviet republics by 1993. Documented evidence pointed to connections of some sort with the Madonia and Troia Families of Palermo, the Santapaola Family of Catania, the Cuntrera Family of Siculiana and Caracas, the Morabito Families of Catania and Calabria, the Licciardi clan of Naples, the American mafia's Biondo Family in Detroit, and the Gambino Family in New York. Their partners in the Cali cartel were present, too.

Nobody in authority could determine how many were actually on the Russian scene or, with a few interesting exceptions, what they were doing there. Italian investigators looking for the tracks of Italian crooks in Russia and East Europe found little more than tantalizing traces. According to Criminalpol's Alessandro Pansa, they were "probably not ready to invest millions of dollars in a wildly unstable Russian economy." They were investing *fake* dollars, he said. This enabled them to pick up raw materials, real estate, factories, and antiques without spending a dime. More than a billion and a half counterfeit dollars in $100 bills were *confiscated* in Italy in the single year of 1992.[50] Several billion more were adding to Russia's torments by the year's end. Not all were Mafia made, but Dr. Pansa told me forged $100 bills were one of the Mafia's biggest earners all over the ex-Soviet bloc—Poland, Hungary, Romania, Czechoslovakia, and Bulgaria.

Apart from counterfeit money, the Italians were doing scams:

ruble swaps, food for precious metal swaps, credit card frauds, EC subsidy frauds, and straight swindles. In Poland and Hungary they were shipping girls into slavery; in Romania they had a child adoption racket.[51]

Pansa's men could ascertain only two hundred such cases, plainly not the whole story. Nearly all the instruments needed to detect foreign criminals were lacking in these countries; the fallen Soviet empire was a perfect place for them to hide. There were undoubtedly more of them in the ex-satellite states than the record showed.

"All kinds of criminals started to come here in 1992—that was the year the dam broke," said Andrzej Kowezsko, head of Interpol in Poland.

> This is their contact country, where they meet to discuss their business—Italians, Colombians, Turks, and Russians.
>
> They don't hurt Poles, so it's almost impossible to get them into court. For instance, the Russian mafia just stops Russian tourist buses at gunpoint and collects five dollars a passenger, like checking tickets.
>
> The Sicilian Mafia doesn't come to commit crimes. It's only interested in laundering money. We caught two of them when another one came up from Palermo to torch their place. . . .
>
> The Colombians see a whole new situation here— they can use Polish camels to move cocaine instead of going the old Balkan route. It's not against Polish law to *possess* any amount of cocaine, so how do you catch the camels? But the Colombians do money, too. . . . We cops in Poland have no way to check the money's provenance. They can transfer it out of the country—you can get any bank documents you want here if you pay enough—or they can invest it. God knows, we can't trash investments. Now criminal interest in Poland is growing. They come here to start producing synthetic drugs themselves. We think the Italians or the Dutch,

maybe both, are getting into it. That's our nightmare.

If you're a foreigner and you buy a villa here, you're a nobleman. You have flowers in your garden, you give candy to kids, then you open a little factory, you provide jobs, you pay taxes. You say you're processing vegetables, and you're probably making amphetamines; they have no smell. But how can we tell? We cops get no information from the West saying you have dirty hands.

We have no laws, we have no surveillance in hotels. We don't have the mentality. The public doesn't *expect* us to deal with such things. When we get around to looking, they'll be far, far ahead of us.[52]

Czechoslovakia was in much the same predicament. "We've been isolated, under glass. Now with open borders we get whatever the rest of Europe gets: A wave of crime is advancing on us," said Czechoslovakia's police chief, Miroslav Opravil. "They're all here: the Sicilians, the Camorra, the Colombians, the Yakuza, the Yugoslavs, the Russian mafia, the Ukrainian mafia, the Uzbekis, the Turkmenis, the Afghanis, the Chechen—a very dangerous mafia, the Chechen. They seem to have divided the territory; they don't penetrate each other's turf," he went on.[53]

Like the Chechen, the Sicilian Mafia and Camorra were buying real estate, cafes, and casinos in Prague, each carefully keeping off the other's territory.

"Some very suspicious Italians have settled here. They bring in tax and financial specialists to launder their money, and they're laundering plenty," declared the head of the Czech financial police.

They're all doing it. The Medellín cartel tried to launder three hundred million through Czech banks, and they got away with $100 million. Our banks don't ask the origin of their money. This is a paradise for them. We know of certain Italians who are using straw men to buy their own banks in southern Bohemia; that's the best place for laundering.

We have no laws to stop them. Soon they'll start to
influence politicians. Then they'll block legislation. So
we're racing to get the laws. The question is who'll be
quicker. I think they will.

As a new Mafia hinterland grew discernible in the East, an old one
long and resolutely overlooked in the West began to emerge as
well.

Around Christmas time in 1992, Belgian police came across a
huddle of wretched Africans from Burkina Faso waiting to be
smuggled into Italy. A ring of camorristi had flown them to the
Belgian capital of Brussels where they needed no entry visas. They
were supposed to go on to Naples by taxi, for $500 apiece.[54] The
Camorra was going to put them to work in its underground factories in Naples, turning out a fair share of the world's counterfeit
goods, worth an amazing $80 billion a year.

(Apart from forged dollar bills, the Camorra's products included
fake Rolex watches, Vuitton luggage, Scotch whiskey, and Chanel
perfume, for which the bottles were made in Italy and Spain, the
labels in Holland, and the contents in Mexico.)[55]

The Camorra and the Mafia were both moving African illegals
through Belgium where they did a considerable amount of business. Indeed, a "Mafia milieu" had managed to "penetrate and
conceal itself in the highest realms of Belgian industry and finance
. . . including advanced technology and armament," warned an
eminent judge, Jean-François Godbille, in 1989. He received a
brushoff from an incredulous Belgian parliament at the time. Three
years later, however, he was heading a national commission to
combat a *"Mafia des negriers,"* running a colossal slave market in
Belgium and northern France.

The ring worked out of a stupendous castle in Charleroi, owned
and expensively restored by an unemployed Sicilian laborer. The
real owner was Pasquale Cuntrera of Sicily, Venezuela, and Aruba,
whose base in Belgium went back many years.[56]

From their castle in Charleroi, the Cuntreras' men were farming out ten thousand black Africans to construction companies all across the country. Seven people were murdered for nosing around, including a young reporter for Charleroi's *Nouvelle Gazette*.[57] His killer presumably slipped back to Sicily; nobody of importance in the ring was ever caught.

Brussels, seat of the European Community, also turned out to be a drug traffickers' haven. Foreigners and citizens alike had a sacrosanct right to privacy there: no phone taps, no bugs in the wall, no electronic devices tracking a suspect van, and not many bank controls, either. Therefore the Sicilian Mafia and the Cali cartel were using Brussels as headquarters for a huge cocaine ring. French police learned of it when they seized six hundred kilos of the ring's cocaine—a record haul—coming over the Spanish border at Perpignan, on the way to Milan.[58]

France was worse off, if anything. Though long occupied, the country was stunned to discover "disquieting signs of a growing Mafia presence" in 1993. "The Italian Mafias" considered this a "territory to colonize," a place to put its money and men, reported a special French parliamentary Anti-Mafia Commission.[59]

Don Michele Zaza, the ranking Camorra boss, incorrigible drug trafficker, and longtime Italian fugitive, was "the best example of their colonization efforts," the commission said.

"A scent of the Mafia" emanated from French holdings bigger than Zaza's very considerable holdings, however. One, a development project for a golf course, hotel, and two hundred villas, was financed through 150 Dutch companies largely controlled by shell companies in the Channel Islands.

Several other mega-investments were being made by an Italian millionaire named Giancarlo Casaccia, "known to the Italian police for illicit money dealings." Based in the principality of Monaco, Casaccia belonged to a financial consortium of thirty companies in France, Monaco, Luxembourg, and Panama, specializing in real estate. Through two intermediaries, he was investing, the Commission said, on behalf of Carmine Alfieri, topmost Camorra boss, and Alfieri's number two, Pasquale Galasso, a *dollar* billionaire.

(Galasso, arrested in Italy in 1992, confessed to thirty-two homicides and a working arrangement for shared payoffs with several Italian politicians of cabinet rank.)

According to the Commission, Casaccia's projects included a thirty-story tower in Beausoleil (Alpes-Maritime), an eighteen-hole golf course in Pierrevert (Alpes-de-Haute Provence), and a projected $30 million residence complex around the golf green. Even more ambitious was a joint project with the mayoralty of Orange for "the most important urbanization plan ever undertaken by the city"—the restoration of its historic center and a new satellite quarter giving on to the national autoroute, with apartment buildings, offices, and a grand deluxe hotel.[60]

The Commission said that one of Casaccia's subcompanies, Transimmo, had paid sixteen million francs (around $3 million) for thirty-five thousand square meters of the land—nearly three times its market price (six million francs).

Buying real estate for more than its worth was the classic mark of the money launderer. All the Italian Mafias were investing heavily for this purpose in France, and not just buying but building. Sicilian mafiosi in particular were actually financing a third of all the new construction on the French Riviera; so the parliamentary commission learned from Judge Giovanni Falcone. Full-page ads in the Italian press offered stupendous villas and high-rise condominiums on the Côte d'Azur for low, low prices.

Several other avenues were open for laundering in or through France. Four-fifths of all casino receipts along the Côte d'Azur were of Italian origin, for instance.[61] Monaco, though subject to bank controls for French citizens, offered complete bank secrecy for anyone else. Shell companies of every description found it "a particularly choice place to launder capital," the Parliamentary Anti-Mafia Commission said. Best of all was the island of Sint Maarten (St. Martin), on the way to becoming the world's second Mafia state.

A Sicilian mafioso named Rosario Spadaro held the Dutch side, allegedly laundering for fellow Italians, Americans, and Colombians. The proceeds were "passing unhindered to St. Martin" on the French side, and on into France itself. This capital was "absolutely opaque," said Jacques de Larosière, governor of the Bank of France.

Like Germany, France was beginning to feel the Mafia's sinister powers of corruption—its ability to seduce and manipulate French middlemen, bankers, and politicians, to contaminate whole economic areas, and to pass as legitimate. "France is not safe from the Mafia," the Parliamentary Anti-Mafia Commission concluded. "The Mafia is not folklore. The Mafia is a model of the future for organized crime. France has no immunity from Mafia-type organizations. . . . There is no part of our territory or sector of our economy that could not interest [them]."

By a hair, in 1989, the American mafia had failed to lock into a peculiarly alluring sector of the French economy. A U.S. corporation strongly suspected of mafia financing offered $178 million for the most advanced industrial incinerator in France, but was turned down.[62] The Americans were moving rapidly into other crime business in Europe: gambling casinos in Germany, export-import scams in Russia, laundering everywhere. But garbage was a kind of statement for America's Cosa Nostra Families, their way of staking out territory on the Continent as they had done all across the United States.

They had rarely ventured across the Atlantic since the days of Lucky Luciano. Now they were joining the rest of the underworld in Europe. The rest of the underworld had joined them in America long before.

CHAPTER SEVEN

In America

"This is gonna be a Cosa Nostra till I die. Be it an hour from now, or be it tonight, or a hundred years from now, when I'm in jail. It's gonna be Cosa Nostra."[1] So John Gotti said before a judge sent him up for life. The perceived wisdom today is that he was wrong, but the facts suggest that he may have been right.

Cosa Nostra's end, predicted regularly in America for half a century, *ought* to be near. Over a thousand of its members and associates have been indicted or imprisoned since the 1980s. Its entire governing commission has been convicted. The biological solution awaits its geriatric bosses. Practically all its top patriarchs are behind bars for good anyway, including Gotti himself.

Their younger successors are inexperienced, brash, incautiously greedy, several generations removed from the old mafia culture, and bereft of historical memory. Their discipline is poor. Their humus, the Italian-American community, is washing away into the mainstream of American life. Their hold on the streets seems to be weakening since they lease out rackets to others. Their nerve appears to be slipping, in that they kill less than some of their ceaselessly multiplying and recklessly violent rivals. On the other hand, they are killing each other off more persistently than they have done in decades.

"This is the twilight of the mob. It's not dark yet, but the sun is going down," one expert announced.

Yet for the FBI, Cosa Nostra is still "the most serious organized crime problem in the United States." The crime ring that has outlived every other in America since the 1890s is still recruiting, still creaming 20 percent off the top of all new construction in New York, still doing nearly everything it has always done, in the areas that have always been its strongholds.[2]

FBI field officers report that Federal prosecutions have "had little impact on Cosa Nostra's overall activity" in Detroit, "no impact" in Los Angeles, "little effect" in Chicago; that its activities "do not appear to have diminished" in Miami and "remain relatively unchanged" in Kansas City; that the Genovese Family has "a huge operation" in New Jersey where its structure "remains intact."

Nationwide, the organization "remains particularly strong in Chicago, New England, southern Florida, Las Vegas, Atlantic City, and New York City," the FBI says.[3]

"In the universe of organized criminal groups, the racketeering activities of La Cosa Nostra are the most protracted and sustained, the most impacted and entrenched, the most expansive and profitable, the most corrosive and deleterious to legitimate sectors of society, the most resistant to enforcement efforts generally, and the most resilient to the aftermath of any single enforcement effort," observes the FBI's New Jersey office.[4]

THE SICILIAN MAFIA

Second only to this seemingly unsinkable organization is its big brother from Sicily. An independent entity in America since the 1960s, Sicily's Cosa Nostra was supposed to have been finished there halfway through the 1980s when its heroin network was cracked in New York's Pizza Connection case. Actually, it has been "growing precipitously," says the head of the FBI's organized crime section, Jim Moody.[5]

It may become a graver menace than its American counterpart, warned Attorney-General William Barr in 1992. "I've said this privately, and I've said it at the cabinet table. We are facing a tremendous challenge from the Sicilian Mafia, one that could dwarf La Cosa Nostra here in the United States. We may be at the beginning of a more serious threat from organized crime than ever before," he told a reporter for the *Legal Times*.[6]

There were clear signs by then that the Sicilian Mafia was rapidly colonizing the American underworld. Its men have been arriving legally; visas are no longer required for Italian nationals. Keeping away from big cities inhabited by the American mob and knowledgeable cops, they have been fanning out over the countryside like KGB moles. They settle into small towns, file for citizenship, go into business, and win the community's respect. Their names and faces are unknown, and they have no rap sheets in America.

The harder the law bears down on the American mafia, the more Sicilian mafiosi arrive. The FBI thought there were a few hundred of them in the late 1980s. By 1991 it was speaking of three thousand, not counting members of the Camorra and 'Ndrangheta, "noted with increasing frequency." By the end of 1992 it was estimating "between ten and twenty thousand members and associates."[7] That is roughly the size of the American mafia itself: two thousand members, some twenty thousand associates. A second Mafia as large as the first, accountable to Palermo, has calamitous implications for the United States. These are the soldiers formed during Totò Riina's long and violent reign, veterans of Sicily's Great Mafia War, interlocked with the world's biggest crime syndicates, brutalized to a degree that frightens even their American cousins. They are already drawing the American mafia into their planetary orbit—notably in the sack of Russia—and they can undoubtedly give it lessons in the art of wielding power.

"If you want your Cosa Nostra to be as successful as our Cosa Nostra, you oughtta use Sicilian methods, like killing judges and cops," advised a prize Sicilian trafficker in New York.

Relations between the two mafias have always been mysterious, at times unfathomable. By mutual agreement they have been separate and distinct for some forty years; neither can intrude on the other's sovereign territory. Actually, the Sicilians have occupied several of the Americans' exclusive enclaves since the 1960s and poached all over their criminal preserves.

For the Americans they are the "zips," "geeps," "fuckin' siggies," secretive, predatory, resented, and detested. John Gotti, then the highest boss in the land, had raged against the Sicilians in an exchange with a couple of his soldiers recorded by the FBI:

> FIRST SOLDIER: They're opening up all over the fuckin' place, these zips, ain't they? There's three of them right on this avenue here. They all make money. . . .
> SECOND SOLDIER: If they run a game, you know, Johnny [Gotti] will go along with another game. . . .
> GOTTI: They're not gonna play nothin'. . . . I got four thousand guys I'll send from every neighborhood, I'll put in there. . . . Let 'em come ahead. Let's see what they'll do.
> FIRST SOLDIER: They make like they don't understand, the motherfuckers. . . .
> GOTTI: They don't understand what they don't wanna understand. . . . They go around with hundreds of thousands in their pockets, and you're going around with your hat in your hand. . . .[8]

Yet the Sicilian Mafia's top emissary to the United States was taken into New York's Gambino Family with "five, six, seven of his crew" in the mid-1970s; a decade later he was elevated to the rank of *capodecina* by John Gotti himself. "You knew then that I made a mistake," Gotti said to his *consigliere*, Sammy "The Bull" Gravano, who so testified at Gotti's trial in 1992:

> He's discussing the liaison guy from Italy to here who we believe might be a made member of our Family and made in Italy and have one foot here and one foot in Italy, and he's doing business.
> John Gotti said: "If it's true, if it's him, the liaison guy is getting whacked. . . ." He meant, "If the liaison guy

is a made member with us and he has a foot in Italy and he's doing drugs, he's gonna get whacked." . . . The liaison guy is getting whacked because they don't belong to us. That's their crew. . . .[9]

The liaison guy did not get whacked, however. Early in 1987 five different *capos* from New York's five mafia Families sat down with him in the back room of the Cafe Giardino, his Brooklyn seat. John Gotti himself drew up in a limousine to call on him soon afterward. From then on he was wintering with Gotti in Florida and seeing him in New York once a week.[10]

His name was John Gambino, eldest of the three Gambino brothers of Brooklyn and Cherry Hill, New Jersey, who had come over from Sicily in 1974. Though a distant relative of the late Carlo Gambino, boss of the most powerful Family in America, he answered to the Cupola's innermost circle in Palermo.

Arrested in New York on the day that General Manuel Noriega of Panama was arraigned in Miami for collusion with Colombian cocaine cartels, John Gambino received barely a mention in the press. But he had done more than the General to feed America's drug habit.

Tons of heroin had been shipped to him directly in Brooklyn since the 1970s, from Sicilian refineries "transforming and selling heroin to the United States silently, intensively, and continuously," wrote an Italian magistrate. Billions of narcodollars in need of laundering had been entrusted to him, and through him to the Sicilian Mafia's banker in New York, Michele Sindona.[11]

In fact, John Gambino could not possibly be whacked, as Gotti discovered when the secrets of Cosa Nostra's previous top boss—the one Gotti got rid of, Paul Castellano—were revealed to him. John Gambino was the diamond point of the whole Sicilian Mafia heroin operation in the United States and guarantor of its longstanding arrangements with the Americans.

The deal, made at a summit meeting in Palermo's Grand Hotel Des Palmes in October 1957, allowed the Americans to divest themselves of the risks in dealing heroin while collecting a share of the profits. The Sicilians took exclusive charge of import and wholesale distribution. The Americans received a rakeoff per kilo and announced that they were out of the drug business—officially, right after the Palermo summit, at their historic Appalachin congress in upstate New York.[12]

Whether or not this was an early sign of the Americans' decline, as some maintain, it marked the beginning of the Sicilians' ascendancy. Once installed in America, they could not be dislodged. Nor, for all their incursions, could they be molested.

They might be feared and disliked, but they were needed—are needed urgently today. American bosses habitually dodge their own ban on drugs by investing money in Sicilian deals. More and more of their soldiers are risking an in-house death sentence to work with Sicilian traffickers. Many Families, running to flab, are in search of more backbone and muscle. For an aging organization tormented by the law and beset by new young rivals, the Sicilians have come to mean fresh blood and the saving strength of ancestral Mafia tradition. Compared to their American cousins, they are still the keepers of the ancient Mafia code, however they may have trashed it. Thus, a growing number of Sicilians "made" at home are getting made in the United States as well. Several have become *capos* in American Families. One has taken over a Family altogether.

Spicy evidence to this effect dropped into the lap of FBI agents in Medford, Massachusetts, in the autumn of 1989. Twenty-one members of Boston's Patriarca Family gathered there on a Sunday to induct four new members. An FBI bug picked up every word as a Patriarca captain administered the ritual oath: *"Io, Carmen, voglio entrare in questa organizzazione. . ."*

The oath giver, a Sicilian Man of Honor named Biagio DiGiacomo, had to explain from time to time in strangled English. "Put your hands out like this, Carmen, and when I read it to you, repeat after me and then go like this, boom, boom, boom," he said, preparing to draw blood from Carmen's trigger finger. He continued:

"If I said you must kill a police informer, would you do that for me on behalf of our organization?"

"Yes, I would."

"You would do that?"

"I would do that."

"This thing of ours, we would be delighted to have you . . ."

Then DiGiacomo continued in Sicilian: "I swear to enter this organization alive and leave it dead." In English, he went on, that meant, "We get in alive in this organization, and the only way we gonna get out is death, no matter what. It's no hope, no Jesus, no Madonna, nobody can help us if we ever give up this secret to anybody. . . . This thing that cannot be exposed. . . ."[13]

The Patriarca Family inducted several more Sicilians in 1992; bugged repeatedly and mercilessly by the FBI, it is plainly in need of their reviving presence. New York's Lucchese Family has sworn in an unregenerate Sicilian drug trafficker, Enzo Napoli. The Philadelphia Family, an exceptionally riotous lot, has actually come under a Sicilian's rule.

The Philadelphia Family has dominated crime and politics in much of Pennsylvania for some seventy years, but it started to fly apart when its longtime boss, Angelo Bruno, was shot dead with a sawed-off shotgun in March 1980. A month later Bruno's consigliere was tortured, stabbed, and shot to death. A few months afterward his chief loan shark was found stuffed into two green plastic garbage bags. At year's end his successor was blown up by a bomb packed with nails.[14]

The perpetrator, Nicodemo Scarfo, ordered the murders of nineteen more members after he took over—this out of forty in all, replaced by his own men. Ruling with a flamboyance and raw violence much like John Gotti's, Scarfo met much the same end. He was tried for criminal conspiracy and a continuing criminal enterprise—ten homicides, five attempted homicides, extortion, gambling, narcotics—and jailed for life.[15]

The fact that he left the Philadelphia Family in shambles does not altogether explain why the highest echelons of America's Cosa Nostra sent in a Sicilian Man of Honor to replace him. The reputed new boss, John Stanfa, once drove for Angelo Bruno, but he is still a "zip." Born and made in Sicily, he communicates regularly with Palermo's top bosses and is part of their crowd in the United States.[16] Nevertheless, the Gambino Family sent Stanfa down from New York, John Gotti backed him, and Cosa Nostra's national commission even authorized him to swear in a few more Sicilians. Decisions like these are not made casually.

Philadelphia is where the American mafia is "the *second* most serious problem, *after* the Sicilian Mafia," says the FBI. Sicilian drug traffickers infest the city—indeed, they own the whole northern half of it. Angelo Bruno, Sicilian-born himself, turned over the north side long ago to John Gambino and his brothers in nearby Cherry Hill, New Jersey.[17] It is in Philadelphia that the two mafias may decide to remarry after nearly half a century apart: a union of imperial grandeur for the international underworld and a nightmare for American authorities.

There could hardly be much doubt about where such a marriage might lead. "Them fucking zips ain't gonna back up to nobody. . . . Those guys are looking to take over everything. You give them the fucking power . . . they'll bury you. They don't give a fuck. They don't care who's boss. They got no respect," a Bonnano Family captain observed some years ago.[18]

Invited to rejuvenate the American organization, the Sicilians may well end up running it. They will be on their way if they can infuse a once-illustrious American Family with fresh strength.

"A reorganization and perhaps a return to tradition is taking place in the Philadelphia Family and others as well. . . . What is developing may signal a new trend for the organization and operation of La Cosa Nostra," says the authoritative Pennsylvania Crime Commission. "If Stanfa is successful . . . we may see a powerful confederation of Sicilian Mafia members with the remaining Family veterans. Cosa Nostra may emerge as far more powerful, effective, and insulated from law enforcement. The metamorphosis in the Philadelphia Family may represent the future of Cosa Nostra."[19]

This was the attorney general's bad dream: the emergence of a hydra-headed criminal monster in America that would certainly dwarf La Cosa Nostra as we know it.

Never again, the FBI vowed in 1991. The mafia, as if designed by some diabolical hand, seemed impervious to everything the law could throw at it. The United States could not let that happen again.

Apart from redoubled efforts to eliminate the mafia itself, the main thrust of FBI strategy now was to "ensure that no other criminal organization can ever achieve a comparable level of power."

Heartfelt agreement came from Assistant Attorney General Robert Mueller, testifying on the Hill. "For most of the last thirty years we've played catch-up in eradicating what is still this country's most serious organized crime problem—La Cosa Nostra. We will not repeat that mistake. We cannot stand idly by while newer organized crime groups invade our society," he told a Senate committee.[20]

But American society was invaded already, by the same forces advancing on Europe, working both continents as one. Though far ahead of others in trying to cope with them, U.S. law enforcement agencies still cannot bridge what is known as the "technology gap" between the crime syndicates' capabilities and their own.

To deal with more than a thousand organized gangs is overwhelming—Hispanics, Asians, West Indians, Mexicans, African-Americans, California's Crips and Bloods, motorcycle gangs such as the Pagans, the Bandidos, and Hell's Angels. These can be nationwide, disciplined, heavily armed, and lethal. Jamaican Posses rampage through thirty-five states, pushing nearly half the crack sold in the country. Hell's Angels have thirty-five chapters in the United States and as many again abroad, in Canada, Britain, Denmark, Germany, France, Brazil, New Zealand, Russia, Japan.[21]

But they are no potential Cosa Nostras. Most of them hire out to Cosa Nostra or pay it tribute. Hell's Angels are its "working partners," the FBI declares. Cosa Nostra's Chicago Family employs Mexicans, Puerto Ricans, and Colombians. New York's Families collect a tax from Cubans handling the numbers game in Harlem and Russian crooks in Brighton Beach. The Philadelphia Family collects a street tax from any criminal band trying to work there.

What worries Washington is an alarming invasion by Cosa Nostra's true peers—the Triads, the Yakuza, and the Russian mafia, the largest organizations in the crime business. The Triads have four times as many members and helpers as their American counterparts, the Yakuza five times as many, the Russians over a hundred times as many, more and more of whom are drifting into the United States. Any one of the three in league with either of the two mafias in the United States would be a fright story, and they are all in league with both. Such concentrated criminal strength is beyond anything in American experience—in any country's experience, for that matter.

With a statesmanship yet to be achieved by the United Nations, these titans of the underworld have been sharing resources, personnel, and protective cover for years, peaceably and to their mutual benefit. They all "pay tribute" (taxes) to the American Cosa Nostra, the FBI says. In exchange they "utilize Cosa Nostra connections to penetrate the country's law enforcement and judicial communities through long-established Cosa Nostra contacts."[22] The fact that Cosa Nostra gives them access to its private collection of corrupt judges and cops suggests extraordinary levels of complicity.

As far back as 1984, witnesses summoned by President Reagan's Commission on Organized Crime described some of their operational links. A compulsive Japanese gambler told how the Yakuza ran its high-stake games in New York, for instance:

Q. Were all of the people operating these games Japanese?

A. No, some of them Italian.

Q. How would the games run?

A. Different people sell drinks, but Italians were in the back room and approved play on credit.

Q. How was the credit collected?

A. If I pay in two, three weeks, nothing happen, but if you took longer, I would be visited by someone from the game. They say they hadn't seen me for a while, and they hope to see me soon.

Q. The people who came, were they Japanese?

A. No. Italian-American.

Q. Did the Japanese carry weapons?

A. No.

Q. Did the Italian-Americans carry weapons?

A. Yes.[23]

A Chinese witness at the hearings told of ongoing collaboration between the Triads and the Sicilian Mafia in New York. First, the Sicilians had asked the man's Triad boss to open a letter of credit for them in Taiwan, covering the cost of a heroin shipment from there. Then they gave him a suitcase full of cash to be laundered and delivered to Italy. Finally they asked him to "bring a letter over to Hong Kong" for "a very wealthy Chinese gentleman wearing a very expensive gold Rolex watch," who provided them with a new heroin supply line.

Back in New York, the witness received a classic Sicilian warning: "He said that you know that I am very powerful in this country, and I hope you don't betray me or be unfaithful to me."[24]

Those were early days. The Triads had only a modest share of the heroin traffic then; the Yakuza were barely recognizable to the average law enforcer; and the Russian mafia was just getting started on multi-billion-dollar scams which, "for imagination and gall, rival anything La Cosa Nostra could ever have done," observed a harried California detective.

THE TRIADS

Today, the Triads are second only to the mafia as a menace to American society, and they are the mafia's best friends. Those in Philadelphia's Chinatown buy their video poker machines from the Lucchese Family in New York and the De Cavalcante Family in New Jersey. Others pay percentage points on their gambling take to the Family in Chicago, buy guns from New York's five Families, and import loan sharks from the Patriarca Family for their Manhattan gambling dens.[25]

The more heroin they bring in, the more they rely on their old Sicilian colleagues. Chinese traffickers are too exposed outside their community to distribute several tons a year—enough for the better part of half a million addicts. As usual, the Sicilians are moving it wholesale for them.

"Is the Sicilian mob still doing what it always did in Brooklyn? Sure it is," says the Brooklyn district attorney's special assistant, Douglas Le Vien. "People think it's the Triads because so much heroin comes from Southeast Asia. But believe me, the Sicilians are still big in dope," declares the FBI's Jim Moody.

Many disparate Chinese are in the drug business—indeed, in every kind of crime business—but it is the Triads who rule over America's Chinatowns. More than a million and a half people live under their dominion—the largest Chinese population in the West, exceptionally conscientious and hardworking, exploited methodically and frightened into silence.

Those in charge are the cream of Triad society in Hong Kong and Taiwan. The Sun Yee On and Wo Hop To operate all over Southeast Asia. The 14K runs most of the Triads' European heroin trade from Amsterdam. The United Bamboo Gang has entered into a formal pact with the Yamaguchi-Gumi, leader of Yakuza society in Japan.[26] Whether through fraternal tongs or on their own, these are the top four in control of gambling, usury, prostitution, and extortion in the Chinatowns of San Francisco, Los Angeles, Portland, Denver, Houston, Phoenix, Chicago, Boston, Philadelphia, Atlantic City, and New York.[27]

Four out of five Chinese merchants pay them protection money on a sliding scale—$200 to $750 a week per restaurant table in San Francisco. A recalcitrant owner might lose his restaurant or be beaten unconscious or be sliced with a hundred cuts of a razor and hung on a meat hook. Law enforcement could never get far past the barriers of culture, language, and fear in these Chinese settlements. But the Triads are on the loose now, "expanding rapidly outside the Asian community . . . growing exponentially in sophistication and power," say Federal authorities.[28]

Like the Sicilian Mafia, they are diversifying: laundering drug money, swindling insurance companies, defrauding banks, passing counterfeit currency, cleaning up with fake credit cards. (Triads in Hong Kong and Singapore make half the world's forged credit cards.)[29] Virulent Asian street gangs under their influence— the Ghost Shadows, the Flying Dragons, Born to Kill—are burglarizing homes, terrorizing the inhabitants, threatening to slaughter the children, raping and occasionally murdering the women. "It has happened in Washington, D.C.," a shocked Senate Committee on Investigations was told by the FBI.[30]

Caught in this second game of catch-up, Federal agents can see the enemy's troops multiplying before their eyes. For the Triads on the ground, America is the natural solution to the vexing problem of vacating Hong Kong. Before the Crown Colony reverts to China in 1997, the Triads are racing to bring over money, fellow members, and a whole conscript army of illegal Chinese immigrants.

An astonishing $3.8 billion in currency was transferred from Hong Kong to the United States in 1991—up 540 percent. How much belonged to the Triads was impossible to say. A lot, the Senate committee thought. A surge of illegal Chinese immigration started around that time. In the entire decade of the 1980s, Triad "snakeheads" and associates had smuggled 108,975 Chinese illegals into the United States. They were bringing in 80,000 a year by 1993.[31]

American agencies have identified at least sixty different routes of theirs by land, sea, and air. Thirty-seven shiploads were on the high seas at once in 1991. Twenty-four carrying human cargo were intercepted off the island of Manhattan over the following year, and at least as many again off San Francisco. One syndicate bought six blocks of two hundred tickets each for a European airline to get his customers as far as Central America where a chartered 707 waited to make the final run.

At anywhere from $30,000 to $50,000 a head, the smugglers are grossing over $3 billion a year, not counting heroin picked up in Thailand on the way. This is practically found money involving next to no risk: The United States has granted refugee status to any Chinese requesting it since the 1989 uprising in Tiananmen Square. "No one loses because we don't prosecute and we don't deport Chinese. All they have to do is get there, and they can stay forever," said a U.S. immigration officer in Southeast Asia.[32]

Most passengers haven't a prayer of paying for their passage, especially coming from dirt-poor regions such as Fujian. "If you have $30,000 and live in Fujian Province, there is no reason to leave because you are one of the richest people there," the immigration officer observed.

Those who fail to pay generally end up in brothels, sweatshops, or the steel grip of a drug ring—expendable chattel, bonded slaves. Before getting there, they may be "bound and handcuffed in some apartment, fed infrequently, beaten, tortured with claw hammers and lit cigarettes, and held until payment is made," a New York detective has testified.

"What if the full fee cannot be paid?" a *Time* reporter asked Big Boss Ma, a champion people smuggler in Thailand. "That is very dangerous business," he replied, inasmuch as the debt "is turned over to the Mafia in the United States and Europe, or the Yakuza in Japan."[33]

THE YAKUZA

The Yakuza, or Boryukudan, have nothing like the Triads' ethnic hinterland in America, but they have an unnerving unseen *presence*. Their main pursuits in the United States, as in Europe, are by definition not often discussed: corporate blackmail and enormous capital investment.

Nobody knows how many billions of dollars they are laundering through the U.S. economy, how many of Japan's giant companies they are holding for ransom in New York or California, how many U.S. companies may be falling victim to the provocative wiles of their *sokaiya*. Investigators have enough evidence to believe that the Yakuza have a massive subterranean operation going in America. "Insurmountable difficulties" lie in the way of proving it, says the Senate Subcommittee on Investigations.

Tracing the source of Yakuza funds is next to impossible in Japan, which has total bank secrecy, and identifying Yakuza gangsters is scarcely easier. Since they have been known to sue the Japanese National Police for releasing information to U.S. officials, not much help comes from those quarters.[34] They can no longer be spotted by their once distinctive markings, either. Airport cops everywhere have learned to look for the elaborate body tattoos and missing finger joint that once gave them away. But the Japanese government is paying for cosmetic surgery now to conceal the one and replace the other, in hopes of persuading them to go straight.[35]

It is mostly through their cruder criminal ventures that American police are getting on to them—gambling, pornography, arms, and drugs. Here, too, they might pass for the well-heeled Japanese tourists on whose backs they ride, if not for their ties to Cosa Nostra. The Yakuza have been dealing with Cosa Nostra since the 1960s when they first turned up as waiters, cooks, and dishwashers in Hawaii, the westernmost point of entry to the United States. They are more than worthy partners. Compared to the Yakuza, said a U.S. Air Force veteran who smuggled guns for them, "the American mafia is kind of like—it is kind of funny to say, but it is like a kid's game."

The two have always traded in guns and dope. American guns sell for ten or fifteen times their cost in Japan, where they are banned. "Ice" or crystal methamphetamine, the Yakuza's specialty, comes back in exchange by way of Honolulu where it is now the drug of choice. Increasingly, Yakuza traffickers are bringing in heroin and cocaine, too.

But gambling is the real bond among them. Perennial favorite of the underworld, this is arguably the fastest way to take in cash, slip dirty money into the laundry, and trap clients into borrowing at outrageous interest rates: 1 percent a day for a high-roller from Japan. Japanese businessmen love to gamble in New York, Atlantic City, or Las Vegas, where the Yakuza deliver them in luxury package tours and the Mafia provides the facilities, supervises the play, bankrolls the losers, and sends around the collectors. Those who try sneaking back to Japan are merely putting off the day when a Yakuza hood comes along in Tokyo to make them pay up, on the Mafia's behalf.[36] (Recently a Brooklyn wiseguy forgot a suitcase containing $80,000 and a list of Japanese who owed in Las Vegas, with their phone numbers in Japan.)

Yakuza racketeers would have liked to buy Las Vegas if the American mafia hadn't owned it. Short of that, their associates began by leasing a restaurant and spa in the city's Tropicana Hotel in the 1970s, picked up two more hotels with casinos attached, and then started on a $600 million resort project near Las Vegas. They went bankrupt on that but not for want of capital. Yakuza associates were investing as much or more in several similar projects at the time.

In 1991, for instance, the Yamaguchi-Gumi showed up on the tiny Pacific island of Tinian, off Saipan. Through a Tokyo-based company, ASA Development and Investment Corporation, it proposed a $300 million project for a hotel and casino there—to develop tourism, the company said.

Tinian, an inconvenient five thousand miles or so from American shores, isn't even on the map, but it is a U.S. trust territory with all the resulting entitlements. "The Yakuza think this is a great idea. . . . This is their chance to get U.S. passports and launder money," said Frederic Gushin, director of Tinian's Casino Gambling Control Commission, who turned them down.[37]

Under a less vigilant authority, the Yamaguchi-Gumi might have bought the Pacific island of Tinian, just as Sicilian Mafia Families have bought Aruba. In fact, Yakuza associates have bought a sizable chunk of Hawaii already and a disquieting amount of choice real estate on the American mainland.

According to "Mr. Bully," a confidential witness for the Senate committee, the Yakuza probably own "close to fifty major properties in Hawaii," including several golf courses. All are fronts for their money laundering, he said.

"Mr. Bully" claimed that Yakuza associates used an intricate web of shell companies to buy the famous Pebble Beach Country Club in Monterey, California, for $841 million in 1990.[38] Over half a billion dollars' worth of other Yakuza assets were traced by the Senate committee in Hawaii, Nevada, Arizona, California, and New York. These included a bundle of shares in Christies' Auction House, owned by a Yamaguchi-Gumi associate known as "The Snake," according to the Senate Committee Report. Apart from buying into the company, he had invested $80 million in paintings by Picasso, Van Gogh, and other masters.[39]

The Senate committee took a year to uncover this much, a fraction of the Yakuza's camouflaged capital in America, beyond which came the insurmountable difficulties. Any number of American businessmen might welcome their discreet offers of investment capital, no questions asked—even the brother of the President of the United States. In 1991 the Kyodo News Service reported that Prescott Bush had received a quarter of a million dollars as a consultant for a Japanese company called West Tsusho. On his advice, it was claimed, and with his guarantee for half the sum, the company had invested $5 million in two American ventures: Quantum Access, a Houston-based computer software firm; and Asset Management, a "business development consulting firm" employing Bush himself as senior adviser.

West Tsusho, authorities said, was the overseas investment arm of Susumu Ishii, number two boss of the Inagawa-Kai, one of the mightiest Yakuza bosses. It was for questionable loans of $180 million to Ishii that the world's largest brokerage, Nomura, very nearly crashed in 1991. Much of its money went into Susumu Ishii's investments in the United States.[40]

There is no evidence that Bush knew this. But what of those who do know and don't say—American companies eager for capital from anywhere or Japanese companies serving as Yakuza conduits in America? The Yakuza's piratical *sokaiya* (corporate blackmailers) have been nosing around the American scene since the 1970s.

A *sokaiya* famous for blackmailing a hundred companies in Japan came close to capturing the City Bank of Honolulu in 1978. Several of America's biggest corporations were approached or targeted over the next few years: AT&T, IBM, General Motors, Dow Chemicals, BankAmerica.[41] The strongest pitch came from the star practitioners who raided Paribas in France, the Rondan Doyukai.

In 1982, the Rondan Doyukai's boss showed up at a Chase Manhattan Bank stockholders' meeting in New York. Presenting himself as "a representative of your stockholders from Japan," he expressed "sincere admiration for your high dividends" and bowed out. Chase heard no more from him, perhaps because *The Wall St. Journal* warned "The *Sokaiya* Are Coming!" in front-page headlines.[42]

Although America's blue-chip corporations do not appear to have been bothered since, the same cannot be said for Japan's blue-chip corporations in America. Leaders of Japan's hundred-billion-dollar-a-year trade with the United States, they have in effect been financing Yakuza expansion in America for almost two decades. Describing their inaugural meeting with the *sokaiya* in Los Angeles in 1976, the authors of the book *Yakuza* wrote:

> According to police sources, fifty Japanese executives filed into one of the ballrooms of the Biltmore Hotel in downtown L.A. They were the top-ranking officers of the largest Japanese corporations operating on the West Coast, and they had come to pay their respects to a group of visiting *sokaiya*.
>
> Police at the same time observed *sokaiya* Masato Yoshioka making a tour of Los Angeles to present himself at Japanese-owned banks, conglomerates, and securities investment firms . . .
>
> Although the businesses were reluctant to talk about the incident, informants revealed that, as in Japan, it was cheaper to pay up than risk the consequences.[43]

Around the time of that *sokaiya* visit nearly a quarter of a century ago, a young U.S. Federal Attorney called Michael Sterett warned, after coming upon the Yakuza in Honolulu, "There are now shadow governments in the United States and Japan that collect their own taxes, make their own rules, and enforce their own laws. An alliance between the Yakuza and U.S. organized crime means that drugs and guns and huge amounts of money will be moving across the world accountable to no one but the mobs themselves. It means an international shadow government."[44] He did not get much attention in those days. "No one in Washington had ever built a career on chasing crime around the mid-Pacific," the authors of *Yakuza* noted.

THE RUSSIAN MAFIA

The Russian mafia's appearance on the American scene was not sudden but long overlooked or underrated. A small number of Russian crooks were cheating tax collectors of around $3 billion a year in bootleg gasoline by the time they were caught at it in 1986.

Their leader, a true son of the Thieves' World named Marat Balagula, had made a fortune in Soviet Russia in the mafia of the Brezhnev era. He had left behind "the charmed life of a high-flying black marketeer" in 1977 because "he had read about capitalism and knew he could do well over here," a business associate told *Vanity Fair* magazine.[45]

Like many others in his line of work, Balagula had gotten a visa as a persecuted Jewish refugee from Odessa on the Black Sea. He really was Jewish, unlike a number of fellow crooks getting in with forged papers to that effect—Chechen, for instance. He had served the Nomenklatura much too well to be persecuted, however. Before long he became *consigliere* to Evsei Agron, reigning boss of the Organizatsiya in Brighton Beach, Brooklyn, known as Little Odessa by the Sea. Brighton Beach had nearly half of all the Russian émigrés in America—some thirty thousand out of seventy thousand, due to double and more by the early 1990s. Most, like the boss of Brighton Beach himself, were there thanks to a 1974 U.S. law favoring Soviet political refugees.

Agron, an ex-Soviet convict who carried around a cattle prod to keep his subjects in line, had a hearty band of five hundred thieves in the purest Russian sense.[46] Their income from shakedowns, arson, fencing, counterfeiting, burglary, armed robbery, gambling, prostitution, fraud, smuggling, drug running, arms running, contract killing and so on was approaching $100 million a year by the mid-1980s.[47]

Russian gangs loosely associated with Agron's Organizatsiya were doing exactly the same in Los Angeles, San Francisco, Philadelphia, Chicago, Dallas, Miami, Boston, and a dozen other cities in America and Canada.[48] Described by a senior FBI agent as "very violence prone," they were in fact the most brutal, remorseless, and wholly frightening criminals that America had ever seen; and their ranks were growing fast as the tide of Russian immigrants mounted.

Mingling with the newcomers were fresh forces from the Soviet underworld and its patrons in the professions, the military, the KGB. Many were hardened criminals who had spent years in harsh

Soviet prison camps, incurable troublemakers handpicked by the KGB to be dumped on the United States. Others were Jewish reinforcements from the Ukrainian mafia, and their impostors, arriving with a ready-made international network. Before hitting the United States they had gone first to Tel Aviv and then to refugee camps in Vienna and Rome where "they made contacts with Italian Mafia people who told them who to see in the United States," says the editor of New York's Russian-language newspaper *Novoye Russkoye Slavo*, Alex Grant.[49]

A Russian immigrant describing the pattern of one she had known in the old country told the Russian-speaking scholar Lydia Rosner:

> He was a thief there. When he left, the day after he left,
> they came to arrest him. But he had paid for documents
> to get out. He went to Israel and then to Italy. He was
> involved in narcotics there. My daughter had grown up
> with him, and she found him again here in New York.
> He was robbing again, and he had diamonds and gold.
> He went back with them to Germany. . . . He got mar-
> ried, and he travels the whole world.

For these criminals, as indeed for any new Russian immigrant, perceptions of law and justice had been shaped in a lifetime under totalitarian communist rule. All found the American justice system "nonthreatening and inefficient," Rosner wrote. Criminals in particular found it laughably so.

American prisons held no fears for survivors of the Soviet gulag. American courts presuming a defendant was innocent until proven guilty were simply not serious. An American cop who had to read you the Miranda Act was "Mickey Mouse," in Rosner's words. "They feel we are pussycats, and the United States is one big candy store," said a New York detective monitoring their network.[50]

This was the legacy inherited by Marat Balagula in 1985 when he succeeded to the throne in Brighton Beach after Evsei Agron was shot dead. Balagula was not only more worldly and imaginative but more literate. He had a graduate degree in economics, and he was not the only one. "John Gotti doesn't have college-educated people and trained military officers like the Russian mafia does," the FBI's Jim Moody observed.

Balagula and his crowd had been working the gas tax scam for several years by then, with Cosa Nostra providing the cover. The deal had been negotiated on Long Island in 1982 with a captain in the Colombo Family, Michael "Sonny" Franzese, and his associate, Larry Iorizzo.

"The Italians thought the Russians were good guys, not too greedy, reliable, innocent. So they made the agreement. The Russians gave the Italians a rakeoff, and the Italians gave them security plus custody of corrupted cops," explains Alex Grant.

Specifically, the Russians were paying a "family tax" to New York's Gambino, Lucchese, Colombo, and Genovese Families— two cents out of the twenty-eight cents a gallon in Federal and state gas taxes that they were pocketing—in exchange for which they received Cosa Nostra's tolerance and protection. "The mafia and the Soviet mob—it gives a new meaning to détente," observed NBC's Tom Brokaw.

The gas tax scandal, as this ongoing scam has come to be called, shows that not everything American is necessarily the biggest and best. Although many like to think the American mafia dreamed up the scheme, it clearly came as a surprise to John Gotti in 1986. "I gotta do it right now! Right now I gotta do it!" he was heard to exclaim when told of it.[51]

Actually, a Russian "petrol mafia" was already working a crude version in Baku, Azerbaijan, when the Russians cut their deal in New York. "The town pumps in Baku sold gas for unrecorded cash," wrote Russian journalist Arkady Vaksberg. In America, however, the Russians developed a much more sophisticated model, the most brilliant ever sprung on U.S. revenue men, known as the daisy chain.

Simple in conception and dazzlingly intricate in execution, the scam rested on the fact that the law required gas taxes to be paid not at the wholesale terminal but at the pump. The daisy chain consisted of numerous shell companies starting at the wholesale terminal—often in South America or Africa—passing the gas along from one to another in fake paper transactions until the trail was irretrievably lost. The dummy company at the end of the line then sold the gas to retailers at a discount, with forged tax receipts. At the first sign of an approaching tax inspector, the dummy company folded its camp chair and moved on.

Nobody in America had ever invented such a faultless money-making scheme: "A hell of a lot less risky than dealing in drugs and just as profitable," a Federal prosecutor observed.

Gas retailers faced with cut-rate competition were forced either to go along or go under. Even the giant Getty Oil went along.[52] Countless others fell into line as the racket spread from New York to the rest of the East Coast to the Midwest to the West Coast.

The Federal government was losing a billion dollars a year, and state governments across the country another two billion. Cosa Nostra's four Families in New York were collecting over $40 million a year without lifting a finger. The Russians and their close mafia confederates were sending hundreds of millions to the laundry, in Panama, Austria, and Russia. They were planning to buy up oil terminals all over Eastern Europe to assure a cheap and steady supply when the long arm of the law reached them.

Discovering the scam did not stop it. Balagula, picked up at the Frankfurt airport in 1989 after visiting thirty-six countries as a fugitive, is doing time now. Sonny Franzese has done his, and Iorizzo is in and out of the Witness Protection Program. But the scheme is so profitable that it "continues to flourish throughout the nation," law enforcement officials say.[53]

Despite over a hundred bootleg gas convictions, the Justice Department still has several hundred investigations under way from New York to Los Angeles, some dating back to 1983. "We could be investigating this forever," said the chief of a rackets bureau in upstate New York.

U.S. authorities were slow to see something more than "just a guy with a brilliant idea" behind the gas scam. As late as 1989 the Senate Subcommittee on Investigations did not include the Russian mafia on a list of "nontraditional crime groups" that did include the Jamaican Posses and the Bloods and Crips.

By then the Organizatsiya was showing up in a multitude of

counterfeit currency cases, forged icons, fake Fabergé antiques, fabricated credit cards (American Express) and bank checks (Citibank), nationwide burglaries, jewelry heists, and a multitude of other scams including at least one more in the billion-dollar range. "The Russians add a zero to anything that anyone else thinks of," said an FBI special agent in New York.

Their billion-dollar scam in California was the largest health insurance fraud in U.S. history. A fake medical clinic was used to front the operation in Los Angeles, luring patients to mobile "diagnostic centers" by promising free checkups, persuading them to sign over their insurance claims, and billing insurance companies for $8,000 to $10,000 per patient. Some fourteen hundred insurance companies paid out on the phony claims. The companies were hurting so badly that health insurance premiums went up throughout the state of California.[54]

The small group pulling this off consisted of a David Shmushkevich from Brighton Beach and girlfriend, two doctors, a lawyer, and five others. Shmushkevich alone was charged on 175 counts of mail fraud, money laundering, racketeering, and conspiracy, for which he faced 1,980 years in jail.

That was in 1991, by which time the Soviet Union was breaking up and the Russian mafia had joined the planetary crime club. The Organizatsiya in America, although still a loose association of crooks, was now hooked in solidly to the Sicilian and American mafias, the Colombian cocaine cartels, and its own mother cell in the old country. Its ranks were swelling with thousands of new arrivals from liberated Russia, some of whom were "probably younger than Marat, tougher than Marat, and smarter than Marat," said Marat Balagula's lawyer.[55]

Numerous Chechen were among them, the embodiment of their rising expectations. "I want to send my son to Harvard and own a Rolls-Royce," one said.

By 1992 the FBI was setting up a Federal Task Force devoted solely to the Russians. The DEA broke a Russian ring bringing in heroin from Poland for Sicilian mafiosi in New York—a "small part of a growing Russian involvement in heroin smuggling and distribution," a spokesman declared.

The Immigration Service, Secret Service, and Internal Revenue Service were all watching a two-way traffic between Brighton Beach and Moscow. Contract killers were flying in from Moscow or St. Petersburg or the Caucasus to do a quick and inexpensive turn-around job—fly in, hit, fly out—for the Organizatsiya or the American or Sicilian Mafia or even ordinary Russian émigrés. "If you're a Russian shop owner, you don't go to the local mafia boss to complain anymore. You just call Russia and ask them to send a hit man," said Alex Grant.

America's Russian criminals were returning to their homeland to work a whole new set of crooked deals, often in partnership with their American and Sicilian counterparts. "They go to Moscow all the time," said an investigator studying the Brighton Beach crowd.

Police were overwhelmed by such goings and comings in a closely sealed criminal society whose language and customs they did not understand. "It was hard before, but this is ridiculous," observed an agent tracking émigré crime.

By 1993 the Russian mafia's parent export-import companies in Berlin were known to have daughter companies in New York, Los Angeles, and Miami; doubtless there were others, still unknown. "These are storefront companies, moving Soviet raw materials and finding buyers across the United States. They have lists and will deliver," the FBI's Jim Moody told me.

This was the key to an operation that had mystified the police of America and Europe since that momentous year 1990, luring the entire international underworld to Moscow, culminating in the biggest swindle ever perpetrated anywhere, exposed in Russia but almost nowhere else in January 1991.

PART IV

The Great Ruble Scam

CHAPTER EIGHT

The Buildup

As the winds of freedom swept across Soviet Russia in 1990, traces of an apparently senseless traffic in rubles appeared in America and all over Europe.

The ruble was not and is still not a convertible currency. Its buying power was nil in the West and virtually nil in the Soviet Union, where hardly anything buyable was worth buying. Exporting it was strictly forbidden anyway; getting it back into the country seemed next to impossible.

Nevertheless, massive shipments of rubles *in cash* were sighted in Poland, Germany, Holland, Belgium, France, and Italy—trainloads, truckloads.[1] "Russian currency was sold off by the aircraft container. Dozens of such containers were flown to Zurich and then delivered to clients by truck," wrote the president of Russia's Center for Global and Strategic Studies later.[2]

A "solid European bank" offered an American investor a billion dollars' worth of rubles "with official letters guaranteeing their reentry into the Soviet market," reported Eugene Milosh, president of the American Association of Exporters and Importers. "There are rubles out there trying to find a home; there's a lot of hanky-panky going on," he declared.[3]

Several signs suggested an intense criminal interest in this traffic. The Sicilian Mafia in particular was found to be investing heavily in rubles; so were Colombia's cocaine cartels. The international underworld's designs on Russia were emerging even before the communist state gave way. Nothing came of such discoveries, however.

In Belinzona, Switzerland, late in 1990, an undercover narcotics agent was approached by a notorious Turkish heroin trafficker, Hamza Türkeresin, trying to peddle rubles packed into a cargo container. Türkeresin was the Milan point man for the Turkish mafia in Istanbul, wanted in Switzerland for a one-hundred-kilo heroin shipment seized on the way to Italy. On occasion he moved cocaine in Europe for Pablo Escobar's Medellín cartel. More closely, he worked with the renowned Italian drug trafficker Santo Pasquale Morabito.

Morabito, also operating out of Milan, ran a powerful Mafia Family in Catania and an 'Ndrangheta offshoot in Calabria. Earlier that year he had bought seventy billion rubles in cash—$4 billion worth on the black market by late 1990—hoping to turn a profit by reselling them for hard currency.[4]

On Morabito's behalf, Türkeresin offered the Swiss undercover agent a sample 100,000 rubles, saying there were billions more where they came from. The agent bought them and referred the case to Geneva.[5]

In Geneva, Judge Jean-Pierre Trembley ordered the arrest of five men representing a German fugitive, Andreas Behrens, wanted for laundering several million narcodollars through Canada for Pablo Escobar. They were a Colombian, a German, and three Argentinian money changers who had been meeting at the Hotel Century in Geneva, trying to broker a swap of Morabito's seventy billion rubles for $4.6 billion, fifteen times below Russia's official commercial rate of one ruble for $1.20.[6]

Judge Trembley could not locate the rubles, reportedly left in a container at Brink's in Holland. Whether or not the judge looked that far afield, an open question, he finally released the suspects. "I just couldn't believe that anybody in his right mind would swap narcodollars for rubles that nobody can spend," he said.[7] Yet huge swaps were being made by men who were anything but mentally retarded.

Shortly before Morabito's ruble deal was uncovered in Switzerland, a TIR truck stuffed with rubles was detected traveling across the Italian north. Italy's High Commission to Combat the Mafia had spotted it, I was told later by the head of the commission, Domenico Sica.

"The truck was moving around the area from Bologna to Verona to Rimini," Sica said. "We never caught it, so we couldn't count the rubles. How do you count a TIR-full of banknotes, anyway? But they must have amounted to hundreds of millions or billions. We knew from phone intercepts that a German national named Ulrich Bahl and his Sicilian wife from Catania, Ludovica, were selling them in blocks, and the Soviet embassy was involved."[8]

The phone taps had revealed a master criminal ring at work, the High Commission told a judge in Palermo to whom it passed on the case. "A vast criminal organization, dedicated mainly to illicit financial activities on Italian territory and abroad, is operating in collusion with Mafia groups in Palermo, Catania, and Trapani, laundering the money of Mafia Families [and] converting their capital into rubles through Swiss banks," the High Commission wrote.[9]

Though the High Commission's tip led eventually to a hot criminal case in Palermo, the ruble side of it was never fully explored, nor was it connected to a sizable Mafia ruble deal the year before.

In 1989, Palermo's San Lorenzo Family alone had bought 500 million rubles—a good year before the ruble went into a free fall.[10] The San Lorenzo Family ranks high in the Mafia command. Its boss, Mariano Troia, was reportedly in line to become *capo di tutti capi* after Totò Riina's arrest.[11] The fact that he had bought half a billion rubles was beyond understanding in Sicily in 1989.

The intermediary in the deal turned out to be Ulrich Bahl, the German national found selling blocks of rubles around Bologna a year later. His wife's maiden name was Morabito; Santo Pasquale Morabito, brokering seventy billion rubles in the north, was her father.[12]

Thanks to the tip from High Commissioner Sica, Ulrich Bahl was spotted in Sicily again at the end of 1990. This time he was at the center of a case pointing investigators beyond Italy to Germany, Austria, Switzerland, Holland, America, Bolivia, Panama, Yugoslavia, Hungary, Romania, Bulgaria, and Russia.

Police closed in first on a pizzeria in Palermo's Mafia-infested district of Santa Maria di Gesù, where three Men of Honor were printing $20 million worth of fake hundred-dollar bills with the aid of a Macintosh computer.[13]

Two Germans were caught with $1.5 million in Freiburg, Germany, over the next weeks. Three Sicilian mafiosi were arrested in Switzerland. Ulrich Bahl, trying to hawk $2 million of the fake bills, was picked up by the U.S. Secret Service in Phoenix, Arizona. With his arrest, another ruble deal—this one for $40 million—fell through.

Bahl, allegedly in the helicopter business, was juggling prodigal sums in mysterious conferences with international bankers, moving at frenetic speed from one sumptuous hotel to another, traveling by private plane to and from Palermo, Bologna, Milan, Miami, Vienna, Zurich, Munich, Amsterdam, Budapest, Bucharest, Sofia, and Belgrade. His main connections in Sicily were with Ciccio Madonia's Family in Palermo and Nitto Santapaola's in Catania. On their behalf he was trying to unload stolen, forged, or irregular bank checks, government bonds, and illicit currencies amounting to 500 billion lire, close to half a billion dollars at the time.

A good share of this was in Bolivian traveler's checks for 1.15 billion pesos—$220 million—a payment for moving cocaine. Bahl had trouble with the Bolivian pesos since the checks were out of date, but he did fairly well with the rest in Switzerland (Credit Suisse of Bern, Banca Svizzera Italiana of Zurich); Germany (West Bank of Hamburg, D.S.K. and O.S.K. Bank of Munich); and the United States (First Union Bank U.S.A., Barnet Bank of Miami, American Express in New York).

Meanwhile, Bahl was arranging a major arms deal for his Sicilian connection with a state factory in Yugoslavia. The initial shipment in what was to be a regular monthly supply included one hundred Kalashnikovs, two hundred Russian Tokarev pistols, ten silencers, one hundred grenades, night sights, bazookas, and munitions. All was ready for the passage through customs in Milan (a pushover by arrangement, the Sicilians said) when fighting broke out in Croatia and the deal collapsed.

During the same month of December 1990, the DEA's Rome office advised police in Palermo that Bahl was bringing down $40 million for the Madonia and Santapaola families, with which they were going to buy rubles.[14] The dollars were the laundered proceeds of the Mafia's stolen checks, wrote investigating magistrate Agostino Gristina. "This capital, converted through Swiss banks into rubles and, successively, into certificates for *gold* rubles, was to be used to buy dollars, arms, and drugs in Miami, Florida," he said.[15]

The Soviet gold ruble was legal tender abroad, guaranteed by the Soviet Central Bank for commercial use, freely exchangeable at the official rate of $1.20 per ruble. The common ruble, forced into its free-fall halfway through 1990 (as we will see), was selling for around six cents on the black market when Bahl arrived with the dollars.[16] Forging the papers to turn a common ruble into a gold one was tricky but possible with connivance on the Russian side; Russian crooks were adept at this. So, barring unforeseen complications—Bahl's premature arrest in this case—the Sicilian Mafia's leading Families, their German confederates, and their Russian accomplices stood to turn $40 million into $600 million.

Judge Gristina had no idea of the gold ruble's possibilities in 1990, nor did any investigator I questioned in Italy or elsewhere in Western Europe even a year afterward. Nor did I.

Much the same puzzle faced a judge in Rimini on Italy's Adriatic coast. Several months of wiretaps in the autumn of 1990 had led Judge Roberto Sapio to arrest a ring of fourteen money launderers, overheard as they discussed heavy transactions in lire, dollars, Swiss francs, deutsche marks, Algerian and Libyan dinars, and rubles.

They had exchanged "masses of rubles—trainloads, billions," their leader admitted later to the judge. Several Mafia bosses were among their clients. Santo Pasquale Morabito, for one, had sold a hundred million rubles through their network; a noted Sicilian mafioso called Tommy Marsala had bought half a billion for the Lebanese Druse chieftain Waled Jumblatt.[17] The Sicilians were using several different channels to tunnel their way into Russia.

This particular ring was led by an elderly, suffocatingly pious fake *monsignore* named Roberto Coppola, who had phony credentials from the Sovereign Military Order of Saint John of Jerusalem, Knights of Malta. Over the previous year he had collected eighteen *authentic* diplomatic passports as ambassador extraordinary or plenipotentiary, endowing him with "full powers" to "spread charity in the world" or "develop economic and financial activities" for his honorary homelands. As he said himself on a tapped phone, he was laundering politicians' secret funds. ("You understand, this money is from rakeoffs for Algerian politicians, and these politicians have to get the money back in francs or Italian lire or Algerian dinars. . . . So they say they'll give a discount of 20 percent," he explained to an associate.)[18]

Along with Algeria, Antigua, Bulgaria, Equatorial Guinea, Fiji, Gabon, Israel, Romania, and the Solomon Islands, "Monsignore" Coppola had credentials from the Soviet republics of Russia, Bielorussia and Georgia, and the Leningrad region. His Russian Republic credentials had been signed by Boris Yeltsin and his foreign minister, Andrei Kozyrev, in October 1990. "Listen to this! Twenty minutes ago I was named ambassador of Russia!" Coppola exulted over his tapped phone. "Congratulations!" said his interlocutor.[19]

Three months later—on January 28, 1991—Coppola was passing on more exciting news to his associates. A phone intercept by police in Rimini caught the conversation, reported as follows to Judge Sapio: "G. calls His Excellency [Coppola], who informs him that the Russian embassy is selling two thousand tons of gold, and there would be a 1 percent profit. He asks G. if he has the possibility of buying any. G. says yes, and they agree to phone each other the next morning."

Two thousand tons of gold was worth $22 billion—more than the entire package of international aid for the Soviet Union proposed at a G-7 summit that autumn. Such quantities could hardly have hit the meticulously regulated world market without causing total disruption. Nor was so much likely to have been amassed abroad, still less sold, all at once. Nevertheless, a "package" worth $12 billion was said to have moved out of the U.S.S.R. by the spring of 1991, "bypassing normal export channels," reported the *Manchester Guardian*.

The following September, Soviet economist Grigori Yavlinski told leaders of the G-7 meeting in Bangkok that his country's gold reserves, thought to be between 2,000 and 3,000 tons, were down to 240 tons. In November, Western analysts were shocked to learn that *all* the reserves in the Soviet Central Bank were missing. "Not a gram of gold remains; the vaults are empty," said Gosbank director Viktor Geraschenko.[20]

Who in the Rome embassy had asked Coppola to sell all the gold in the Soviet Treasury?

In January 1991, the Soviet embassy in Rome still belonged to the central Soviet government, as it would until the U.S.S.R. disintegrated at the year's end. On the other hand, "Monsignore" Coppola had credentials from the government of the U.S.S.R.'s Russian Republic. Therefore, the answer could point either way.

The mystery of the missing gold still haunts investigators in and out of Russia; none of it has ever been recovered. One way or another, however, the vanished gold was entwined with the scandal that rocked Russia in the same month of January when the huge subterranean traffic in its currency culminated in the Great Ruble Scam.

CHAPTER NINE

The Deal

Criminal Case No. 18/5922-91 hit Russia with hurricane force in the winter of 1991 but soon subsided. It took an effort of will to believe that the Russian government had made a deal with a bunch of international con men to swap all the rubles in circulation for black market dollars. The story seemed preposterous. Politicians claimed it was a frameup; nobody went to jail for it; the foreign press largely ignored it.

But the story was true. Exposure was not the end of it, either. Negotiations were resumed and new deals were struck—are still being struck. The same "businessmen" are running fabulous joint ventures in Moscow to this day.

These men were only part of the story. While they were in it for money, others were in it to manipulate the politics of a dying Soviet state. In the end, the case that shook Russia turned out to be an enormous and almost indecipherable conspiracy in which elements of the KGB, in collusion with the international underworld, set out deliberately to destabilize the Soviet Union's currency, almost certainly with the tacit consent if not active participation of the Western intelligence community.

What they did together, or helped greatly to do—some intentionally, some otherwise—perfectly reflected the teachings of John Maynard Keynes."There is no subtler, no surer means of overturning the existing basis of society than to debauch the currency. The process engages all the hidden forces of economic law on the side of destruction, and does it in a manner which not one man in a million is able to diagnose," Keynes once wrote.

Though the criminal forces involved were only one of the hidden forces on the side of destruction, they opened the way to the ongoing and relentless sack of post-communist Russia. The magnitude of their operation is a measure of the great new spaces open to international crime with the end of the communist era and of the apathy or dangerous self-absorption or diplomatic cowardice allowing the spaces to grow.

The fact that scarcely anyone outside Russia has heard of the Great Ruble Scam may be explained partly by its seemingly unbelievable details, but partly, too, by Western reluctance to touch exquisitely sensitive political nerves. The scandal involved the new as well as the old Nomenklatura—far more the new than the old. Western governments rejoicing in the collapse of the evil empire wanted to assume, and to all appearances did assume, that all the evils in an emerging democracy emanated from politicians identified with the fallen communist state. Not one was prepared to acknowledge indelicate evidence to the contrary.

The story broke in the first month of the year the Soviet Union died. Tensions were building toward the abortive coup of August 1991, foreshadowing the union's death at the year's end. Mikhail Gorbachev was struggling to hold the fifteen republics together. Boris Yeltsin was straining to free his Russian republic from the Kremlin's hold. The secret agreements coming to light that winter had a lot to do with the implacable enmity growing between these two men.

On January 23, 1991, a British businessman named Paul Pearson was picked up at Moscow's Sheremetyevo Airport. In his briefcase was a signed contract endorsed by the government of the Russian

Republic for a swap of 140 billion rubles for $7.8 billion. No wonder people later disbelieved. One hundred and forty billion rubles was the sum of all Russian cash extant at the time, worth $224 billion at the commercial rate and around $10 billion on the black market by January 1991.

The deal seemed to make no sense for the Russians, and hardly more for their foreign partners. "Who in his right mind was prepared to part with a fortune in solid U.S. dollars for bales of colored paper?" asked a Western reporter much amused at the thought.[1]

Unamused, the Russian Republic's Supreme Soviet formed a Commission of Inquiry headed by a staunch Yeltsin supporter, Alexander Pochinok, who said the commission "should not cast doubt on the government's probity." Simultaneously, the Soviet Union's prosecutor-general appointed a famous and incorruptible investigator—Vladimir Kalinichenko, hero of the assault on the Uzbek mafia in the 1980s—to handle Criminal Case No. 18/5922-91.[2]

Despite the friction between their respective sides, both turned up more or less the same astonishing information on the Russian end of the deal. Without outside help, however—and there wasn't much—they could learn little about the Western characters concerned or the secret consortium in the background or a covert traffic in rubles reaching from Poland, Germany, Belgium, Italy, Austria, Sweden, and Switzerland to the United States, Turkey, and Singapore. Certainly they had no knowledge then of the international underworld's avid interest in the ruble, dating back a good year or more.[3]

Many of the missing facts fell into place for me in two years of exceptionally difficult investigation. They are not complete, but they are verifiable.[4]

The final report of Russia's Commission of Inquiry, published on March 1, 1991, revealed not just the criminal designs of the foreign parties to the deal but the alarming innocence of the first freely elected government in the Soviet Republic of Russia: Boris Yeltsin's, voted in the previous summer.[5]

Beginning in that summer of 1990, the report said, three obscure Western "businessmen" in succession made nearly identical propositions to Yeltsin's government. All three, "in close liaison," offered to buy 140 billion rubles or more for $7.8 billion and up. All held out radiant if elusive prospects of feeding and clothing all Russia by earmarking the dollars to bring in Western consumer goods. In exchange they wanted permission to keep the rubles in Russian bank accounts, and government licenses to buy raw materials with the rubles for export—duty-free, tax-free, and under state protection.

The first businessman to appear, in August, was a "John Ross" of New York, who turned out to be Zubok Jan Semyenovich of Ukraine, twice convicted of theft there before heading for the United States. Owner of a small condom factory with six employees in New York, he presented himself as the president of "New Technology and Production International." By the time he was found out, he had signed a Protocol of Intent with Russia's prime minister, Ivan Silaev, to exchange 300 billion rubles for $50 billion.[6] The deal included a state license "to buy and export raw materials, waste materials, precious metals, etc., without paying duties"—$480 billion worth, at the commercial rate.[7]

Next, in October, came a Leo Emil Wanta who, when asked for credentials, proffered a signed photograph of President Reagan and said he belonged to "the President's Club" (meaning he had contributed $50,000 to a presidential campaign). His outfit was the "New Republic Financial Group," incorporated in Appleton, Wisconsin, and registered in Vienna, Austria, with a declared capital of 500,000 schillings ($17,000).[8]

Received in the best Moscow circles, Wanta proposed a swap of $5 billion for 140 billion rubles—an outrageous 28 to the dollar, well under half the black market rate—rising over a period of five years to $50 billion for 300 billion rubles (the "John Ross" proposal). This extravagant arrangement would have been beyond the means (and comprehension) of the biggest Western banks. Nevertheless, Prime Minister Silaev asked President Yeltsin for "the necessary authority to sign the appropriate agreements."

Wanta, the "foreign partner," would spend the dollars to import

Western goods for "an emergency saturation of the consumer market," the prime minister wrote to Yeltsin. In exchange, Wanta was "requesting an immediate line of credit of 140 billion rubles for investing in the economy of the Federal Soviet Russian Republic and purchasing raw and other materials."

"I believe that it is possible to provide the credit indicated from the funds of the [Russian Federation's] state budget," continued Silaev. It was "feasible" to "control and coordinate" the ruble funds through a joint venture allotting 25 percent of the shares to the Russian government and 75 percent to Wanta, he concluded.[9]

In other words, Leo Wanta would control both the dollars and the rubles.

Whether or not Yeltsin consented personally, his closest adviser, Gennady Burbulis, did so implicitly: The proposal was referred to him, and he did not object. In fact, the Commission of Inquiry found an agreement already drawn up by Silaev's cabinet, accepting Wanta's offer.[10] The agreement fell through, or seemed to, when the U.S. State Department warned that Wanta "had major debts and some credit card problems." ("I confronted him in November 1990, and he fled," said the chief investigator, Kalinichenko.)[11]

Just as Wanta was falling from grace, a Colin Gibbins of Great Britain appeared. President of an unknown South African–based "Dove Trading Company," he had talked his way into a signed 140-billion-ruble contract and an authorized Russian bank account when his partner, Paul Pearson, was stopped at the airport. The signatory on the Russian side was an A. A. Sveridov, regional deputy from Chelyabinsk, at the center of Russia's military-industrial complex in the Ural Mountains. He signed on behalf of an improbable "Ekho Manufacturing Ecological Company" and a dubious charity called Eternal Memory to Soldiers, representing a brand-new foundation named Revival of the Urals Countryside. According to the Commission of Inquiry, Sveridov "never intended to revive the Urals," nor did he have any money. Russia's deputy prime minister, Gennady Filshin, had arranged to provide the rubles from the state budget.

Gibbins had faxed his proposal to Prime Minister Silaev, who consulted his ministers of trade, foreign economics, and foreign affairs, and passed the proposal on to Deputy Prime Minister Filshin, who gave his blessings to an arrangement just like Wanta's. Gibbins, acting for an unnamed investment consortium, was to deposit $7.8 billion in a Swiss bank while a credit line of 140 billion rubles would be opened for him in a Russian bank. Both accounts would be under Gibbins's control; he had this in writing.

The contract was flagrantly illegal: Only the Soviet Central Bank could handle foreign currency transactions of any size. The Commission of Inquiry found nine other violations of the law as well, enough to incur a death sentence for "large-scale speculation" under Article 154 of Russia's still valid criminal code. (The death sentence was abolished at the end of that year.)[12]

Nonetheless, Deputy Prime Minister Filshin had directed Russia's Foreign Trade Ministry to "render assistance and support for the contract" and instructed the director of the Moscow Inter-Regional Commercial Bank to open the necessary ruble account (No. 713713). The documents prepared by the bank director for this last were "an obvious forgery," the commission declared.[13]

Summoned to explain himself before the Parliament, Filshin claimed that the deal would not really cost Russia anything since it was actually "a version of the Marshall Plan." Gibbins was going to spend his dollars to "saturate the Russian market" with 700,000 tons of meat, 300,000 tons of butter, and other "top quality" Western goods, Filshin asserted; and he was going to spend his rubles to "invest and reinvest" in the Russian economy, thereby "supplying the population with goods of primary necessity."

"This kills two birds with one stone: On the one hand, consumer demand is satisfied, and on the other, additional financial resources are poured into industry and agriculture," Filshin maintained.[14]

In reality, Gibbins had expressed only an unspecified "readiness" to spend his dollars on imported food supplies, and no readiness whatever to invest his rubles in industry and agriculture. He was just after the currency, he said under interrogation. "One of his clients" had asked him in June 1990 to "buy a great sum of Soviet rubles."

"We planned to swap currencies in a straightforward credit transfer. A consortium of European and Canadian banks was involved. It is no different [from] arranging to buy traveler's checks," said another of his partners in Johannesburg, David Frye.[15]

It remained for the Commission of Inquiry to discover that Gibbins was a professional con man. Interpol had had an international arrest warrant out for him since 1984 when British customs discovered that he had smuggled the world's fastest video camera to the Soviet Union: the Imacom 790, ten million frames a second, capable of filming the heart of a nuclear explosion.[16] ("Nobody seemed to know a thing about Gibbins, so I thought I'd give Interpol a call," said Alexander Gurov, then head of the Interior Ministry's Sixth Department and a commission member.)[17]

Yet the Russian government would not give up on the Gibbins proposition even after losing Gibbins. Here, the commission must have flinched at what it found. For within five days of the con man's exposure in Moscow, Russia's deputy minister of trade, Vladimir Kozlov, was meeting with the same "businessmen" in Zurich, Switzerland. The commission knew only that the meeting was held, since Kozlov confirmed it. The details were given to me by British authorities tracking the fugitive Gibbins.

The talks started in Zurich's Hotel Savoy on January 28, 1991, and lasted through early March, these sources said. Nine or ten Russians showed up with Minister Kozlov, presenting a "fantastic" shopping list for the first billion-dollar installment, including frozen chickens and Tampax—so said Colin Gibbins's partner, David Frye, who was there.[18] Also attending was Gibbins's other partner, Paul Pearson, fresh from his brief detention at Sheremetyevo Airport.

Others present included Gibbins's predecessor in the negotiations, Leo Wanta of the "New Republic Financial Group"; two American confederates of Wanta's named Jack Tremonti and Martin Gulewicz; a Vladimir Rozenberg and an Igor Chernyafsky, described by a British paper as emanating "a whiff of brimstone"; and a mysterious Omar Khan.[19]

Several more represented seemingly unknown trust companies:

Golden Eagle of Zurich; Van Lynch of Knightsbridge, London; Eurofin of Geneva; and Balaton N.V. of Holland, which in a fax to Dove Trading earlier in January had "reiterated that our funds are in place to effect this exchange with additional rollovers [that is, repeat orders] of up to 500 billion rubles or more."[20]

The meeting was inconclusive. The Russian contingent was apparently unable to scrape up the rubles at that stage. The buyers seemed to be getting cold feet, and Leo Wanta, a dominant figure in the whole affair, seemed to be getting nowhere. To all appearances, he dropped out of the game.

Upon unraveling this much of the story, the Commission of Inquiry delivered its devastating opinion: The Gibbins contract was "a fraud . . . that could give rise to uncontrollable financial processes and provide conditions for grave financial sabotage," it said.

The unidentified "buyer company" behind Gibbins "could use its ruble account to make massive purchases of raw materials, recyclable products, and fixed assets—the whole national wealth—at extremely low prices. With privatization of state enterprises on the way, this could even result in the loss of the Republic's economic sovereignty," the report concluded.[21]

The commission did not suggest any arrests (since the contract was never consummated) but recommended that Deputy Prime Minister Filshin be dismissed for "incompetence, negligence, insincerity . . . and deliberately misleading the commission." In a decree signed by President Boris Yeltsin, Russia's Supreme Soviet fired him.

The staggering swaps sanctioned by Yeltsin's government were not necessarily, or not only, for personal gain. This was government policy. Russia's leaders were desperately pressed for dollars, and not just to feed and clothe their people: Boris Yeltsin's most passionate objective that winter of 1991 was to build up a war chest, assert Russia's independence, fight free of Gorbachev's rankling authority and Soviet control.

Unlikely to get enough dollars through conventional channels, his ministers had turned to the other kind, sadly unaware of the sharks circling in the outside world. If some in his cabinet were undoubtedly on the take, others were mercilessly gulled.

Yeltsin had personally authorized such black market swaps as the only practical way of luring foreign capital to his bankrupt country. His prime minister, Silaev, had actually issued a decree to "promptly implement such government agreements with several foreign companies."[22] The decree provided explicitly that foreign firms bringing in Western food and goods in exchange for rubles were "authorized to sell goods and services in the Russian Federation's territory without middlemen for rubles"; they were entitled to "protection of [their] subsequent investments in industrial and trade projects" and were "allowed to buy on license, for Soviet money, and to export without paying duties, a strictly limited range of raw and other materials, waste products for recycling, products made of precious metals, etc. "[23]

Western businessmen usually had no such privileges.

Silaev's "ideologist," former Deputy Prime Minister Filshin, conceded that he had "spent a long time" formulating these plans.[24] In fact, he had begun negotiations almost directly after the Yeltsin government came to power in the summer of 1990. "Gennady Filshin's program of fantastic currency transfers was a substitute for all programs and reforms of the Russian government until it collapsed with a crash," observed the London daily, *The Independent*.[25]

Far from being punished when caught out, Filshin was promoted directly after being fired—to the lucrative post of foreign trade minister; from there he went on to head the Russian Trade Mission in Vienna, where he has remained.("We shall preserve Filshin for Russia," Yeltsin had declared.)[26]

Once the deals came to light, however, a shocked public could scarcely believe the appalling sums and sleazy foreign interlocutors. The idea that Russia's leaders could have signed the country away—and to such swindlers—seemed so incredible that many thought the KGB must have set them up. Suspicions grew when, less than a week after the case was blown, the Soviet Union's hard-lining Premier Valentin Pavlov ordered the recall of all 50-

ruble and 100-ruble notes, the largest in circulation at the time. Yeltsin's government was to blame because of the Gibbins deal, he said.

Pavlov denied that his order was meant to wipe out popular savings, although it very nearly did. He insisted that its primary purpose was to stem an uncontrollable flow of rubles to the West and "a river of dirty money" coming back by the winter of 1991. The 140-billion-ruble deal was just one of several amounting to hundreds of billions more, he told the press. The Moscow Commercial Bank had offered to sell 20.5 billion rubles to the Bank of East Asia, for instance. A "Spartan International Company" had ordered 100 billion rubles by mail.[27]

Predictably, the communist premier spoke of an imperialist plot. Western banks were conspiring to dethrone Gorbachev and derail the Soviet economy, "flooding the country with billions of rubles hitherto stashed abroad, triggering hyper-inflation and a financial catastrophe," Pavlov alleged.[28] Western diplomats dismissed the charge as "bilge" or "xenophobic rubbish"—Britain's foreign minister called it "manifestly dotty"—but Pavlov was not far wrong.

The flow of rubles out of Soviet Russia was heavy enough to suggest a conspiracy, and a lot of it was moving through Western banks. It was moving through Russian banks also, however. Everybody with any rubles to speak of was racing to exchange them illicitly for hard currency, starting with those who had the most: communists on the way out, politicians on the way in, and the Russian mafia.

As one, they all turned to the same bunch of international con men.

A year after the case of the 140 billion rubles was presumably closed, a providential hand led me to a man with personal knowledge of the whole affair. Rather, he came to me.

Mr X., a hearty American with a springy step, an easy smile, and a forthright clear-eyed stare, was a private investment banker operating at the outer edges of the law in Europe. After reading an article of mine on the case of the 140 billion rubles in the *Corriere della Sera* of Milan, he looked me up.[29] Mr. X. had played a considerable part in the ruble scam, dealing with the major players. Whether through pride or a bad conscience—his motives grew somewhat clearer later on—he wanted to tell me how it had really worked.

There were four main characters besides himself, he said. One was a Finnish national operating out of Helsinki named Michael Preisfreund, for whom Mr. X. acted briefly as fiduciary banker. The others were Leo Emil Wanta and his two confederates, Jack Tremonti and Martin Gulewicz.

Preisfreund, "six feet five and straight as an arrow," elegant in "a wardrobe that smacked of Savile Row," was brilliant, handsome, charismatic, said Mr. X. "He was fluent in German, Swedish, French, and Italian [and Finnish, presumably] and passable in Spanish, Danish, and English; and he was incredibly astute about Western economics and politics." Since the Preisfreund family had been suppliers to the Russian navy for two generations, Michael "knew most of the powerful men in the old Russia and had access to the highest levels of Russian governmental and military personnel," Mr. X. explained.

Leo Emil Wanta, born in Appleton, Wisconsin, was a fifty-year-old, heavyset snake oil salesman, as Mr. X. described him. Starting out in the pinball machine business in Menomonee Falls, he had gone on to "work credit card and many, many other scams," said a senior FBI official.[30]

For the U.S. Secret Service, where the files on him are a yard long, he is a "flim-flam artist," convicted in Switzerland for money laundering involving the Charleston Bank in Panama, deported to the United States to stand trial for tax evasion and wanted in Austria for aggravated fraud arising out of events going back to September 1990, just as he was moving in on the Russian government.[31]

An eclectic trader, Wanta faxed offers to a worldwide clientele in the summer of 1990, including one million atropine sulfate tablets from Germany; ten million jute sandbags from Saudi Arabia;

twenty million cartons a month of tax-free Marlboros from the Ukrainian capital of Kiev; and two million gas masks from the U.S.S.R. "while the supply lasts."[32] Apart from miscellaneous goods, Wanta was trading not just in rubles but in lire, yen, pesetas, deutsche marks, Swiss francs, pounds sterling, and Singapore dollars for commissions up to 14 percent—the clear mark of a money launderer.

Jack Tremonti came from Detroit, which has an American mafia, a Sicilian Mafia, and a Ukrainian mafia.[33] Whether a made man, a mafioso wannabe, or simply someone who moved in the circles of the heavily Sicilian Biondo Family, he was "a macho mafia asshole—he's got the walk, he's got the talk," said Mr. X. Tremonti had been convicted in 1976 on three counts of theft and interstate shipment of stolen goods by a Federal court in Grosse Pointe, Michigan. (The FBI referred him to the U.S. attorney in Los Angeles for suspected money laundering late in 1991, but the charge was dropped.)

Martin Gulewicz, an ex–football player closely associated with Tremonti in Detroit, was "pure rotten bad," in the view of Mr. X. A Federal court in Grosse Pointe had convicted him for drug trafficking in 1987.[34]

For the purposes of the ruble scam, Wanta worked through his "New Republic Financial Group" and something called "Anthem." Tremonti was president of a "Global Tactical Services" based in Duncan, Oklahoma. Gulewicz was with Tremonti. Preisfreund, like Mr. X, worked prudently out of countries sanctioning such ruble traffic. He worked through a "Transatlantik Foundation" in Lettstrasse 37, Vaduz, Lichtenstein.[35] Preisfreund also had a subsidiary "Consulting Liberty Company" based in Founex, Switzerland, and an "Amberhaven Ltd." working on commission in Geneva.

Together, these four and Mr. X. cut the black market price of the ruble in half within three or four months—from around ten to the dollar in May 1990 to eighteen to the dollar by the end of that summer.

Obviously they weren't the only ones in what became a colossal ruble traffic. The Soviet Communist Party alone is thought to have transferred the better part of its assets abroad through dozens of channels beginning that year. Any number of other Russians were also trying to swap rubles for hard currency. "We found out that 100,000 dummy accounts were used to export rubles through the banking system. As soon as our bankers saw these illegal accounts, they went crooked, too," says the Russian prosecutor-general's serious crimes investigator, Boris Uvarov.[36]

But Mr. X.'s group set out deliberately to manipulate the market from the start. What they did was not necessarily illegal. In fact, at least Mr. X and Preisfreund were careful to stay within the law and only operated out of countries where such ruble transfers were legal. Michael Preisfreund started the run on the ruble in May 1990, Mr. X. told me. From Helsinki, Preisfreund began by offering blocks of rubles "in manageable amounts, a few hundred million at a time," for discreet sale abroad. His faxed offers gave potential customers a choice: "external rubles," meaning bank-to-bank transfers or cash shipped out of Russia with bank letters guaranteeing their reentry; or "internal rubles," meaning certified checks or cash deposits in Russian banks such as Promstrojbank or Vnesekonombank.

"Michael told me that he had all the quantities of both internal and external rubles, and could provide any amount of ruble bank checks that could be exchanged internally or externally, but *additionally* that he could obtain the Soviet finance minister's authority that the checks would be honored in Russian banks!" Mr. X. wrote in a long fax answering some of my questions.

At first Mr. X. thought Preisfreund was merely managing the old Nomenklatura's flight capital. The Soviet Union was crumbling. It would be plausible, therefore, for officials in the old regime to squirrel away hard currency for a rainy day or perhaps an eventual triumphant comeback.[37]

But Preisfreund's offers were escalating rapidly. By July 1990 he was faxing customers in Geneva, Munich, London, Vienna, and Hong Kong interested in a "minimum of two billion Soviet rubles" up to "twenty billion in five-billion rollovers." His first big customer was Jack Tremonti. His second, for ten billion rubles, was Leo Wanta.[38] "I'll take all the rubles you got," Wanta said.

Like Wanta, Preisfreund was buying as well as selling. While this could have been "pure currency speculation," it suggested that Preisfreund might in reality be "attempting to manipulate world ruble prices," said Mr. X. The proposition appealed to Mr. X. strongly. He insists that what he did from then on was done strictly on his own, which is hard to believe. The ability of three or four characters to mount such a planetwide operation, their extraordinary impact on what was still a world superpower, and their singular immunity from beginning to end suggest the guiding hand of not just one but several intelligence agencies. Every secret service has its own private agenda, usually incomprehensible to any but its adversaries in the game. Whether Eastern or Western, they all use criminals to serve their ends: in the drug trade, the arms trade, the laundering business, the manipulation of international politics.

The KGB, for one, played some role in this instance, not just limited to Colin Gibbins, as we will see in chapter 11. Its interest in this matter is still unclear. Possibly it wanted a cheap ruble to stave off Soviet Russia's radical reformers: create runaway inflation, stir popular unrest, force a tough repressive policy on Mikhail Gorbachev or force him out. Or else a deviate wing might have wanted a cheap ruble to buy up Russia's natural resources and make a pile of money—just as the Russian mafia and its international partners did. Whatever the reasons, there are grounds to believe that the KGB did form an underground network abroad in the autumn of 1990, to "develop commercial undertakings with broad possibilities for entering international markets." Coded cables to that effect were discovered two years later. Judging from scandalous revelations in 1993, the old Nomenklatura invested billions of dollars in such ventures abroad.[39]

It is difficult to imagine that Western services, the CIA in particular, would be unaware of what was going on. The Soviet Union was collapsing, a fate ardently desired by the Western intelligence community for half a century. As John Maynard Keynes had written, there was "no subtler, no surer means" than debauching its currency to finish it off. Somebody in some Western intelligence service must have read Keynes. Nevertheless, I have no evidence that Mr. X. was prompted or pushed. He is plainly proud of what he did, insists that it was not illegal—strictly speaking, it wasn't—and *wants* his role to be known, as he told me in a long written explanation.

His motive was patriotism, he wrote. Watching Michael Preisfreund in operation, he saw a chance to give the tottering Soviet regime a final shove:

> I knew there would be a possibility of a Western privately orchestrated economic Jihad that could help crush the communist ruling powers by destroying their unstable ruble. Unilaterally and privately, I decided to play a catalytic role to crash the ruble.
>
> [That summer] I set up the tracking of internal and external ruble supplies, and how the exchange rates could be artificially manipulated on paper, this *in spite of all racketeers* [his italics]: the Preisfreunds, Wantas, Tremontis. Let them profit if they could; I was after Ivan's jugular.
>
> The flood of paperwork generated by the profiteers enabled me to implode the ruble whenever I could. Did I have any impact? Only history will be the judge.[40]

History would have a hard time judging who among the known players deserved how much of the credit or blame for what followed. Their dealings were full of mysterious characters, obscure investment foundations, and cryptic messages. Here are some samples of the faxes whizzing around the globe:

Preisfreund was looking to buy 500 million Soviet rubles to or through a Robert Hutschenraiter of Augsburg, Germany, and selling a billion to 2.6 billion rubles to a Franz Mikulits of Impex GMBH in Vienna.

Preisfreund's Consulting Liberty Corporation was offering to buy a billion rubles from a Comalco International via Anker Bank in Geneva.

Preisfreund's Transatlantik Foundation was buying a billion rubles from a Georg Horvath of Unitrade in Riemerling, Germany.

Preisfreund's Amberhaven was negotiating 5 billion rubles through the Atlalanos Ertekforgalmi Bank in Budapest; offering 700 million to a Van Moer, Santerre & Cie in Brussels; buying 50 million from a Faisal Finance in Istanbul via Impex in Vienna; buying 1.2 billion through a prominent Swiss lawyer in Chiasso named Francesco Campana, acting for, if not with, Jack Tremonti.

Leo Wanta was offering eight billion rubles to Volksbank in Bonn for $544 million—a "first tranche," according to a fax from a bank officer; selling 9.63 billion rubles to a Noweka Co. through the Regio Bank in Basel, Switzerland; selling or claiming to sell 30 billion to the French bank Paribas, of which 20 billion appeared to be confirmed by the bank's director-general for foreign relations, M. De Montpellier.

Wanta was looking to buy 3 billion rubles in cash from a Sofidad in Geneva (the "French group," said Mr. X.); offering "up to 3 billion internal rubles" from his account at the Metishe Bank in Moscow; selling 50 billion external rubles to a Corep-Gestion, Sari corporation (apparently through the good offices of "the India ministry et al."); and bidding for "100 billion clean, clear, good, legal, bundled, counted, verified, packed, and stamped Russian rubles" from a Starl AG in Vaduz, Lichtenstein.

(Apart from his Metishe Bank in Russia, Wanta was using accounts with Credito Italiano in Milan, Swiss Banking Corporation in Geneva, Anker Bank in Geneva, the Dutch Algemeine Spaar in Brussels, Zentralsparkasse und Kommerzialbank in Vienna, Creditanstalt Bankverein in Vienna, and Citibank in Milan, New York, and Los Angeles.)

Jack Tremonti had dozens of supposed buy/sell deals going with Wanta and Preisfreund as well as outsiders, including an offer of "up to ten billion internal Russian ruble bank drafts" to a Basar Ltd./Presto AB in Istanbul and Stockholm. (Basar Ltd. was "the Turkish group—very big, very serious," Mr. X. said. AB appeared to be the Avenue Banque on the Champs-Elysées, where Wanta had another of his numerous bank accounts.)[41]

One of Tremonti's offers to Preisfreund's Amberhaven Ltd., for half a billion rubles, came in an interesting letter from Sofia, Bulgaria. Tremonti had been bounding up and down so often on a Balkan cargo plane that "my appearance now resembles a basketball," he wrote. He was not offering external white checks or promissory notes, he said. He *was* offering internal white checks. "However, as any good smuggler can tell you, 'nothing is impossible.' . . . Now, let's you and I knock the flies off and find solutions to this valid transaction. I believe we are all singing out of the same hymnbook, but one of us is tone deaf."[42]

Some of their transactions had to be genuine and legal, judging from estimates of the rubles draining out of Russia between the middle and the end of 1990. "Billions of Russian rubles were purchased by Westerners at most favorable prices," said Leonid Fituni, president of Russia's Center for Global and Strategic Studies, later. "Tens of billions" was the estimate of the Soviet Central Bank.[43]

"I figured around seventy billion rubles were trading on the world market by late autumn of 1990," Mr. X. told me. That would have been around half of the national currency in circulation.

Looking back, the deputy head of the Russian Interior Ministry's Sixth Department, Gennady Chebotarev, conceded this. "We can agree with the figure of seventy or maybe eighty billion," he said.[44]

On the other hand, the paper trail was full of phony transactions never meant to be consummated. There is no evidence that the companies or individuals at the receiving end of these faxes were involved in the scam or knew its nature. Many of the several hundred faxes I saw were purely invented buy/sell orders for astronomical figures—one of Wanta's was for 500 billion rubles—sent in icily professional prose, with occasional grammatical lapses. In fact, Mr. X. explained, Wanta and his confederates were working the fax and phone methodically to force the ruble into a free-fall on world money markets, and Mr. X. was helping them. "We were beating the ruble down with paperwork, proposing false deals at low, low prices," he said. ("Leo, I desperately need phone, fax,

Former Prime Minister Giulio Andreotti (left) with his longtime spokesman in Sicily, Salvo Lima, known now to have been a made member of the Mafia. Lima was shot to death by a Mafia hit team in early 1992 when he could no longer deliver judicial protection for Mafia bosses. (Publifoto)

Pasquale Cuntrera, the most powerful of the three Cuntrera brothers, who directed the Sicilian Mafia's North American heroin trade from Caracas, Venezuela, for nearly a quarter of a century. He is photographed here in the VIP lounge of Rome's Fiumicino airport, following his expulsion from Venezuela in October 1992. (Mario Proto)

The bold and inventive Marat Balagula, who towered over the Russian mafia in Brighton Beach, Brooklyn, during the 1980s.

Judges Giovanni Falcone (left) and Paolo Borsellino, intimate friends and staunch allies, both murdered by the Mafia in Palermo in 1992. (Publifoto)

Russian mafia boss Evsei Agron, who wielded a cattle prod to keep his Brighton Beach subjects in line until his murder in 1985.

Mr. ███████████
AMBERHAVEN LTD.
July 9, 1990
Page Two

However, as any good smuggler can tell you "Nothing is
impossible". We will instead have the **PROMSTROJBANK**
issue a letter that the checks are unencumbered.

Now: "Let's you and I knock the flies off", and find solutions
to this valid transaction. I believe we are all singing out of the
same "hymn book", but one of us is "tone deaf".

Respectfully submitted.

Jack Tremonti

Jack Tremonti/ by ███████████

A piquant phrase in Jack Tremonti's letter to Leo Wanta, offering to sell
500 million Russian rubles on deposit to his account
in the Promstrojbank in Moscow.

ХИМБАНК

COMMERCIAL BANK OF CHEMICAL INDUSTRY OF RUSSIA
COMMERCIAL STOCKHOLDING BANK-"HIMBANK"
20, MJASNICKAJA STREET, 101851 MOSCOW, RUSSIAN FEDERATION

Issuing Office:- OFFICE FOR INTERNATIONAL AFFAIRS
111 ALEXANDER STREET, ROCHESTER, N.Y. 14620-1105

Letter of Indemnity/Guarantee

Guarantee No. NB	US	Dollars
	Rochester, New York	of April 1993.

As security for a credit which you will grant to   we
Commercial Stockholding Bank "HIMBANK", Rochester, New York office, hereby
irrevocably undertake to pay you on first demand, irrespective of the validity and the
effects of the above-mentioned credit relationship and waiving all rights of objection and
defences arising therefrom, any amount up to   million   hundred thousand
dollars ($), INCLUDING PRINCIPAL, INTEREST AND OTHER CHARGES, in
lawful currency of the United States of America. Upon receipt of your duly signed
request for payment by duly encoded telex stating that the amount claimed has become
due to you by the end of the term, 12 months and 5 days from the date of issuance,
April 1993. Your claim will be considered as having been made once we are in
possession of your written request for payment or the telex to this effect.
The total amount of this indemnity will be reduced by any payment effected
hereunder.
Our indemnity is valid until   April 1994 and expires in full automatically if your
claim has not been made on or before that date, regardless of such date being a banking
day or not.
This arrangement is governed by the laws of the United States of America.
For and on behalf of COMMERCIAL STOCKHOLDING BANK "HIMBANK".
MOSCOW, RUSSIAN FEDERATION.

....
authorised signature   authorised signature

STATE OF NEW YORK
COUNTY OF MONROE
On the 06th. day of April in the year 1993, before me personally came Terry John
Archer and Hector Rodriguez Laureano to me known to be the persons described in
and who executed the foregoing Letter of Indemnity/Guarantee and agreement,
and who severally acknowledged to me that they executed the same.

Notary

The mysterious "Himbank" of Moscow and Rochester, New York,
offers its credentials.

Mr. X explains his "unilateral and private decision . . . to crash the ruble" in a fax to the author.

New Republic/USA Financial Group, GES.m.b.H
Kartnerstrabe 28/15 Telefon: 414 738 0229
A – 1010 Wien, Austria-Europe

03 OCTOBER 1990

URGENT >>>>>>>>>>>>>>IMMEDIATE RESPONSE APPRECIATED

BANQUE PARABAS   CC –
ATTN: MR. DE MONTPELLIER
TFAX – 331 429 81144
BANK CODE – 30026
BRANCH   – 00140
TELEX   – 280263/210041   REF: JACQUES SCHULTZ

DEAR GENTLEPERSONS:

HOLDING FOR IMMEDIATE BANK TO BANK EXCHANGE –

    •TWENTY BILLION EXTERNAL RUSSIAN RUBLES
    TITLE OF OWNERSHIP, COUNTED/VERIFIED
    SWISS PRIME BANK, ETC.

    USD 6.85/100 SUR – FOB: GENEVE BANK

    TOTAL VALUE   – US$1,370,000,000.00

    BANK CLOSING   – 03 OCTOBER 1990

    ROLLOVERS   – YES, ADDITIONAL SUR 50 BILLION TODAY
                      AND TOMORROW.

The mighty French bank Paribas is offered 20 billion Russian rubles from the American Leo Wanta in 1990. The price, $1.3 billion, was about half the going rate on world money markets at the time.

Orlando Cediel Ospina-Vargas of Colombia, better known as "Tony" Duran, photographed secretly during his stay in Rome in the autumn of 1992, to negotiate a top-level partnership between the Sicilian Mafia and Colombia's main cocaine cartels. (Mario Proto)

Leo Wanta, the American snake-oil salesman who stormed world money markets to crash the ruble in 1990–91.

John Galatolo, proudly displaying his marlin on the island of Aruba, where he negotiated a historic deal on the part of the Sicilian Mafia with representatives of Colombia's Medellín cartel in 1987. (Police Photo)

Salvatore "Totò" Riina, the Sicilian Mafia's fearsome capo di tutti capi, photographed on the day of his capture after twenty-three years in hiding. The portrait on the wall above him is of General Carlo Alberto Dalla Chiesa, murdered by the Mafia in 1982. (Publifoto)

ПОСТАНОВЛЕНИЕ

ВЕРХОВНОГО СОВЕТА РСФСР

(.зультатах депутатского расследования
[..в заключении соглашения между россий-
скими организациями и иностранными фирмами

The Russian Parliamentary report on the 140 billion ruble scam: front
pages and signatures of Commission members for the final report dated
February 27, 1991.

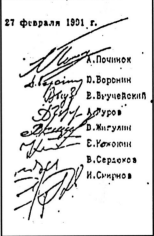

Diplomatic credentials
for Roberto Coppola,
according him "all aid
and protection in his
international activities in
the interests of the
Federal Socialist Soviet
Republic of Russia,"
signed by Boris Yeltsin
and his Foreign Affairs
Minister, Andrei Kozyrev,
on October 10, 1990,
and later withdrawn.

New Republic/USA Financial Group, GES.m.b.H
Kartnerstrabe 28/15 Telefon: (414) 738.0229
A ~ 1010 Wien, Austria-Europe

25 SEPTEMBER 1990

CONFIRMING

PREPARED FOR: MR. AVEL DE MILLER AND ASSOCIATES
STARL AG VADUZ
ATTN: MR. AXEL DE MILLER

IRREVOCABLE/CONFIRMING PURCHASE ORDER NO: SUR/90.EXT.04

WE, NEW REPUBLIC/USA FINANCIAL GROUP, GmbH, ARE READY, WILLING AND
ABLE AS A USDOLLAR PROVIDER WITH GOOD, CLEAN, CLEAR AND LEGAL USDOLLARS
TO EFFECT THE IMMEDIATE EXCHANGE(S) OF EXTERNAL RUSSIAN ROUBLES (SUR),
WHICH ARE TO BE CLEAN, CLEAR, GOOD, LEGAL, BUNDLED, COUNTED, VERIFIED,
PACKED AND STAMPED IN 100 DENOMINATION BANKNOTES BY A PRIME/FIRST CLASS
BANK FOR THE AMOUNT OF   100 BILLION   SUR, WITH ROLLOVERS PLANNED
UP TO MAXIMUM AVAILABILITY, UNTIL EITHER FUNDING IS EXHAUSTED.

COMMODITY	: EXTERNAL RUSSIAN ROUBLES - CASH SUR NOTES
EXCHANGE(S)	: TWENTY FIVE BILLION SUR PER DAILY EXCHANGE TRANCHE, CIF: ZURICH, SWITZERLAND.
EXCHANGE RATE	: USDOLLARS SIX POINT SIX THREE PER 100 SUR
MODE OF EXCHANGE	: LETTER OF CREDIT, SIGHT DRAFT AND/OR SWIFT WIRE TRANSFER AGAINST PRESENTATION OF THE FOLLOWING BANK DOCUMENTS:

A. DEPOSIT CERTIFICATES
B. VERIFYING CERTIFICATES
C. REPATRIATION CERTIFICATES

(ALL BANKING FEES/COSTS TO SUR PROVIDER ACCOUNT)

BANKING COORDINATES	: TO BE EXCHANGED UPON SUR PROVIDER RWAD ACCEPTANC OF ABOVE-MENTIONED TERMS AND CONDITIONS THROUGH RELEASE OF ADDENDUM A.
DELIVERY	: IMMEDIATELY VIA PRIME SWISS, AUSTRIAN, N.V., OR OTHER ACCEPTABLE BANKING INSTITUTIONS.
SUR ACCEPTANCE	: SUR PROVIDER TO ISSUE RWAD IMMEDIATELY THROUGH TELECOPIER - (414) 738.7007 USA OPERATIONS, IN FAVOUR OF NEW REPUBLIC/USA FINANCIAL GROUP, GmbH

THANK YOU FOR YOUR RAPID RESPONSE TO THIS PENDING TRANSACTION.

FAITHFULLY YOURS,
FOR AND ON BEHALF OF NEW REPUBLIC/USA FINANCIAL GROUP, GmbH.

By: _____   Telecopiador - (414) 738.7007
L E WANTA, DIRECTEUR-GENERAL, WIEN

LEW/nv

NEW REP... ...SA
FINANCI...
Ltd. Ges... ... AUSTRIA

*An obscure "Starl AG Vaduz" in Lichtenstein appears to be supplying Leo
Wanta with 100 billion "clean, clear, good, legal, bundled, counted, verified,
packed and stamped" Russian rubles, in cash, at 15 rubles to the dollar.*

NEW REPUBLIC / USA FINANCIAL GROUP, LTD.
2101 NORTH EDGEWOOD AVENUE
APPLETON, WI, USA 54914
TELE/FAX: (414) 738-7007

04 FEBRUARY 1991   REF/NIDETZKY GROUP

PREPARED FOR: CONFIRMATION - DO NOT DUPLICATE

EL-SIRAAT TRADING INTERNATIONAL (INC) [MANDATED AGENT]
IMPORT - EXPORT - COMM. REPS   ATTN: MR. FAISAL S. KHAN, ES
112 LAKEVIEW TERRACE, OAKLAND, NJ, USA 07436-0000
CONFIRMING IRREVOCABLE CORPORATE PURCHASE ORDER No. AU.910116.75(2X)

THIS DOCUMENT WILL CONFIRM THAT, NEW REPUBLIC/USA FINANCIAL GROUP, LTD.
GmbH, IS READY, WILLING AND ABLE TO BUY/SELL/EFFECT *2000* METRIC TONS
OF AU BULLION METAL, WITH ROLLOVERS UNDER GOOD LONDON DELIVERY (GLD), WITH
USDOLLAR FUNDING BASED ON DAY OF EXCHANGE - SECOND LMER FIXING, FOLLOWING
THE COMPLETION OF ASSAY AND VERIFICATION OF AU METAL.

COMMODITY   : AU BULLION IN 74 KG BARS, 999.5/1000 FINENESS
HALLMARK   : INTERNATIONALLY ACCEPTED HALLMARKS
QUANTITY   : ** 2000 ** METRIC TONNES, WITH ROLLOVERS
DELIVERY   : PER ACCEPTABLE LIFT SCHEDULE TO BE DETERMINED

USDOLLAR PRICING   : GROSS DISCOUNT: 3.25 % NET DISCOUNT: 3.00 %

TRANSACTION CODE   : AU/POL.91.SBC   SECURITY CODE: GEVERS/LEON

DOCUMENTATION   : CERTIFICATE OF ORIGIN   EXPORT LICENSES
                      CERTIFICATE OF OWNERSHIP   WAREHOUSE RECEIPTS
                      CERTIFICATE OF ASSAYER
                      TAX EXEMPTION CERTIFICATES
                      VERIFICATION OF FREE OF LIENS AND ENCUMBERANCES

LOCATION   : SECURITY VAULTS - KLOTEN, SWITZERLAND

PAYMENT TERMS   : TWO BANKING DAYS AFTER COMPLETION OF ASSAY AND THE
                      PRIME BANK DELIVERY OF DOCUMENTS.

NEW REPUBLIC/USA FINANCIAL GROUP, LTD GmbH, STANDS READY TO RECEIVE YOUR
PRIME BANK TESTED TELEX OF AU METAL AND ACCEPTABLE LIFT SCHEDULE, WHEREAS
OUR CLOSING BANK WILL CONFIRM USDOLLAR FUNDING. UPON AU SELLER GROUP
ACCEPTANCE VIA YOUR RWAD, PRINCIPALS TO EXCHANGE PRIME BANKING COORDINATES
TO FINALIZE THIS SPECIFIC AU TRANSACTION.

VALIDITY OF THIS METAL PURCHASE ORDER IS FOR FIVE (5) BANKING DAYS, UNLESS
AU METAL PROVIDER CONFIRMS READINESS AND AVAILABILITY TO OUR PRIME BANK
COORDINATES.

FAITHFULLY YOURS,
FOR AND ON BEHALF OF NEW REPUBLIC/USA FINANCIAL GROUP, LTD GmbH

By: _____   TELEFON: (414) 738.0229
    USA AUTHORIZED SIGNATORIE - L E WANTA

LEW/nv   NEW REPUBIC/USA
                                         FINANCIAL GROUP
                                         Ltd. Ges.m.b.H - AUSTRIA

Leo Wanta announces that he is selling 2,000 tons of gold in February 1991. An El-Siraat Trading International Corporation in Oakland, New Jersey, is among his prospective clients.

PROCURA DELLA REPUBBLICA

PRESSO IL TRIBUNALE DI

C O M O

SEZIONE DI POLIZIA GIUDIZIARIA

SEGUITO PREGRESSA SEGNALAZIONE RISERVATA DEL 25.3.1992.

AL SIGNOR PROCURATORE
DELLA REPUBBLICA C/O
IL TRIBUNALE DI C O M O
Dr. Romano DOLCE Sost.

I sottoscritti ufficiali ed agenti di P.G.:

- Mar.Magg. MERLI   Gianpietro
- VBrig.   LAGIOIA   Giovanni
- App.sc.   ERDAS   Antonio

         Si evidenziano di seguito gli elementi informativi, ulteriormente sviluppati, pervenuti per il tramite dei vari organi collaterali ufficiali in ordine al traffico clandestino di materiale radioattivo ed altro che verrebbe perpretato sistematicamente da una organizzazione internazionale con ramificazioni anche in Italia.

Tali materiali (Plutonio, uranio, mercurio rosso ed armamenti di vario genere) verrebbero contrabbandati nel territorio nazionale (in transito) per mezzo di intermediari.

La mente dell'organizzazione si identificherebbe nel tale Alexander Viktorovitch KUZIN, nato a Voronjez (ex URSS), il 15.07.1956 e residente a Vienna 1° distretto, Brandstatte 3/16 e presso KOCH 80, Herlerstrasse 91/2, dove abita anche la moglie Nadezhda NIKOLAEVNA, nata il 16.05.1956.
Dal settembre 1991 domiciliato a Belgrado, via 29 Novembre 128.

Il KUZIN risulta essere in possesso dei seguenti passaporti:

- ordinario jugoslavo nr.CA831821 rilasciato dalle Autorità della Repubblica Serba il 20.9.1991;

- CK-I nr.493737, rilasciato dal Ministero degli Esteri dell'URSS il 26 marzo 1990.

Secondo il Ministero degli Interni dell'URSS, KUZIN, presidente della ditta cooperative di Stato "BIOCOR", farebbe parte di una banda di criminali con collegamenti in campo internazionale e serebbe coinvolto in truffe e rapine commesse in Russia.

Avrebbe interesse (50%) nella ditta "KUZIN SYSTEMS" con sede a Vienna, 5000 Koch 80, Herlerstrasse 103-106 e a Colonia (Germania). Giunto a Vienna il

            - segue -

Report to Judge Dolce of Como by Italy's judicial police regarding Aleksandr Victorovich Kuzin and his connections to "a clandestine traffic in radioactive materials . . . perpetrated systematically by an international organization with branches also in Italy."

computer links, etc. Please help soon, so we can slay the dragons!" he wrote to Wanta that fall.)

A "ruble mania" ensued in the summer of 1990, wrote a reporter in Washington. "The fax machine and international direct dialing combined with the age-old lure of instant wealth to create a global frenzy."[45] The reporter thought it all came to nothing, and nobody else in Washington seemed to notice it.

Afterward, if not beforehand, however, somebody somewhere in the West must have noticed this killer attack on a disintegrating Soviet state—since it worked. A nonconvertible currency in an unstable country has few defenses on the free market. In a blizzard of paper leaving a trail from Seattle to Singapore, the Wanta crowd kept offering to buy or sell billions of rubles dirt cheap until the price they had in mind—around eighteen to the dollar—was accepted as the right one by the summer's end. Then they went after all the rubles in Russia.

"John Ross" made the first pitch in August 1990, but Wanta was the central figure. Colin Gibbins, who horned in on the bargaining in Moscow, merely "tried to steal the rubles," Wanta wrote to Mr. X. "He was just trying to do a mirror image of the New Republic deal. New Republic offered real $ for rubles. . . . NR are the only good guys."[46]

As the whole troop went for Ivan's jugular, Wanta insisted he was on a crusade to "rescue Boris" by plying Russia with food and consumer goods. "What a laugh," Mr. X. recalled. "The real game was to grab the bulk of the Soviet currency and the natural resources while the country was falling apart."

Plainly the KGB knew but didn't tell, waiting to do exactly what Boris Yeltsin said it did—frame him. Colin Gibbins, who took the fall, had been smuggling hi-tech weapons for the KGB. According to Gibbins's partner David Frye, the KGB actually sent him in to set up Yeltsin.[47] Once he received a signed contract from Yeltsin's cabinet, the KGB promptly tipped off the airport police to pick up his other partner, Paul Pearson, and then hustled Gibbins off to safety in South Africa. (Insistent requests by the British for his extradition since then have been denied.)

But Gibbins was almost irrelevant to the case of the 140 billion rubles. So was Mr. X., in the way that mattered most—the money. The one who mattered was Leo Wanta.

The Russian government never dropped Wanta. Barely a week after the Gibbins deal was exposed in January 1991, Wanta sent a fax thanking Deputy Prime Minister Filshin "for the invitation to work further on the documents." Filshin helped him get a visa, despite the cloud over his head.[48] Over the following months he negotiated a government sanctioned food-for-petroleum swap for fifty billion rubles, by his own account.[49] The figure has not been confirmed, but the deal has. The deal was completed in the last days of 1991 when there was no longer a good excuse for doing government business with an egregious crook: The Soviet Union had just perished, Russia was a free sovereign state, and Boris Yeltsin had no further need of a war chest.[50]

Nonetheless, Wanta was still running his government approved joint venture in Moscow when I went back there in the summer of 1992.[51] And he was in and out of Moscow the summer after that, by which time investigators of several countries were looking into his multifarious activities.

Italian investigators were interested in Wanta because he was thought to be among the suppliers of Russian weapons and nuclear materials to a ring of international traffickers, including members of the Italian Camorra. Several of the ring's couriers were caught that summer with samples of radioactive cesium-133—first in Geneva, and then in the northern Italian city of Vicenza.[52] With the arrests in Vicenza, Italy's interest in Wanta was spreading to America. Apart from cesium-133, the couriers picked up in Vicenza had brought in certificates of deposit amounting to $25 million, issued by the American subsidiary of the Commercial Bank of the Chemical Industry of Russia.

This was the mysterious Himbank, in vernacular English, with headquarters in Moscow and a branch in Rochester, New York. The Rochester branch, which according to the FBI was apparently doing no legitimate business, was evidently a new laundry service devised by Russian and American currency traders.[53] The $25 million worth of Himden's CDs, the first found anywhere, were going to be exchanged for narcodollars in Italy, to be redeemed for laundered money in Russia or the United States, investigators believed. Evidently the two mafias were launching a portable washing machine.[54]

Meanwhile Geneva's chief investigating magistrate, Judge Jean-Louis Crochet, had flown to Moscow to confer with Russian mafia hunter Vladimir Kalinichenko about Wanta's murky currency dealings. The two men were "working to solve a money-laundering mystery that originated in Russia," wrote the director of the Russian Academy of Science's Center for Global and Strategic Studies, Leonid Fituni, afterward—the seemingly forgotten 140 billion ruble scam, in fact .[55] It was while comparing notes on Leo Wanta that the Swiss judge and the Russian investigator came upon explosive indications of a possible connection between the great ruble scam and Russia's missing gold.

In the very days when the 140 billion ruble contract was being signed, January 1991, Leo Wanta was storming the world market with faxed offers to sell two thousand tons of gold.[56] How much might be coming from Russia was not known, but the extraordinary and plenipotentiary ambassador of the Russian Republic in Rome, "Monsignore" Roberto Coppola, was offering exactly two thousand tons of gold at exactly the same time.[57]

Interpol Moscow had noted Wanta's almost daily phone calls to Coppola from Moscow between January and June 1991—the same period when two thousand tons of Soviet gold somehow disappeared. It had even queried Washington about the "close contacts" between this pair.[58] (Indeed, Mr. X. told me, "Roberto Coppola was the source of all the gold that Wanta was offering.") Obviously the pair could have been pushing the gold for the Soviet Communist Party, the group in the best position to smuggle two thousand tons out of the Central Bank's vaults and out of the country in 1991.

Nevertheless, the Wanta link was bound to suggest a different possibility. According to the Moscow daily *Kuranty*, Judge Crochet and Kalinichenko strongly suspected that the gold might have been pledged as security for the 140 billion ruble swap, for lack of enough rubles to satisfy the Wanta crowd's faceless investors.[59] Furthermore, they thought the unknown investors behind the front men were probably criminals who saw Russia as a miraculous solution to the problem of their drug money. By then, police were "pretty sure about the identity of some suspects," Judge Crochet told the press on returning to Geneva.[60] Certainly he and his Russian colleagues had learned enough to believe that this seemingly preposterous ruble scam probably served as the original model for the most fabulous money-laundering machine ever invented.

"International organized crime got into the whole gigantic fraud to launder narcodollars," Kalinichenko declared.[61]

Were these criminals in their right minds? Yes, indeed.

CHAPTER TEN

The Payoff

On November 16, 1991, Boris Yeltsin's chief of foreign relations, Valery Grishin, announced that the Russian government was "closing the petroleum faucet."

Planned oil exports for that year had been set at 61 million tons, but export licenses had been issued for considerably more than twice as much (150 million tons). Domestic fuel supplies were running desperately short. Therefore, all permits for exporting crude were suspended. "We cannot permit sales of so much petroleum abroad; we are dramatically in need at home," Grishin said.[1]

A month later—on December 20, 1991—Leo Wanta set up his food-for-petroleum joint venture in Moscow. A "safe custody" bank account in dollars and rubles was opened at the Status Credit Bank jointly by Wanta and his partner in "Asian-Europa Development Pte Ltd.," Kok Howe Kwong of Singapore. Kok Howe Kwong had been Wanta's "consultant" throughout the year when he was beating the ruble down on world money markets and peddling Russian gold by the ton. By the time the two hit Moscow, Russia must have looked to them as a chocolate mountain might look to a wondering child.

Despite the government's new edict, Wanta appeared to have no trouble shipping petroleum. Its price had gone up in the year since he had made his 140 billion ruble pitch. Even so, he could buy a ton for $26 in rubles and sell it for $140 in the West.[2] Asian-Europa Development had a right to do this, as long as it undertook to import Western goods in exchange. Any foreign company bringing in Western food or consumer goods was entitled to export licenses for petroleum or other natural resources. Under the guidelines established by Russian premier Silaev in 1990 (see Chapter 9), such phenomenal transactions were tax-free, duty-free, and legal.

The purpose was still to attract foreign capital of whatever provenance, and since serious capital was still holding back, the benefits were going largely to illicit capital. It was impossible to say how many villains besides Wanta had similar deals. There was no public record of all the foreign companies granted such privileges or of who in the government had granted them; and no one appeared to be keeping track of them. Several ministries could issue export licenses. None seemed to be held accountable.

During that same month of December, for instance, Russia's first deputy economics minister signed new export licenses for an unknown "private charity" to ship out ten million tons of petroleum and ten million tons of petroleum products at a potential *net* profit of around $2 billion. Although the faucet was supposed to be off, no harm came to him.[3] Such was the Russian scene by the end of 1991 that nobody could tell if the private charity was Russian or foreign or both.

As early as the previous spring, the deputy chief of Russia's Sixth Department to Combat Organized Crime, Gennady Chebotarev, had submitted this confidential report to Interpol's world headquarters in Lyon:

> Strong mafia groups, in association with business circles and various government establishments, are committing large-scale unlawful export-import transactions with foreign partners at the state's expense.
>
> Their activity usually involves raw materials. Using

bribery and corruption of government officials, high-quality materials are exported as "waste." Strategic raw materials are passed off as low-quality materials. Titanium is reworked and exported at scrap metal prices. . . .

The high price of nonferrous and precious metals and alloys on the Western market has brought a dramatic increase in the export of such materials. Organized groups also engage in direct smuggling of Soviet currency through criminal avenues.[4]

That was in April 1991. A year later Chebotarev told me of "great sums going abroad through transactions with the Sicilian and American mafias." Raw materials were draining out of the country at a terrifying rate, he said, "tons and tons a day, every day, every hour" of petroleum, nickel, cobalt, aluminum, roller steel, exported as "scrap metals" or "waste."[5]

On the day I talked with Chebotarev, ten tons of copper pipe were stolen from a single enterprise. Reports were coming in that month of a military transport plane flying out from Chelyabinsk with forty tons of copper, of gangs stealing close to a ton of cobalt from the "Severonikel" combine, stealing sixty-seven tons of bronze in the Magadan Oblast, stealing the rare earth metals tantalum and indium from the Yaroslavl radio plant—all for export.[6]

In a single two-day period, customs officers at one border crossing detained *and released* a ten-ton shipment of calcium carbide from Karaganda, sixty tons of fuel oil from Nizhnegorod, two freight cars with fifty tons of benzene from Kirishi, and a railroad tanker of gasoline hitched to other freight cars loaded with sugar, paper, shampoo, rugs, children's clothing, rescue rafts, Caterpillar tractors, and an asphalt road roller.[7]

Over just two months in 1992 a massive police operation called "Operation Trawl" *captured* $180 million worth of resources on their illegal way out of Russia: 18,700 tons of rare metals, 731,500 tons of oil, sixty-five thousand cubic yards of timber, and a wide range of weapons including one Mi-8 helicopter, one armored per-

sonnel carrier, five thousand missiles, and ten million bullets.[8]
Capturing this much was some indication of how much was getting away.

Above all, the petroleum faucet could not be closed, whatever the government's decrees.

"Oil. That is what bothers us most. We have had great losses in all strategic materials, but the oil matter is utterly catastrophic," said the respected journalist Mikhail Gurtovoy, appointed that spring to head a special government commission fighting economic crime. He continued,

> What has actually happened? The big Western companies who treasure their reputation were in no hurry to invest money, so they waited. But a swarm of scoundrels who very quickly found a common language with our oil generals came running. . . .
>
> All these joint ventures couldn't drill or develop anything, not that they ever planned to. One was supposed to drill a specific number of boreholes and pump out 649,000 tons of oil. Not a single borehole was drilled, but they're contracting for the sale of 700,000 tons. What is this, a new invention—pumping oil out of undrilled boreholes?[9]

Measures designed to deal with such illicit exports were consistently toothless. A parliamentary Oversight Committee had undertaken to take a closer look—"open up quite a few black holes"—in the autumn of 1991 but had no power to impose any form of punishment.[10] The Department for the Struggle Against Corruption of the Ministry for Security (formerly the KGB) could only impose "administrative penalties"—this when "the illegal issuance of export licenses is the basic source of income for corrupt officials," the department's director said.[11] Government inspectors in Gurtovoy's own new anti-corruption commission could only monitor and report what was there to see. They had no authority to investigate actively or make arrests; often, for lack of government funds, they were not even paid.[12]

In any event, Russia had no custom controls on its borders with other ex-Soviet republics, no laws on procedures for confiscating contraband, and no laws to punish corruption. Most of its resources are still crossing freely into the now sovereign Baltic states over unmanned frontiers—or "transparent borders," as Yeltsin has called them. Thus Estonia, which has no copper, has become the world's leading copper exporter.[13]

On the very day the Russian government announced the drastic cut in oil exports, it issued a decree abolishing all requirements for registering foreign investments, all curbs on exporting or reinvesting the profits, and all restrictions on foreigners wanting to open ruble bank accounts.[14] A decree issued the previous spring—in May 1991—already allowed companies to be formed with 100 percent foreign capital, permitting them to export and import without normal licenses, exempt from taxes.[15] If these steps failed to lure many legitimate foreign investors, to whom Russia still looked too chancy, they obviously heightened its attractions for the other kind of investor.

The last restraints were falling away for representatives of Palermo's San Lorenzo and Madonia Families, Catania's Santapaola Family, Aruba's Cuntrera brothers, the 'Ndrangheta's Morabito Family, the Camorra's *magliari* ("sweater peddlers"), the Colombian cartels, and the whole array of operators like Leo Wanta. "A number of facts" now confirmed their presence in Russia, wrote the Russian Academy of Science's Leonid Fituni. The Sicilian Mafia, the Camorra, and the 'Ndrangheta had all "established their business ties with organized crime in the ex–U.S.S.R." by 1991, he said.[16]

The Sicilian Mafia had been "storing huge amounts of rubles in Palermo" for its entry into Russia. The other two had made "their first contacts in March and June 1991 in Warsaw, which were later continued in Moscow." Instead of moving in on their own hook and using hard currency, they "preferred to buy through Russian proxies or front companies, with rubles," Fituni noted. Illegal operations with rubles were proving to be "extremely lucrative," he declared.[17] "Western mafias" had in fact found "an ideal combination of conditions in Russia favorable for broad-scale money laundering," thanks to "legal chaos, transparent borders, widespread corruption, and market naïveté."

Apart from buying natural resources from the largest store in the world, their rubles could buy arms, nuclear materials, antiques, authentic icons (of which 24 million—80 percent of those registered—had already been stolen and smuggled abroad),[18] high-tech industries such as chemicals and oil extraction, citizens' vouchers to acquire privatized factories and real estate, and politicians in charge of such things.

In addition, they could diddle, con, and swindle an inexperienced and undefended public. Here, Leo Wanta could serve as an example for all.

Within a week of launching "Asian-Europa Development" in December 1991, Wanta was somehow involved in a sixty-six-billion-ruble swindle through Russia's Central Bank: thirty-six billion on December 26, 1991, soon followed by another thirty billion.

His implacable Russian pursuer, Kalinichenko, discovered the scam involving "transfers." The word *transfer* in today's Russia covers a multitude of tricks to swap rubles for dollars and vice versa, move them in or out of the country (mostly out), and cheat on the deal wherever possible. In this scam, the Central Bank was at once the swindlers' victim and their accomplice. Someone in the bank agreed to let them exchange sixty-six billion of its clients' rubles for $660 million: one hundred rubles to the dollar, half the going black market rate at the time. (The black market ruble was in a constant state of decline at this point.) They sold the rubles to American buyers at fifty to the dollar, amounting to $1.2 billion, and split the difference with a banker friend.[19] The former KGB official who had been director of the Central Bank throughout the great ruble scam, Georgy Matyukhin, resigned shortly afterward "for health reasons."

Another transfer scam involved a joint venture calling itself "DiP Sovgroup" in Moscow and "D&P Group Inc." in California. Both were headed by a Ukrainian émigré named Alexander Dokiychuk, an old-time associate of Wanta's.[20] During the very weeks of the sixty-six-billion-ruble bank swindle, Dokiychuk's American D&P Group received a credit of $1 billion in rubles from the Russian Foreign Trade Bank, for which Dokiychuk undertook to bring in the equivalent in Western computers and food aid. The credit was endorsed by Vice Premier Gaidar in a directive "On Attracting Preferential Credits From U.S. Banks." The Russian Foreign Trade Bank gave an advance deposit of nine billion rubles to Dokiychuk's DiP Sovgroup in Moscow for the purchases. When no computers or food aid had arrived three months later, an angry would-be customer tipped off the press. Dokiychuk then repaid the 9 billion rubles, without interest. Meanwhile he had converted the rubles to dollars and lent them out short-term to dollar-hungry Russians at 40 percent interest. Since inflation was running to around 20 percent a month in Russia at the time, a ruble would cost him 60 percent less by then. Thus he could buy the rubles back for a third of the dollars he had bought them with in the first place.[21]

Wanta was believed to be in on this deal although his name did not come up, Kalinichenko told me. He and Dokiychuk were "part of the same crowd," backed by an invisible army of foreign investors working dollar-ruble "transfer" deals ever since. Some were straight swaps, with the Wanta crowd creaming 3 percent off the top. Others involved a Russian version of the loan-back: Russian bank credits in rubles, unsecured, pledged as security for an American bank loan in dollars, lent in Russia at high interest or simply made off with.

This last was a favorite among swindlers. One Moscovite presented a document to a U.S. bank showing he had an impossible seventeen billion rubles in his Russian account. He received a $2 million loan from the U.S. bank and "went off in an unknown direction," said an officer of Russia's Sixth Department.[22]

Mostly, though, people like Leo Wanta were doing the big straight swaps. Like an underground clearinghouse, they were collecting the rubles from Russian enterprises and rounding up foreign buyers. "Hundreds of Russian firms chip in the rubles to get hard currency that isn't taxed away by the government; without people like Wanta, they'd be paying thirty cents on the dollar to the Central Bank. They're dying to do it; Wanta could line up a hundred billion rubles in a week," Kalinichenko said when we met again in the summer of 1992. He continued,

> The dollars do bring goods into Russia—sold at Western prices—and the rubles don't even leave the country. But the point is that *the Western investors own the rubles*. They come and buy *anything* in rubles—petroleum, precious metals, mines, real estate, factories. . . . This is American mafia money now, and Italian and Russian mafia money. Wanta and others like him work with Russian mafiosi abroad and with Sicilian mafiosi. They do swaps for Russian firms without documents. Their guarantee is the mafia structure on the Russian side and the Western side.[23]

For all the colossal wealth they are draining out of Russia and everywhere in the ex-Soviet commonwealth, these consummate criminals are never caught. Indeed, the more they take, the more they appear to be protected—*cosseted*—at the highest government levels. Leo Wanta is an egregious example. But the one who towers above all others is Marc David Rich, the most notorious swindler in American history.

A fugitive from America since 1985, Rich faces a 325-year prison term in the United States on fifty-one charges of racketeering, mail and wire fraud, tax evasion on $100 million of unreported income, and trading with the enemy (Iran, during the hostage crisis). The FBI has offered a $750,000 reward for his capture. These facts come from a report entitled "They Went Thataway: The Strange Case of Marc Rich and Pincus Green" in which the House Committee on Government Operations reviewed his criminal history.[24]

Since Rich is now a naturalized and unextraditable Swiss citizen, holding Spanish and Israeli passports as well, he roams the world at will. Much of his time was spent in Russia until recently. A longtime dealer in petroleum and many other commodities, Rich had operated on Soviet territory since 1983. An irate Special Commission there had once obliged him to refund $20 million of "surplus money" he had picked up in deals with the former Soviet government.[25] As the Soviet regime was falling, he hooked into Istok, a joint venture sponsored by the new regime in Russia and founded by the country's first ruble millionaire, Artjom Tarasov. (See Chapter 5.) With Istok's help, Rich got four million tons of petroleum out to Western Europe in 1990, at a profit of around half a billion dollars.[26]

Head of the second largest commodities firm in the world, Marc Rich & Co., he quickly became Russia's largest provider of grain— five million tons a year—and largest raw materials exporter. That made him the largest single beneficiary of Prime Minister Silaev's guidelines for foreign investors. By 1993 his yearly turnover on ex-Soviet territory ran to $3 billion, up half a billion over the year before. Only a tenth of this went into Russia's treasury. His three huge joint ventures in Russia, for crude and refined petroleum, were touted as the nation's most "capital-intensive" foreign investments. The intensive capital was mostly Russian, however. Nobel Oil, largest of the three, was funded with just half a million dollars in dollars and the king-sized balance in rubles (thirty billion).[27] All three ventures were exempt from standard export duties on crude oil.

In a full-length TV film that he commissioned and paid for, Rich presented himself as "a man whose every thought is for the good of Russia." Hogwash, said Moscow's Interpol chief Vasiliy Ignatov. Marc Rich was charging world prices for the grain he brought in, Ignatov explained. In exchange he was shipping out not only a sea of petroleum but four-fifths of Russia's exported aluminum (worth around $700 million), nine-tenths of its exported zinc, and quantities of nickel, ferro-alloys, carbon, copper, and molybdenum—all bought for rubles, at bargain prices.[28]

According to *Forbes* magazine, Rich had "stunning contracts" with the former Soviet Republics by 1992; his profits on Russian oil and aluminum alone were "a factor of two to three higher than the average profits on the world market." The Russians were "losing about thirty percent on this trade," said the director of Britain's giant corporation Lonrho.[29]

Similar stories were coming out of Ukraine and, more spectacularly, out of Kazakhstan, whose government accused the Balkhashmed factory there of selling cathode copper to Marc Rich & Co. in massive quantity at far below "universally recognized discounts" on the London market. The factory—Marc Rich's primary partner in Kazakhstan—was also accused of keeping "concealed profits" in Marc Rich bank accounts all over Europe.[30] Even as this came to light, Kazakhstan's president Nursultan Nazarbayev was cordially inviting Marc Rich to expand operations in Kazakhstan.[31]

In Moscow, meanwhile, an Interpol Red Alert warrant issued in 1992 appeared briefly to be having some effect. "The Russian government vowed to suspend its ties with Marc Rich & Co. pending a thorough investigation," *The Wall Street Journal* reported. This "was never followed through," however, the paper noted.[32] With the warrant out, Rich left 150 assistants to run his Russian affairs and withdrew to his home beyond the reach of Interpol and the FBI, in the tranquil Swiss town of Zug.

The Russian government was more generous than ever in his absence. On January 25,1992, the Ministry of the Economy and the Ministry of Fuel and Power agreed jointly to give him export permits for 2,616,000 tons of heating oil and 1,530,000 tons of diesel fuel for the year 1992.[33] Did Russia's governing politicians know who they were favoring in the person of Marc David Rich? "Sure they did," says *Izvestiya*; the KGB's dossier on him went back a decade. Yet he led the lengthening list of criminals who continue to ransack Russia systematically, often in direct collaboration with the politicians who run it.

Unlike America's early robber barons who stole but *built* something, who enriched the country as well as themselves, nearly all of those stripping Russia of its natural and man-made resources simply take the money and run. The highest aspiration of a Russian mafioso today is to grab as much as he can as fast as he can, get it into a Western bank, and take off for America. Much the same goes for a Sicilian or American mafioso, who comes in to make a quick killing with rubles and clears out again with his rubles changed back into laundered dollars. Together they account for much of the illicit capital gushing out of Russia, approaching $20 billion a year by 1992.[34]

Why is the Russian government giving away the resources it owns to a bunch of proven crooks? The likely answer, the payoff, would be no more unusual here than anywhere if not for the staggering size of the sums.

Early in 1993, Russia's vice-president Alexander Rutskoi disclosed that the illicit flow of raw materials abroad in the single year of 1992 had amounted to $17 billion. Although Rutskoi was then on the way to becoming Boris Yeltsin's intractable enemy and was himself no better than he should be, his estimate was accepted by all top Russian leaders at the time.

"It would be enough to get that money back; we wouldn't have to ask for foreign financial aid," he said. Actually, it was more than enough: The world's seven most industrialized countries, the G-7, had pledged $13 billion of aid for the year 1993.[35]

Instead of giving any money back, Italian crime groups were flooding Russia with counterfeit dollars that winter, forged well enough to pass almost anywhere. These were now used to finance their purchases of privatized enterprises, real estate, petroleum, titanium, uranium, plutonium, missiles, MiGs—assets worth billions of dollars for which they were literally paying nothing.[36] The forgeries came forcibly to police attention late in December 1992 when Moscow police captured four Italian "tourists" after a shootout in the center of town. They were not only bringing in $1.2 million in forged hundred-dollar bills to buy arms, including a missile ramp, but preparing to fence two stolen Italian certificates of deposit for a million dollars each. Pledged as security for a loan from a Russian bank, these could have stripped the bank of around two billion rubles at the end of 1992.[37]

In the same month of December, Russia's Ministry of Security cracked an international ring preparing to pump in another $11 million of fake hundred-dollar bills. One in every ten U.S. dollars circulating in Russia was counterfeit by then, the Ministry calculated—one billion in an estimated ten billion.[38] That alone could be enough to devastate the Russian economy if it weren't so blasted already.

Nothing in history compares to this cancer consuming the largest country in the world. Devoured by criminal predators and rampant corruption from within and without, Russia seems helpless to save itself. Certainly the West has not done much to save it. From a position of averting their eyes and hoping this would all go away, Western leaders are shifting to one of open resignation.

"There's no point in handing over even $5 billion if it is merely going to end up in the Swiss bank accounts of [Russia's] ruling elite," remarked a senior Western official at the G-7 meeting in March 1993. Britain's foreign secretary Douglas Hurd warned at the same meeting against "putting huge sums of money into a pocket with holes in it."[39]

Rather than write Russia off for its sins, Western governments might consider how they have failed it by refusing to notice, still less address, the worst of its numberless afflictions. This sickness cannot be contained by quarantine. For every Leo Wanta whose operations may come to light—and he is still operating freely— there are hundreds, perhaps thousands of others. Some may be loners, but the Sicilian and American mafias are there, the Colombian cartels are there—indeed, all the big crime syndicates are there. The capital they are amassing is clean when it leaves the great laundry that Russia has become—billions and billions of untraceable dollars infecting the rest of the world, used to fortify criminal power around the planet, finance the drug trade, and invest in money markets, stock markets, commodity markets, real estate, tourism, transport, and every kind of legitimate enterprise.

Yet what is happening in and to Russia is "not a priority" for Western police, a foremost European police chief admitted to me halfway through 1993. Apart from Germany's BKA, no agency I have questioned in the West keeps a close watch on the crime scene here or anywhere in the ex-Soviet bloc. No Western agency has a workable system for exchanging police information with Russia or the rest of the ex-Soviet bloc. (The first serious effort in that direction, an informal agreement among American, German, Italian, and Russian police, was just beginning to test out at the end of 1993.) No Western country has an extradition treaty with the Russian Republic, in the absence of which the whole international underworld can shelter on its territory while its most dangerous native criminals can find sanctuary anywhere abroad, and do. No Western government has made financial help to Russia contingent on the passage of laws to make law enforcement feasible, which would be much simpler than complying with Western demands for a brisk transition to capitalism. None has acknowledged the manifest collusion between an exponentially growing criminal force and politicians at the highest levels of government.

Several of the most powerful men surrounding President Yeltsin came under formal judicial investigation in Russia itself in the summer of 1993. Breaking the news to the Russian parliament that June, Assistant Prosecutor-General Nikolaj Makarov named Yeltsin's gray eminence, Gennadij Burbulis, along with Vice-Premier Vladimir Shumeiko, Vice-Premier Alexandr Shokhin, former foreign trade minister Piotr Aven, and the supreme chief of information Mikhail Poltoranin. All were accused of "illicit economic dealings with American and European companies for personal gain."[40] The fact that they accused their opponents of the same thing, perhaps with equal justice, was no excuse.

Even then, no Western government cared to confront President Yeltsin with the evidence that his ministers continued to give away more than they were asking the West for—and this to organized criminals, the West's own mortal enemies. Doubtless Western diplomats have kept silent for fear of giving aid and comfort to Russia's unregenerate communists. In the event, they have denied aid and comfort to the diminishing few still trying to save Russia from the mafias that are now "the country's greatest single problem," in Yeltsin's words.[41]

CHAPTER ELEVEN

The Spinoff

Mr. Kalashnikov, inventor of the 53 million assault rifles bearing his name, told reporters at an international arms fair in Abu Dhabi in the winter of 1993 that he dreamed of inventing a new gun that wouldn't kill people.[1] This was not exactly the hard sell his country needed. Russia was trying desperately to fill the black hole down which billions of dollars had disappeared by that winter. Therefore it was storming the market with some of the world's most advanced weaponry—the deadlier the better.

Why not? All arms-producing countries are mean fighters in the world's most lucrative trade. In the Middle East alone, arms contracts amounting to $428 billion were signed between 1991 and 1993, and that was an old market.[2] The collapse of the Soviet Union has been opening new markets all over the map. Even Slovenia, supposedly no part of the war tearing Yugoslavia apart after the Fall, was caught secretly storing a hundred tons of weapons in the summer of 1993. Eleven containers presumed to be packed with blankets for Yugoslav refugees were actually packed with forty thousand 88mm mortars, 10,900 automatic guns, and nearly a million cartridges.[3] The discovery that these were Russian-made didn't mean much in itself. The provenance might have been

Czechoslovakia, Poland, Belgium, Sweden, Italy, Britain, or America. Anybody in the arms trade might turn up in any war zone.

But Russia and its fellow ex-Soviet Republics are not just in the business of selling arms like everybody else. They own one of the two largest conventional and nuclear arsenals on earth, and except for the most apocalyptic of atomic weapons, it is out of control. All the familiar evils of the arms trade are compounded by the anguishing frailty of these governments, the appalling corruption pervading them, the misery weighing down their people, the undiminished force and indecipherable designs of the KGB, the regnant Russian mafia, and its formidable confederates in the international underworld.

Despite Russia's reassuring words to the West, its military arsenals can almost literally be sacked at will. "Weapons, like all other commodities, have joined a wildly unrestricted market. . . . Wild capitalism means that there is little of the careful official scrutiny of potential buyers that there is in the West. The result is that almost anything can be bought for a price, including radioactive components for nuclear weapons," wrote the president of the Russian Academy of Science's Center for Global and Strategic Studies, Leonid Fituni.[4]

The Russian government "exercises no control whatsoever" over domestic arms sales, meaning any arms that are not sold directly for export, said the deputy chairman of Russia's Military-Industrial Commission, Vladimir Lopatin, in 1992.[5] Factory owners, free to sell for their personal profit, are selling the latest Soviet tanks, rocket launchers, and tactical missiles to local armies, militia groups, front companies, and any other buyers flocking to the domestic market, Lopatin went on. (Holland and Yemen had bought a thousand T55 tanks directly from the factory through Russian front companies that year, reported the Russian business daily *Commersant*. The tanks were being sold by weight: $100,000 a ton.) "The head of a military academy recently bought shares in a military factory by selling some of the buildings of his academy, even though these buildings did not belong to him. And we have dozens of cases like this," Lopatin declared.

With this built-in incentive to increase production rather than convert to civilian uses, military production was in fact increasing. Russia's arms industry spent double the fifty billion rubles allocated to it in the first quarter of 1992, Lopatin revealed. Supposedly the lack of control applies only to conventional weapons, but the borderline is dangerously indistinct. There are no controls on exporting the *critical components* of nuclear weapons if they can be used in legitimate consumer goods as well. Thousands of factories in the ex–U.S.S.R. turn out such dual-use components for ballistic missiles, chemical warfare agents, and nuclear weapons. Numberless Soviet technicians who know how to put them together are migrating to countries offering fabulous salaries. Since these factories don't make complete weapons systems, they don't come under the rules for strategic armament sales and exports."We would have to have people in each and every factory to know what they are doing. This is beyond our means," Lopatin said.

Such critical components are hemorrhaging out of Russia today. Unless Russia imposes strict controls on dual-use exports, half a dozen Third World countries could acquire bombs "Made in the FSU" (Former Soviet Union) within a few years, Lopatin warned.[6] He did not add, though he might have, that it is not impossible—far from it—for the bombs to be acquired ready-made.

Some of the worst nuclear fright stories coming out of Russia aren't true, starting with the one about the terrorists' ultimate weapon—a consummate hoax repeatedly exposed and still going strong.

"The pocket atom bomb is a reality," reported Britain's *Daily Mirror* in May 1993. Russia had developed a nuclear ball the size of a grapefruit, fitting into a briefcase and usable in any common rocket launcher, the paper declared.

Two TV reporters chasing the story for Channel 4 had come upon what was supposed to be the secret ingredient, an amalgam of mercury, oxygen, and antimony called red mercury. American scientists were said to have developed the powder, which Russians had transformed into a heavy liquid capable of provoking nuclear fission in a tiny particle of plutonium. American nuclear researchers at Los Alamos reportedly refused to discuss it, but the director of a Russian company authorized to sell it "to friendly nations" didn't mind. "The world is in great danger," he advised the reporters. Nuclear bombs "the size of a biro [pen]" could be made with red mercury."Eighty micro-bombs could wipe out Moscow," he told them.[7]

Red mercury was selling for up to $375,000 a kilo on the black market when this story appeared. A Russian–United States joint venture called Alkor Technologies Inc., formed in St. Petersburg solely to produce it, claimed to be raking in a billion dollars a year.[8] The product seemed to be worth every cent. Apart from provoking nuclear fission in plutonium, red mercury was presented as a remarkably versatile substance used to make microchips for high-tech computers, fabricate banknotes, improve aerial radar, produce intelligent bombs, increase the precision of missile guidance systems, cool off atomic reactors, and "revitalize atomic warheads impoverished by disuse."[9]

Hundreds of salesmen were crisscrossing Europe and America with ten-gram samples. One was a notorious right-wing Italian terrorist named Marco Affatigato, working out of an impressive office in Valence, France, that offered "diverse services for enterprises." (He claimed to have official licenses from Russia and Ukraine.) Buyers were lining up from Libya, Nigeria, Saudi Arabia, Syria, Lebanon, South Africa, Argentina, Pakistan, India, Germany, Canada, and the United States.

Police and intelligence services everywhere had been braced for just this kind of traffic since the fall of the Soviet Union. Traffickers moving red mercury were sighted all over. The Czechoslovak Interior Ministry mounted a sizable paramilitary operation at Ostrava Airport in 1991 to intercept a $20 million shipment from Russia, which failed to arrive.[10] Similar unsuccessful raids followed in Hungary, Bulgaria, Poland, and Italy over the next year. Half a dozen red mercury salesmen picked up in Italy provided hair-raising descriptions of their product.

At the height of an international police alert, in April 1993, Russian Vice-Premier Alexander Rutskoi dropped his own bomb in Moscow. Charged with investigating corruption—a job he lost soon after he spoke—he accused Boris Yeltsin's closest adviser, Gennady Burbulis, of a gigantic scam. Burbulis had given an exclusive license for the export of red mercury to a small company in his hometown of Sverdlovsk, Rutskoi alleged; and the company had made $3 billion on it.

"How is it possible that a little Siberian company with a capital of thirty thousand rubles can be authorized to export ten tons of red mercury bringing $300,000 a kilo on the international market? And why did this need a secret directive?" he demanded. And he answered: "Because this is a pure fraud, designed to carry out an international financial scheme. Because red mercury does not exist. Because it's all a trick to cover exports of platinum, beryllium, osmium, uranium, plutonium. . . ."[11]

To call it merely a fraud was to belittle the gifted minds behind this monumental bluff. There is no such thing as radioactive red mercury. Some combination of antimony and mercury might once have been tried in a Russian experimental plutonium breeder without success, but even this is a guess, by the only expert to venture that far.[12] What the salesmen push is likely a mix of ordinary if toxic minerals or plain water tinted cherry red or common silver mercury in a glass tube painted red (with nail polish, in one instance). It may be mildly radiated if extracted from a breeding reactor or treated to show traces of radioactivity if tested in a laboratory within three days—its shelf life, the time limit unfailingly set for testing. Sometimes it is presented as a camouflage liquid for minute quantities of the real radioactive element: a deadly substance labeled Trans-uranium or Lawrencium 103.

"Lawrencium is a heavy element that does not exist in nature," I was told by an atomic expert at Italy's Alternative Energy Institute. "No isotope in the range of Lawrencium 103 has been identified. Ten isotopes in all have been identified in the range of Lawrencium 253 to 262; one has a half-life of 3.6 hours, the other of 40 minutes." Neither has any practical use, he stated flatly.[13]

The Russian analyst at the U.S. Bureau of Mines in Washington guffaws when the subject of red mercury is mentioned. So do colleagues at the International Atomic Energy Agency in Vienna where hardly a day passes without a phone call inquiring about it. British customs agents say they've been hearing of red mercury for ten years but have never seen it.[14] Nevertheless, the traffic in red mercury is real and intense, an elaborate cover masking an underground traffic in platinum, beryllium, deuterium, scandium, cesium, strontium, uranium, plutonium: the true fright story.

Perhaps the most frightening part of the story is the public's ignorance of its dimensions. A solid wall of secret agents—good guys and bad guys, Eastern, Western, Southern, and Northern—blocks the view. Secret agents have always been entangled in the arms traffic, traditionally their murkiest domain. The power it signifies and the money in it draw them irresistibly, for whatever enigmatic objectives: political, operational, frequently venal.

Adversaries in their private wars, they are often allies in frustrating the police and the courts. Here they can count on the discretion or collusion of potent politicians and party financiers, corrupt public servants, bankers who are all business, and diplomats piloting their ships of state through tricky international waters.

This was bad enough when they were merely dealing with conventional weapons. Today, however, secret agents of every variety are active and prominent players in the nuclear arms traffic, aside from, and often in connivance with, its con men and crooks. Therefore, it is extremely difficult to uncover the truth about nuclear leakage from Russia. The dimensions of this terrifying traffic are systematically obscured. Countless cases end with the rumor squelched, the fake reassuringly exposed, the con man bared, the fellow who got away. Reporters trying to sort the facts from the cover-ups are forever at the risk of being misled. Clear instances of nuclear materials actually found and impounded are still rare. But there are such instances.

The evidence has been accumulating since October 1991 when a Swiss national and three accomplices were picked up with 0.3 milligrams of plutonium in Como, on Italy's Swiss border. Even this minuscule sample was three hundred times more than enough to cause cancer in the human body .

The Swiss national was turned over to Judge Romano Dolce, destined to become the first Western magistrate tracking the seepage of Russian nuclear materials. Short, slight, energetic, inquisitive, and determined, Judge Dolce is still threading his way among unfathomable and all but insurmountable obstacles.

His hunt began when, after interrogating his Swiss arrestee, he informed Swiss police of an imminent deal for 29 kilos (almost 64 pounds) of Russian uranium. Six traffickers of various nationality were arrested in Zurich with 100 grams on them; the remaining 28.9 kilos turned up in a parked car in the center of town.[15] The uranium proved to be "proletarian," meaning not enriched. Since Switzerland has no law on trafficking in nuclear materials anyway, the six were released. Actually, "proletarian" uranium was a standard item hawked among others less innocuous by the extraordinary organization Judge Dolce came upon that winter.

The judge had first heard of it not from his Swiss arrestee but from a Swedish businessman named Jorgen Quist Nielsen, a freelance trader marginally involved in what he now knew to be a huge clandestine traffic in red mercury, uranium, and plutonium. "When I realized how dangerous the whole thing was, I decided to come to you," he told the judge.

Nielsen had been referred to a certain Aleksandr Kuzin in Vienna as someone who could sell Russian gold to the government of Kuwait. When they met, however, Kuzin asked Nielsen to find customers for red mercury instead. One thing soon led to another. Nielsen said:

> Kuzin confided to me that red mercury, plutonium, and uranium were coming to him from Russia, from generals and colonels in the army who were exporting it illegally and making a lot of money. I was introduced to Italians who were buying red mercury.
>
> One was Marco Affatigato, in Valence. Another was a "Mr. Corrado," the director of Olivetti in Stockholm, who proposed that I should go to Moscow to meet some-

body in the KGB who would fly me to a contact in Kiev where they make nuclear material. . . . Naturally I played along, but I had no intention of getting into such a risky business.[16]

Jorgen Quist Nielsen's testimony led police to four of Kuzin's agents in Milan where they had arrived from Budapest with two kilos of what passed for red mercury, along with a small quantity of radioactive scandium (a nuclear waste product), and five kilos of plutonium (this last was discussed at length on their tapped phones). They had just given the plutonium to a Libyan agent when they were caught. The Libyan got away—the plutonium went to Libya, Judge Dolce has reason to believe—and, as in Switzerland, the four arrested traffickers were soon released. Incredibly, Italy, like Switzerland, has no law on trafficking in nuclear materials. "I had to dust off a law on 'aggravated contraband' to hold them at all," the judge told me.[17]

By holding them briefly, however, he got another and much more important informant. Dezider Ostragonac, a Viennese electronics engineer, was administrative officer for three of Kuzin's companies, in Vienna, Budapest, and Prague. A firsthand witness, he described a huge multifaceted arms network covering the continent. Ostrogonac's testimony led to the arrest of thirty traffickers all over Europe, including Marco Affatigato in Valence and "Corrado" in Stockholm (who fled to Moscow after being freed with the rest of them for lack of a law to fit their crime).

All worked for Aleksandr Kuzin, whom Ostrogonac identified as a former KGB colonel. He named nine other KGB agents in the same network and five Russian military officers working directly with Kuzin in Vienna, including a certain "Kizow," son-in-law of former Moscow mayor Gavril Popov.[18]

This was an official Soviet operation, Ostrogonac insisted, saying,

> I repeat that the true sellers of red mercury, radioactive and fissile material are agents of the KGB, officers of the Red Army, and high officials of the Russian Government. . . .

I want to make it clear that the clandestine traffic of Soviet armament spreading over Europe for some years—machine guns, fighter aircraft, tanks, red mercury, scandium, radioactive and strategic materials, as well as nuclear warheads and nuclear technology—is all part of a criminal design desired and supported by the Soviet state apparatus. I can say with absolute certainty that this traffic depends on the complicity and decisive participation of the ex–Soviet Republics. The transfer of materials is between state and state, and those managing the traffic are state functionaries.

A traffic involving the entire territory of Europe cannot proliferate without the government's knowledge and consent, to bring in indispensable hard currency—especially dollars—for its disastrous economy. Like hundreds and hundreds of other traders or intermediaries of every race and provenance, my role is to tempt buyers with offers of dazzling profits. When a client is hooked, the KGB demands bank proof that he's solvent. The bank's confirmation goes to Russia by way of its embassies or consulates in Malmö, Sweden, or Bern, Switzerland, or Vienna. When Russian officials send their approval, the material moves on to Iraq, Iran, Israel, Syria, Lebanon, Libya, South Africa, Saudi Arabia, Pakistan, Argentina, India. . .

Ostrogonac plainly believed in the strategic uses of red mercury, as did several other informants who came along. This was the beauty of the scam: With a single superbly constructed lie, red mercury could be sold at a fabulous price in its own right, while serving as bait, or cover, for those interested in the genuine radioactive article.

Despite his falling for the red mercury scam, Ostrogonac's testimony was plausible. The required conditions for a network like this one were described precisely by the Russian Academy of Science's Leonid Fituni in 1993. "It is common knowledge, although never confirmed officially, that an organized system of selling special permissions for the marketing of the former Soviet arsenals was created by the new Russian generals," Fituni wrote. "The leakage of weaponry from the army and KGB [involves] both state companies and obscure front firms operating quite openly. . . . This semi-legal arms trade is controlled by Moscow- and New York-based mafias [in collusion with] corrupt top brass who have literally become part of the mafia," Fituni said.[19]

Everything investigators have learned so far about the Kuzin network matches this generic description.

The Kuzin network operates out of luxurious offices in St. Stephansplatz, the most elegant square in Vienna. Its director, Aleksandr Victorovich Kuzin, was undoubtedly a KGB colonel, rogue or otherwise. Russia's Interior Ministry describes him as the president of a state cooperative called BIOCOR, tied to "a band of criminals with international ties, involved in theft and fraud." Although the Russian government may disown him, it doesn't get in his way. On the contrary, a KGB colonel known only as "Boris" is stationed in his Vienna headquarters, collecting a percentage on sales "for the friends."[20]

"Kuzin Group International," the colonel's parent company, claims to be a holding company representing fifty-seven firms in the West and three hundred "branches and agencies inside the U.S.S.R.," with a global turnover of $4.3 billion. Its prospectus, issued in 1991, states that it employs 46,000 people in the West and 120,000 in the ex–Soviet Union, engaged in "trade of every kind from petrochemicals and fertilizers to computers, sophisticated electronics, diagnostic medical equipment, pharmaceuticals, construction, and many other fields."[21]

Not only does Kuzin Group International "maintain very close relations with the U.S.S.R." but it claims "an active role in the process of converting the Soviet military industry to civilian production." Kuzin Group International has a branch called "Kuzin-Italia" in the northeastern Italian city of Udine, near the Yugoslav border. As registered in Udine's chamber of commerce, Kuzin-Italia has no employees but is nevertheless trading in "ferrous metals, plastics, chemicals for industry and agriculture, textiles, food and agricultural products, building materials, and exports of fresh meat."[22]

Colonel Kuzin has another company in Vienna called Impex, with a branch in Como, Italy. Impex is a foreign subsidiary of what used to be called Kintex, Bulgaria's state-owned company trading in arms and drugs since 1968. Kuzin Group International also has a "daughter-company"[23] based in Vienna called Kuzin Unitrade, which has its own branch in Udine; a Sovitrade in Italy's Adriatic port of Trieste; and Unitrade branches in the German cities of Munich and Cologne. Unitrade is described in Kuzin's prospectus as primarily "directed toward the Soviet market, especially Russia's, for every kind of trade." In reality it specializes in a two-way trade, selling Russian rubles and arms in the West and reinvesting the proceeds in Russian factories and raw materials.[24]

This is where the path of KGB Colonel Aleksandr Kuzin intersects with that of Finland's Michael Preisfreund. Kuzin Group International opened for business in Vienna on May 6, 1990, and Kuzin Unitrade within the same month—the very month Preisfreund got started in Helsinki marketing billions of rubles. The Italian terrorist Marco Affatigato opened his office in Valence that month, to sell not just red mercury but rubles as well, in blocks of five and ten billion.[25] Leo Wanta and Colonel Kuzin were both offering two million Soviet gas masks in the same weeks. AB Invest's client (the "Turkish group") bought ten billion rubles from Preisfreund's confederate in the autumn of 1990 and 544 kilos of red mercury from Colonel Kuzin afterward (for $174,124,800).

Two of Colonel Kuzin's operatives conducted ruble transactions with Preisfreund and Wanta's crowd in the same week of 1990. One was Franz Mikulits of Impex-Vienna, among the four men arrested in Como for flogging Kuzin's plutonium in October 1991; the other was Georg Horvath, who heads Kuzin's Unitrade office in Munich. On July 4, 1990, Mikulits bought a billion rubles from Preisfreund; four days later Horvath sold a billion rubles to Preisfreund.[26]

Apparently Colonel Kuzin was involved with the operators behind the Great Ruble Scam. Indeed, swapping rubles and laundering other currencies are a constant in his multifarious activities. Like others in this roaring ruble trade, he works with international crooks, especially with the Russian and Sicilian mafias whose joint "global network for marketing nuclear components" has been described by Leonid Fituni. (See Chapter 9.) "The Sicilians do a lot of Kuzin's currency deals; they have the money. And they take a lot of his arms, buying partly for themselves and selling the rest," Judge Dolce told me.[27]

The arms are what set Colonel Kuzin apart as a singular menace. In addition to conventional weapons from everywhere in Eastern Europe—Kalashnikovs, mortars, tanks, helicopters, plastic explosives, missiles—the Kuzin network is selling "sizable quantities of extremely potent radioactive material to Middle Eastern and North African countries," says a confidential Italian police report.[28] These supplies usually travel west through Romania, Bulgaria, and the former Yugoslavia to the Italian port of Trieste; through Hungary into Austria; and through the Baltic states to a "Mr. Lindberg" in Finland. Informants speak of storage depots for nuclear materials in Chiasso, on Italy's border with Switzerland, and in Traiskirchen, Austria. Conventional weapons are said to be stored in Trieste, Budapest, the Croatian capital of Zagreb, and, above all, the Czech town of Slušovice, seat of what outraged Czechs call "the communist mafia."

The Slušovice arsenal sounded like pure fiction when engineer Ostrogonac described it to Judge Dolce. This is what he said:

> The largest store of Russian and Czech arms is under a mountain about twelve kilometers from Slušovice. This was an old mine; now it is restored and guarded. Here there are or were antitank missiles, land-to-air missiles, Czech-made Skorpions similar to Israeli Uzis, 200,000 Kalashnikovs with ammunition . . . [and] about two hundred new Russian tanks and thirty old ones, the last time I heard. . . .
>
> Slušovice is owned by a Czech cooperative with around six thousand workers. They have companies all over the world, hotels, computers, farms, food process-

ing—in Egypt, Austria, the United States, Germany, Luxembourg.

These gentlemen of Slušovice are so powerful that the president of Czechoslovakia can't touch them. They have their own police force, "Cubpol," named for their own president, Engineer Cuba. All the big spies and secret agents [of the old regime] work for them. They sell food to Russia, so naturally they're number one in Russia.[29]

I might have been skeptical of this account if I hadn't heard about Slušovice independently; it was the scandal of the day when I visited Prague in the autumn of 1991. The Slušovice cooperative had been the communist regime's horn of plenty. It did have six thousand employees and companies all over the world. Apart from dominating Czech agriculture, it owned food processing and bottling plants, hotels, factories, department stores, even horse racing. It had its own security service, ran its own fleet of trucks, built its own roads.

When the communist regime collapsed, the coop's top managers forced the whole enterprise into bankruptcy, put its funds into their personal bank accounts, and sold its assets for pennies to the private company they hastened to form.

Czechoslovakia's post-communist government did seem unable to lay a finger on them. The chief investigator on their trail, a Captain Zak, had just fled to Switzerland, he said for his life, some said with a share of the loot when I got to Prague. Half a dozen responsible Czech sources told me that the renovated Slušovice company was manned largely by members of the fallen Nomenklatura and ex-agents of the STB, their secret police.[30]

The part of this traffic having to do with nuclear materials was not only full of hopeful liars but of secret agents bumping into one another from every direction. Consequently, there was much confusion about offers flooding the Western market by the autumn of

1993. Actually, German police had confiscated eighteen shipments of nuclear bomb materials from the ex–U.S.S.R. the previous year.[31] "We are getting propositions from Vienna on a daily basis—osmium, cesium-133, scandium. Vienna is the center for this sensitive business," said a German dealer in precious metals.

"Yesterday our undercover was offered forty kilos of plutonium and thirty kilos of enriched uranium," Judge Dolce said on my last visit to Como in the spring of 1993. Only six kilos of enriched uranium would have been enough for an atom bomb the size of the one that fell on Nagasaki. Nothing on that order had been found up to then; only eight kilos had been confiscated worldwide by the American, British, French, Italian, and German services combined.[32] Nevertheless, the material was unmistakably out there.

Kyrgyzstan, a Central Asian republic known mostly for its fruit exports, had actually announced its plans to sell weapons-grade uranium on the world market; it is among the largest producers in the former U.S.S.R.[33] Plutonium, which sells for a million dollars a kilo in the West—fifty times its price in the Urals—was showing up in several places around Europe.[34] The first sizable seizures suggested a lunatic nonchalance in the traffickers' ranks. In January 1992, Austrian police found 2.8 kilos of plutonium-239 hidden in a large metal screw, left in a safety deposit box in central Vienna. "It is true; we have found a sample of plutonium," said the state police official handling the case. The sample matched the much smaller one found in Como a year earlier; the trafficker in charge worked for Kuzin.[35] Then in October a German fire brigade in protective clothing opened a luggage locker in Frankfurt's main railway station and found a simple metal tube containing 20 grams of strontium-90. Another 20 grams of cesium-137 in a similar tube—this one wrapped in a plastic bag—turned up in the trunk of a BMW parked in front of an airport hotel.[36]

These two materials, by-products of nuclear power plants, are among the most volatile and lethal radioactive substances known to man. "The mere thought that cesium was stored largely unprotected in a car makes my hair stand on end," a German nuclear physicist said.

The tip had come from a Swiss doctor, who had treated a Polish traveler for severe radiation sickness. Two other Poles ended up in a special German hospital. All had driven over the border from Poland with the material in their car. One had carried two vials of the cesium in his breast pocket. Samples of cesium-137 and cesium-133, carried just as casually, have been seized several times since then—in Zurich, in Geneva, in the northern Italian city of Vicenza (where the bearer of the cesium was also carrying Himbank's certificates of deposit for $25 million).[37]

Only days after the seizure of cesium in Frankfurt, on October 16, 1992, police in Munich impounded 2.2 kilos of uranium in a parking lot—"highly enriched" this time, according to Munich's customs chief, and carelessly wrapped.[38] In March 1993 a team of *carabinieri* in Turin found 3.2 grams of plutonium-239 packed in yet another plain metal tube. It had been stored under the roof of an apartment house for ten months. The plutonium belonged to an ex-agent of the Bulgarian secret police who lived in the building; Italian detectives had been tracking him since the previous June. The Bulgarian agent had been spotted originally in the same northeastern Italian region favored by Colonel Kuzin, and he had the same sources. The traffic in his case was verified by hundreds of phone intercepts, faxes, letters from Italian companies and banks, and state documents from the ex–Soviet Republics and Bulgaria. The sample under his roof was part of a deal for 62.3 kilos of plutonium-239.[39] The full implications—for the world, not just for Italy—were put to the public by an Italian magistrate who could not be silenced or ignored.

"The collapse of the Warsaw Pact and consequent relaxation of controls over nuclear arsenals have opened dramatic scenarios," warned Judge Pierluigi Vigna of Florence, heading what was now a nationwide investigation into the international arms traffic. We know that Soviet radioactive material is reaching countries interested in making nuclear weapons. There is a very immediate and substantial danger that nuclear, chemical, and bacteriological arms are ending up in the hands of governments without scruples." And he added a concomitant warning. "In Eastern Europe, convulsed by the fall of the Soviet Empire, the Mafia and other organized crime groups are running an enormous clandestine arms traffic. These criminal organizations have formed organic ties and reached worldwide dimensions. They are increasingly militarized, sophisticated, and aggressive. Extremely potent weapons are at their disposal. There is a present and tangible danger that nuclear, chemical, and bacteriological arms may be coming into their possession," he said.[40]

PART V

The Problem of the Solution

CHAPTER TWELVE

Getting the Money

"What bothers us most is when you take our money away. We'd rather stay in jail and keep the money than be free without the money—that's the main thing," explained ranking defector Gaspare Mutolo to Italy's Parliamentary Anti-Mafia Commission.[1]

There in a few words is the problem and the solution, in reverse order. Money is the reason for the big crime syndicates' existence and, like Samson's hair, the source of their strength. Taking it away is the solution. Finding it is the problem. Many countries have by now passed seemingly stringent laws to trap criminal money as it flows through the laundry. With few exceptions, the United States and Australia most notably, the laws don't work. Even those that do are barely skimming the surface. Except for Italy—and this not until 1993— no country has managed so far to seize more than what these syndicates would consider petty cash.[2] The Pizza Connection investigation, which took six years, managed to trace only $60 million of the $1.6 billion known to have been laundered.[3]

The DEA, which leads the world in this field, doubts that it is getting more than 2 percent of the Colombians' cocaine money.[4] France has made only thirteen laundering cases since its strict law was passed in 1990. Altogether they amounted to about 100 million francs ($20 million), an "efficacy rate of 1 percent," said a French senate commission.[5]

A few stark facts suggest the difficulties in the way of doing better.

A trillion and a half dollars a year, a quarter of all the money circulating around the planet, is illicit "gray" money in need of laundering, whatever its provenance—graft, shady business, tax dodging, arms trading, drugs, and other criminal revenue.[6]

A trillion dollars *a day*, licit and illicit, moves in and out of the United States alone by electronic wire transfer. A hundred billion dollars a year changes hands in the American drug trade, and five hundred billion worldwide. Any amount of dollars—even a trillion, theoretically—can be wrapped in paper parcels and sent through the mail with an acceptably low risk of detection. This is widely done nowadays.[7] Any amount can be run through automatic money machines or currency exchange bureaus; a billion pounds sterling passed through just three of the latter in Amsterdam in 1992.[8]

Any amount can be sent from anywhere to anywhere else through an American Express Moneygram. There is no limit on the sum and no possibility of detection since no identification or bank account is required for the sender or receiver. All they need is their own code word. The Moneygram costs more than a postal money order: $150 for every $5,000, which amounts to 3 percent. American Express thought such a costly service would make no sense for money launderers, but 3 percent is ludicrous for Colombian cartels ready to pay 25 percent to launder their money.[9]

Any amount can be wire-transferred bank to bank around the world once it gets past a single bank, "layered" through as many as one or two hundred others until it vanishes for good. Getting past the first bank is the only hard part, and it is getting harder in a number of countries. Whenever a country stiffens up, however, launderers merely move on. The list of places for them to go keeps lengthening; the competition for their business is fierce.

Starting with the letter *A* is the Sicilian Mafia's state of Aruba, whose banking center has come to full flower since independence from the Dutch Antilles in 1986. Apart from impenetrable bank secrecy, Aruba has a model law for the establishment of shell companies, called Aruban Exempt Corporations (AECs). The AECs are not only exempt from taxes but can be formed with only $5,000 in capital and controlled by anonymous shareholders.[10]

Austria, next in the alphabet, has become Switzerland's successor as Western Europe's number one laundry state. Switzerland no longer offers perfect protection for suspect funds. On the contrary, it was the first state to sign a mutual assistance treaty with the United States in 1977, and it has had rather stiff controls since 1989 when it outlawed the laundering of money that stems from a crime.[11] Austria has done nothing of the sort. Bank secrecy is guaranteed by the Austrian constitution and zealously enforced. Consequently there are forty-nine million bank accounts in the country, seven for every man, woman, and child. Nine out of ten are secret numbered accounts. [12]

Austrian banks have no shame. In the autumn of 1992, when laundering had become an acute international concern, they were soliciting questionable Italian patronage openly. "Austria is the country with the best bank secrecy in the world protecting our clients," wrote the Bank für Tirol und Vorarlberg in Linz to potential Italian customers, an easy eighteen miles across an open border.[13]

Anyone in Western Europe has free entry through Germany to the Austrian enclave of Oberstdorf, in the Valley of Kleinwalsertal, accessible only by way of southern Bavaria. Cash can move there by car or truck from anywhere in Western Europe without passing a checkpoint. "You can come to the bank, show just the outside of your passport, and open an account," said the BKA's Jurgen Maurer.

Germany itself was a scarlet sinner until September 1992 when it finally made laundering a crime. Like the others in Western Europe, however, its new law is not only full of holes but in no way affects German bank subsidiaries abroad—in the fiscal paradise of Lichtenstein or Luxembourg, for example, both with wide-open borders. Twenty-three German banks have subsidiaries in Luxembourg (population 359,030), where there are 213 others of various nationalities. Thirty billion deutsche marks ($20 billion) were transferred to the German banks' Luxembourg branches in the last days before January 1, 1993, birthday of the EC's Single Market.[14] Thirty-four brand-new banks of varied nationality had opened for business in Luxembourg since the previous year. Many consist of one room, four telexes, a fax, and a couple of personal computers, all that is needed for certain discreet operations.

The affluent grand duchy of Luxembourg has been leaned on so hard and long that it promised to go straight in 1989. Its law against laundering was "in line with those existing elsewhere," asserted its Monetary Institute, and carried penalties of up to five years in jail. According to the French senate commission cited above, however, Luxembourg's system is still "meant to attract capital like an offshore bank" operating inland—worse, inside the EC. A charter member of the EC, it still "passionately defends its bank secrecy," "closes its eyes" to dubious practices, and "participates in an automatic laundering system of illicit international drug profits on a grand scale," the French commission maintained.[15]

Actually, Luxembourg *tightened* its bank secrecy when it made laundering a crime, imposing a *duty* of confidentiality on banks and their employees. Indeed, its law came close to farce in the case of Frank Jurado, the Cali cartel's Harvard professor caught there by the DEA on his way to Moscow. In January 1993, Jurado came before a Luxembourg appeals court on charges of laundering $32 million. The court upheld his conviction for laundering the money but refused to confiscate the money on the grounds that it did not belong to him. The $32 million had to be returned to the rightful owners, the judge said. The owners were the wife and mother-in-law of Jurado's employer, José Santacruz Londono, who heads the Cali cocaine cartel. The only money confiscated was Jurado's salary: $30,000.[16] (Embarrassment caused Luxembourg to tighten its laws again after this.)

Frank Jurado had been laundering freely in another fiscal paradise inside the EC, the principality of Monaco on the French Riviera. He had various accounts amounting to $55 million at the Industrial Bank of Monaco in Monte Carlo, under names like Bufa, Bula, and Buma. The Industrial Bank, owned by Her Most Serene

Highness Princess Isabelle de Bourbon-Parma, was closed down after several similar cases came to light.[17] Its depositors could find any number of safer havens elsewhere, however.

Much of the literature on the subject refers to some twenty-five "fiscally tolerant states" or regions, such as the Channel Islands, the Caymans, the Seychelles, Malta, Andorra, Uruguay, Hong Kong, and Vanuatu. Actually, the entire ex-Soviet bloc is near or at the top of a much lengthier list.[18] Japan is extremely tolerant fiscally, as are Ireland and Belgium. Furthermore, fiscally tolerant *banks* can be found everywhere. The United States may have the most because it is so big and rich, but the small province of Trapani in western Sicily, among Italy's poorest regions, has 142 lenient banks or bank branches. Trapani also has 102 finance companies (Italy has 28,000), and these are ideal for laundering. Much easier to set up than a chartered bank and more slippery to watch, a finance company will often accept dubious cash simply as security for a loan. That gets the cash into the banking system, the hard part. The loan, never repaid, becomes legitimate capital invested through a dummy corporation in a legal enterprise: a Yakuza golf course in America, a Triad residence complex outside Paris, a high-rise condominium for Don Michele Zaza on the Côte d'Azur.

This method is known as the loanback, and it is very nearly foolproof. French authorities believe it may be largely responsible for the fact that French banks, accepting the creditworthiness of such dummy corporations, are in hock for office-building loans they have issued to the amount of five hundred billion francs— $100 billion.[19]

Obviously the best system of all is to buy a bank outright, as American and Sicilian mafiosi did in Sverdlovsk, according to Russian intelligence. Buying one can be surprisingly easy and is not necessarily expensive. An American company in the business of selling offshore banks in 1991 offered "a fully chartered Private International Bank in the Caribbean . . . plus a Management Subsidiary Corporation in the Bahamas . . . plus connection with a professional Bahamas Management Service—all for $9,900."[20]

The *International Herald Tribune* carries regular ads like this one: "Merchant Bank for Sale. No assets or liabilities. No transfer or qualification requirements. Class A license. Bearer shares. U.S. $10,000." Side by side with such ads are others offering "Second Residence Incognito," "Second Travel Documents, Any Country," "Right of Abode" or "Citizenship" in "Various Countries," together with "ID and driving license."

The operational possibilities here may be gathered from an ad in Moscow's financial weekly, *Commersant*, offering dual citizenship to Russian nationals in the Central American mini-state of Belize for $320,000: no residence required or questions asked.[21] As a former colony in British Honduras, Belize has "privileged" (meaning free) entry to the British Commonwealth, the European Free Trade Area, and the European Community. Thus, a Russian who buys Belize citizenship can not only bank there but travel without visas to Denmark, Norway, Sweden, Finland, Germany, Ireland, Malta, Australia, Canada, Cyprus, Hong Kong, and Singapore.

There are underground laundries that don't even need a Belize or American Express Moneygrams or a fiscally tolerant bank. Enormous sums are transferred from one end of the map to the other through Asia's ancient *hawala* system, on the strength of a phone call, a designated playing card, a fax. A brief message from London produces cash or gold in Lahore or Bombay without going through the monetary system at all. Asian immigrants send remittances to their families this way; Asian drug traffickers launder through the same channels. Together they move between $10 billion and $20 billion a year, relying entirely on trust.[22]

In the days when organizations like the Sicilian Mafia were just beginning to make big money, they could leave it in the hands of a single crooked banker. During the 1970s, Sicily's old-guard bosses chose Don Michele Sindona, the most renowned international banker-crook of our time. After killing off the old guard at the beginning of the 1980s, Totò Riina and his close associates used Sindona's ex-partner and fellow crook Roberto Calvi. Both men ruined thousands of depositors and investors before they went under. The crash of Sindona's Franklin National Bank in New York was the biggest on record in America, entailing a loss of $40 million; the crash of Calvi's Banco Ambrosiano in Milan was the biggest in Western history, entailing a loss of nearly $2 billion. Each of them did as much as any single corrupt banker could do for the Mafia, the Vatican, the Masonic lodge P2, and Italy's political elite. But both tried to take the Mafia's money away and came to a bad end.

By the late 1970s, Sicilian traffickers were clearing around $1 billion yearly in America, largely consigned to Sindona for laundering and investment. Unfortunately, he lost it on his way to jail in 1979, the year he went bankrupt. It is likely, though not certain, that the Sicilians got their money back that summer. While free on bail awaiting trial in New York, Sindona was rigged out in a wig, a false beard, dark glasses, and yellow chicken skin pasted to his cheeks, and smuggled to Palermo. The organizer was Sindona's close friend and financial client John Gambino of Brooklyn and Cherry Hill, the Sicilian Mafia's liaison with its cousins in America. A secret Masonic lodge connected to Licio Gelli's P2 took care of logistics.[23]

Sindona was not kidnapped by communist terrorists, as the press was told then, nor was he in Sicily to organize a separatist uprising, as he claimed later; he was the Mafia's prisoner. "He went broke in the United States and cheated a lot of people, so it was necessary to fake a kidnapping," explained the Mafia's reigning prince at the time to a confidante.[24]

After a month under close guard in Palermo, Sindona arranged to give his kidnappers "compromising documents involving authoritative figures in the Italian political and financial world," said Judge Falcone later.[25] In fact, he offered them the wherewithal to shake down five hundred of Italy's leading businessmen and politicians, his former clients. None has come forward to say if the shakedown happened or not.

The billion-dollar blackmail scam, as this came to be known, was Sindona's last service to the Mafia. Shipped back to New York, he was sentenced to twenty-five years, and a life sentence on top of that in Italy, where he died of strychnine poisoning the day after his trial. Whether he took or was given the strychnine, he had been squeezed dry and tossed away.[26]

Roberto Calvi, working for the Mafia's winning Families, might have hoped for a kinder fate, yet he ended up hanging from a girder under London's Blackfriars' Bridge.[27] Calvi's life was so full of mystery toward the end that any of a dozen theories might have accounted for his death in 1982. The least likely was suicide, the British coroner's verdict. But as Britain's foreign secretary Douglas Hurd admitted when the case was reopened in 1991, Scotland Yard was "moving prudently in an investigation considered very dangerous for the judges, the police, their families, everybody helping in some way to collect evidence of the murderer's guilt."[28] The mystery had been kicked back and forth between London and Rome for ten years. The evidence of guilt came in 1992 from the most credible of all Mafia defectors, Francesco Mannino Mannoia. Calvi was strangled by the Mafia's heroin traffic manager in London, Francesco Di Carlo, Mannino Mannoia said. The orders had come from the Mafia's treasurer and "ambassador to Rome," Pippo Calò.[29]

Like Sindona, Calvi had been embezzling on a monumental scale for years with his fellow Mason in the P2, Licio Gelli. By 1981 he was navigating in such troubled waters for theft and misuse of his bank's funds that he asked for a contact with the Mafia to make a pot of money and get out of his predicament.[30] Gelli was handling Mafia money already for the inner Corleonese circle: Totò Riina, Ciccio Madonia, and Pippo Calò. The money was passed on to Calvi, who lost it in the quicksands of his doomed financial ventures. Once again the Mafia got its money back, partly at least. "Before having Calvi knocked off, Calò and Gelli managed to recover tens of billions of lire," testified the *pentito* Mannino Mannoia. "What matters more, Calò got a weight off his chest—the thought that Calvi had proved to be untrustworthy."

The Mafia's representative in London took care of this personally, according to Mannino Mannoia. "It takes at least three men to strangle a man," he said. "But I never doubted that Francesco Di Carlo had his own hands around Calvi's throat. It is not admissible in Cosa Nostra for a Man of Honor to delegate such an order."[31]

*   *   *

Banco Ambrosiano, Italy's largest private bank, had been looted to the last cent when a Mafia envoy escorted Calvi on his frantic flight to London and imminent death. *"Never forget that an entire organization of friends is working for you, an organization ten times bigger than the Christian Democratic Party,"* the envoy had assured him.[32]

Whatever the role of other sinister forces, the Mafia clearly had a hold all its own on Calvi. Almost certainly its ruling bosses owned part if not all of the half a billion dollars that could not be accounted for after he was gone (not counting the billion and a half he is known to have stolen).[33] Certainly they had gained a murderous grip not just on the banker but on his bank. Nobody had realized how deeply Banco Ambrosiano was immersed in the financial affairs of the Mafia and the whole international underworld.

Combing through Calvi's tangled accounts, for example, investigators came upon one of his biggest international money laundries, operating through a nest of Miami banks. Hundreds of millions of narcodollars had moved out of there, passing through a dizzying succession of foreign banks before ending up at Banco Ambrosiano Overseas in the Bahamian capital of Nassau. Returning from Nassau to the United States in the form of Panamanian investments, the laundered dollars were redistributed from there to international accounts in Nigeria, Venezuela, Luxembourg, Argentina, Egypt, Peru, Belgium, France, Brazil, Uruguay, England, Greece, Switzerland, and Spain (to name some).

In an endless wilderness of ghost companies, shell banks, and anonymous trusts were more than twenty major banks involved in secret dealings with Banco Ambrosiano. They ranged from Banco del Centro in Panama to Banco de la Nacion in Lima, Chase Manhattan in Nassau, Central Bank of Venezuela, Bank of China, the U.S.S.R.'s Bank of Foreign Trade in Moscow, and, inevitably, the Bank of Credit and Commerce International (BCCI).[34]

Although the era of the single crooked banker was over long before these facts emerged, the system perfected by Sindona and Calvi still works. The many legal impediments put in place since their day are the merest beginning of an attempt to crack it. Finding and *taking away* criminal money means making the act of laundering it a crime; catching the cash at its point of entry into the banking system; tracking it through the system if it gets in and tracking it on to its reinvestment in some legitimate enterprise; identifying the mover; identifying the owner behind the mover; identifying the source of the cash; providing the legal instruments to seize the money and arrest the owner as well as the mover; assuring investigations, seizures, and arrests across national frontiers; and doing all this without violating the legitimate individual's right to privacy. Every one of these requirements is immensely difficult. Reconciling the last with the rest may never be possible.

On paper, much of the world has been committed to fight money laundering since 1988. The U.N. Vienna Convention, signed by sixty-seven nations that December, requires ratifying nations to make money laundering a crime; identify bank clients; trace, freeze, and seize the proceeds of drug trafficking; eliminate bank secrecy for such offenses; extradite offenders; and provide mutual assistance for investigations.

The Basel Declaration of Principles that same month committed the central banks of twelve leading nations to identify bank customers and the source of their funds, turn down dubious transactions, and collaborate with criminal investigations "within the maximum limits permitted by domestic legislation."

The G-7 and eight other key nations set up a Financial Action Task Force, GAFI, in 1989 with forty proposals to combat laundering.

The EC directive of February 1990 compelled the twelve member states to outlaw the laundering of proceeds from *any* serious crime, require identification of bank clients, "carefully examine unusual transactions," and "refrain from abetting" them. The EC's Council of Europe Convention provided for "search, seizure and confiscation of the proceeds from crime."[35]

These covenants are revolutionary compared to the inertia prevailing before. But while they have undoubtedly made laundering harder in several major countries, they are only expressions of intent until the signatory states turn them into enforceable law.

The difference between the two may be judged from the fact that the Soviet Union was among the first countries to ratify the U.N. Vienna Convention, in December 1990. Even unrepentant Austria has ratified the Council of Europe convention.

The United States is far out front among countries trying to do better. Having started earlier, ventured further, and spent a great deal more than any other, it is actually getting somewhere. Only Australia, adopting the same bold measures, can say as much. America's first move, the Bank Secrecy Act of 1970, required banks to report cash deposits above $10,000—this on pain of confiscation and prison for failure to comply. Once the law got past eight years of challenge in the courts, the paperwork grew awesome. By 1989 it was up to seven million currency transaction reports (CTRs) a year, reporting on a quarter of a trillion dollars.[36] By then a monumental Federal data bank and an artificial intelligence system called FINCEN (Financial Crimes Enforcement Network) made it possible to track unusual currency patterns even in this colossal mountain of paper.

Although the system costs a fortune, it has produced the biggest hits on record. Operation Polar Cap, the earliest, shut down a Medellín cartel laundry operating in six cities, washing over a billion dollars in cash. Seven hundred other successful court cases were made by 1989, rising to the thousands since.[37]

Nevertheless, the Bank Secrecy Act has crippling limitations. It does not catch deposits of $9,999, for one thing. "Smurfing," or spreading any number of such deposits around, is standard practice. The B.C.C.I. is famous for doing this to recycle General Noriega's money in Panama, and the proceeds of Adnan Khashoggi's arms sales to Iran. The Act doesn't cover the trillion dollars a day in international wire transfers, either, or transactions with foreign banks or branches of U.S. banks abroad. This huge loophole cannot be closed without international agreements, still decidedly rare. A number of governments are willing to sit down and talk now, not just because America is leaning hard as always but because they are genuinely alarmed by organized crime's advancing armies. Nevertheless, there are still profound differences between the policies of the United States and the rest of the world.

The United States goes after every kind of criminal money, including undeclared taxes and flight capital, and this makes other countries extremely nervous. Several have "blocking statutes" to forbid cooperation with American investigators who might like to hunt on their territory; France and Holland are among these. Even U.S. Senator John F. Kerry, a bulldog on such matters, understands the nearly universal reluctance abroad to bear down on truant taxpayers or any citizen's private stash. "Countries like Italy have an enormous tradition of capacity for avoidance of taxation and hiding assets and so forth, and they are not alone. All kinds of countries have that," he conceded at a Senate hearing on foreign cooperation, or the lack of it. He admitted as well that "there is an ingrained feeling in the minds, the psyches of many people, many countries, about the government reaching into bank accounts."

While the feeling is undoubtedly shared by many Americans (although the senator didn't say so), they have learned to put up with some loss of financial privacy in a necessary cause. They seem to be the only ones, or nearly. For fear of reaching too far into bank accounts or into "hidden assets and so forth," most national laws on laundering are doomed to failure in advance. Criminal money goes where undeclared capital goes; not much can be expected of laws designed to search for the one while protecting the other. Nearly all the legislation enacted in recent years is crafted with this distinction in mind.[38] Laundering is outlawed only for drugs and extremely violent crimes—for drugs alone in Britain and France. So many strings are attached as to render even such a modest law essentially useless.

Where American investigators can start with the launderer and track back to the drugs, the common pattern elsewhere is the other way around. The launderer cannot be prosecuted in most countries—or even investigated in some—without proof that he *knows* he is laundering drug money as well as proof that the money does come from drugs. It is nearly impossible to produce proof that will stand up in court on either count, let alone both. In the improbable event of a big launderer coming forward of his own will to help out the police, he might well not know where a particular sum of money came from. Short of happening on the launderer, the trafficker, and the drugs all at once, the police would not be likely to know either. While drug traffickers and their drugs may be seized, therefore, their launderers almost without exception are not.

France, with a highly professional financial force called TRAC-FIN, had simply *detected* thirteen laundering cases from July 1990 to January 1993. French bankers, required to report "suspicious transactions" only if they are drug related, are understandably in a quandary.

Britain has been trying since 1986 to trace up to $2.5 billion a year laundered from the proceeds of its own drug traffic (not counting the proceeds flowing into the city from elsewhere). On average, however, it manages to confiscate only about nine million pounds a year (0.5 percent).[39] The better part of its bank reports on suspicious transactions, now running to four thousand a year, are discarded because the suspect money involves tax fraud or hidden assets, not drugs.[40] For all the reporting, Britain had only twenty-seven money-laundering convictions in court from 1986 to the start of 1993.[41]

Italy, sinking under suspicious transactions, had only 122 such bank reports of any kind from 1991 to 1993.[42] It has made up for this in part with a murderous confiscation law, enabling Italian courts to seize $3 billion worth of assets directly from top Sicilian bosses in the space of a single year.[43] This is something the bosses really mind.

Nevertheless, "confiscation" is still one of those buzz words that make governments nervous. Though several are beginning to show an interest in that procedure, few have actually gone much further than suspicious transaction reports. A primary component of the international community's solemn covenants, this form of policing is no more disappointing than several others.

In many countries, banks are asked only to "know their customers," not who is behind them. A bank's customer is frequently a lawyer or company officer in a country authorizing such front men to act for an unnamed party. Germany's law exempts lawyers, notaries, tax advisers, and certified public accountants from the obligation to identify their clients.[44] Swiss lawyers are notoriously exempt as well. Banks are also asked to keep records of cash deposits over a fixed amount, but the records generally stay in the bank since most countries have no national centralized computers to screen them. Although the records can be consulted, they cannot produce the unusual currency pattern detectible only through a centralized data bank—the flash signal that would tell an inspector where to look.

Some national laws are stricter than others, but launderers are free to pick and choose. In the European Community, for instance, they can operate without hindrance in any of the twelve member states, depending on which has the most lenient laws (or banks or bankers).

"The Dutch have no bank secrets; Belgium does," says Roelof Gerrand, police chief of Tilburg on the southern Dutch border. "Just seven miles across our border is a Belgian town composed of seven banks, two bars, and three houses. They guarantee bank secrecy there."[45]

Should even Belgium fail to please—or Luxembourg or Ireland or free-entry mini-states such as Aruba or Belize or Saint Martin—launderers in the EC can simply pack their cash into cargo containers and ship it anywhere outside EC territory. Agents guarding the European Community's external border only check goods coming into the single market, not goods going out. Just beyond the EC's external border is not only Vienna, but Budapest, Warsaw, Prague. "Anybody can open a hard currency account in a Czech bank. You can bring in cash and deposit it in as many accounts as you like. You can buy kroner and get 14 percent interest, untaxed. You can put it in an investment fund and watch it grow. *Nobody* will inform on any foreigner doing this," said a senior official monitoring investments in the Czech republic.[46]

The last word in comfort for the launderer is the portable washing-machine devised by Russian and American mafiosi. Instead of going to the trouble of buying rubles, the owner of dirty money can simply buy certificates of deposit from a phony bank, delivered to his door. This leaves no paper trail at all.

Whatever else the world may be doing to crack down on the big crime syndicates, therefore, it is failing abysmally to take away their money. It is dangerously deceptive, then, to say that the international community has made money laundering a crime at last.

Although Senator Kerry's hammerhead assault has destroyed the composure of many diplomats, American and foreign, he is an expert at calling a spade a spade. In a thrusting exchange with the U.S. Treasury's assistant secretary for enforcement, Salvatore Martoche, he put this question:

> As an ex-prosecutor, I sit here and I say to myself, "Well, you know it is terrific to call something a crime, but when a country comes along and says, well, we are going to call it a crime, I find it hard to feel that that is sufficient. . . .
>
> What good does it do to make money laundering a crime if there is no enforcement capacity to track who is laundering the money and where it is coming from? My question is really, Are we not at a point where we absolutely know we have got to take considerably greater steps more rapidly in order to buttress the naming of it as a crime?

To which Mr. Martoche replied: "I think we have to face up to some realities here. . . . In international relations the sovereignty of other countries is one of those issues that leads them to resist some ideas simply because they have been proffered by the United States."

Still, he added, "If you are asking me should we continue to do more, you bet."[47]

CHAPTER THIRTEEN

Trust Thy Neighbor (If You Can)

America is decades ahead of any country in fighting organized crime, and it is failing. Western Europe, although beginning to catch up, remains a great place to be a crook. Most other countries, from Russia and Pakistan to South Korea and Japan, are as badly off or worse.

The enormity of the problem is just beginning to register, and with it a sense of doom. Modern criminal power has surpassed the ability of governments to contain it. International organized crime is too big; nobody knows how to deal with it. Perhaps it cannot be dealt with as long as the world is divided into nearly two hundred sovereign states. While the big crime syndicates simply go where the money is, sovereign states cannot do anything simply. If they go down to dismal defeat in the war against crime, it will be largely because they are hampered by all the baggage of statehood—patriotism, politics, accountable governments, human rights, legal strictures, international conventions, bureaucracy, diplomacy— whereas the big criminal syndicates have no national allegiances, no laws but their own, no frontiers.

Obviously the mafias of the world cannot be fought on these terms. The question is how far sovereign states can go toward a planetwide defense against this planetwide assault. Presumably they are moving in that direction. A third of a billion people in Western Europe became one community in 1993. A similar number are entering into a free trade zone embracing the United States, Canada, and Mexico, looking to include the whole of the Western Hemisphere eventually. The six ASEAN nations of Southeast Asia are creating a similar area designed eventually to take in fourteen countries along the entire Pacific rim.[1]

These are the great trading blocs of the future, forming up because single countries cannot compete in the global marketplace anymore. But the member countries are still sovereign states, moving slowly and laboriously toward a distant goal. The most advanced model so far, the European Community, has barely gotten to the point of opening enough space for economies of scale— rationalized production, more consumers, easier communications, faster and cheaper transport. The EC's open market should save a quarter of a trillion dollars a year just by cutting the time a truck needs to cross its territory and the expense of checking cars, passengers, and baggage at what used to be twelve inner borders.

While these are necessary and commendable achievements, however, the EC states have taken a third of a century to get this far, and what they have is no borderless union. Indeed, it is an epic joke where fighting crime is concerned. The baggage of statehood is perfectly illustrated by the fact that the EC's inner borders have gone down for crooks but not for cops. The distinction seems inevitable, if perverse. Crooks are entitled to move around freely in an open market like everyone else, a price to be paid for the market's benefits. Cops are servants of the state—upholders of its fundamental law.

Although united in their pursuit of the market's benefits, the twelve EC states are separate to the point of mutual aversion, even open hostility, where their fundamental laws are concerned. The results are grotesque. The drug traffic within the EC runs to $80 billion a year now. The profits, equivalent to a quarter of the French national budget, represent "a grave danger to democracy," says a special commission of the French Senate. Half the arrests on EC territory are drug related. Its addict population is up to a million;

little Luxembourg has the highest number of overdose deaths per capita on the Continent.[2] Yet no two EC countries have matching laws on the sale, possession, or use of drugs, or on distinctions between soft and hard varieties, or surveillance of suspected traffickers, exchange of police information, controlled deliveries, permissible courtroom evidence, and prison terms. They cannot even agree on harmonizing police radio frequencies, still less on a common policy of extradition among themselves.

In an open space covering half the Continent, therefore, drug traffickers play a running game of tag, jumping through the cracks in the law. Depending on their needs, they choose whichever of the twelve countries is most convenient for banking, laundering, shipping, storing, marketing, networking, hiding out, and, if absolutely unavoidable, going to jail.

Holland, among the most civilized of sovereign states, is their favorite for prisons. Holland sends nobody to jail for more than six years. Those who do go in are lodged one to a cell, and since there are only five thousand cells nationwide, they are assured of early release to make room for others on the waiting list. Those who escape are not pursued, on the grounds that "nothing is more natural for a human being than wanting to regain his liberty."[3] Not many traffickers are arrested anyway, none at all for soft drugs. While marijuana is outlawed in most EC states and much of the world, it is a commercial crop in Holland, worth $100 million a year and expanding. "When the drug networks realize the possibilities of Dutch marijuana, they'll come running," said a senior officer in Holland's Anti-Crime Information Service. They were doing so even as he spoke in 1992.[4]

Marijuana is bought and sold legally in some three hundred licensed Dutch coffee shops known as hash cafes, frequented by customers from all over the world known as drug tourists. Up to a thousand drug tourists a day visit the town with a now famous name, Maastricht, near Holland's borders with Germany, Belgium, and Luxembourg.[5] They come for cocaine and heroin as well as hash, to use on the spot or peddle at home. These hard drugs are illegal in Holland but can easily fall off the back of a truck passing through any part of the country. Drugs in transit "are not a priority for the Dutch police," observed the French senate commission. "Holland is essentially indifferent to the external drug traffic since this does not affect its own citizens. That is undoubtedly why it has become a major staging area for the international drug trade."[6] The staging area serves to supply Canada and the United States going west and anywhere in Europe going east. Such is Holland's indifference to this traffic that only five Dutch customs agents are allocated to go systematically through the manifests of thirty-two thousand ships docking in Rotterdam each year. Of six thousand containers offloaded every day, they were managing in 1992 to check an average of six.[7]

Hard drugs passing through may head for any part of Western Europe without running into a roadblock. Mostly they head for Germany, Italy, and France, all with large addict populations and tough drug laws (France has the toughest on the Continent). Several countries try to limit the damage by keeping their own narcotics agents in Rotterdam—Britain, Germany, Sweden, Canada, Israel, Turkey, Spain, and the United States.[8] Not only are they subject to Dutch law, however, but they are also caught in a web of conflicting laws wherever they turn. The most maddening tangle has to do with the exchange of police information, which is central to everything. If interlocking crime cartels are ever to be driven back, the war starts here. And it is here that the EC states, like all sovereign states, are shooting themselves in the foot.

Most police agencies dislike sharing information on principle, in or out of their own countries. Few have a compelling interest in crimes beyond their jurisdiction. Even within their jurisdiction, what generally matters most is not so much the nature of the crime as the score: numbers of arrests, convictions, citations, commendations, promotions. Sharing information across borders is often restricted by national policy. Some EC states require disclosure in an ongoing investigation; others will not pass on information that might be disclosed to a suspect. Some permit relatively free exchange through authorized channels; others forbid it.

Belgium, for one, allows its police officers to talk only to other police officers, not to customs agents. This alone has been enough to hold up completion of a functioning European Drug Intelligence

Unit meant solely to be a "relay station" for exchanging information within the EC. The very idea shocked EC ministers when it was first proposed. "The Germans are all for it. The Belgians say, 'Let's research it to see if we really need it.' The Greeks say, 'We don't need it.' The Portuguese say, 'We can't afford it.' The Dutch blow hot and cold because of their 'normalization of the drug problem,' " observed the head of Scotland Yard's Drugs Intelligence Unit in 1992.[9] Resistance to this or any proposal for sharing information here or anywhere is often due to small-minded pigheadedness, but not always. One country's deeply felt moral and social values are not necessarily another's. Police agencies are not uniformly high-minded, meticulous, or politically correct. Western and Eastern police cannot easily overcome the distrust accruing from having shared disinformation for half a century.

The most paralyzing issue, and the most sensitive, has to do with protecting personal privacy. Nobody likes Big Brother. Anybody might reasonably want to know who is watching over his or her personal life, how much of it is recorded somewhere, what use can be made of the information, and who can get at it. Regulating such matters in a computerized age is increasingly urgent and unspeakably difficult. Nearly everybody winds up in some kind of data bank today, justly or otherwise. The right to know about a personal dossier cannot be denied. Strictly speaking, the right applies to all, from upright citizens to criminals, however villainous, and other assorted enemies of society. Some governments make no exceptions; some make a few; some make more.

Formally, the EC defends personal privacy without reservations. Its entire program for pooling information to fight organized crime is contingent on accepting this principle. The EC Commission's 1990 directive provides that "every person must be able to know the existence of a computerized file on personal data, its principal purpose, the identity of whoever is responsible for the file, and his habitual address."[10] A demand to see one's own file can be made "at the moment the information is gathered" and must be met promptly; failure to comply carries criminal and civil penalties. No computerized file can be started without the "explicit consent" of the person involved, asked for and given in advance. Consent can be withdrawn at any time. Only secret service files are exempt from this rule.

Past criminal records cannot go into the file. Exceptions may be made for an intergovernmental data bank, but only regarding crimes subject to extradition. Most arrests made in the EC states are national and consequently are not subject to extradition. (Even the extraditable kind are extremely difficult to nail down. Holland will not extradite a Dutch national for a crime committed outside Dutch frontiers. Germany will not extradite a fugitive convicted of Mafia association in Italy. Britain is exceedingly rigid about extraditing anybody. "You can't imagine how hard it is to get a person extradited from the United Kingdom to Germany," said a senior BKA officer.)

The only grounds on which personal files may be withheld from an individual are national security and "preeminent public interest," and this under strict judicial control. Directives like these are referred to in Eurospeak as "ministerially driven," meaning that they are thought up by politicians. Translated into plainspeak, this means that no policeman with a grain of caution will put meaningful information into a data bank.

An Italian cop would crack up at the thought of asking the consent of a Mafia suspect before opening a file, providing his own name and address as he does so. A German cop, on a tight rein already, would be driven to hide behind his desk. "A mental barrier has developed in the minds of our policemen who feel caught redhanded or think they've violated a law every time they exchange information with other authorities," says BKA director Hans-Ludwig Zachert.

Several EC states, notably Germany and France, have data protection laws as strict as the EC directive or stricter. Others tend toward America's early Freedom of Information Act, with a fairly wide margin of governmental discretion. Italy has no data protection law of any sort. The standoff is complete, therefore. Without agreement on this issue among the twelve states, possibly years away, the European Community is incapable of a collective effort to pool police intelligence within its own confines.

The height of its aspirations is Europol, described as the world's first international police force. So far, however, Europol consists of twenty-two policemen encamped on a temporary construction site near Strasbourg whose mission has yet to be precisely defined. When and if the twelve EC states can agree on what goes into Europol's future data bank, thus permitting it to come into existence, Europol will still have no power to investigate, much less make arrests, inflict penalties, or operate in any way across borders. There is no such machinery for law enforcement in the European Community. The Treaty of Rome, on which the EC was founded over three decades ago, gives it no jurisdiction over penal matters of any sort. Accordingly, Europol's sole function will be to coordinate the exchange of police data, essentially as a relay station from one national data bank to another.

Some EC states have excellent data banks: Germany's, Britain's, and Italy's are outstanding. Others have none: Holland considers the very existence of one to be an intrusion on privacy. France has one but severely restricts the input; unless convicted in court, a suspected criminal cannot be listed, for instance. At best, then, the information to relay will be spotty and inadequate. "It will probably be good for catching a husband who isn't paying alimony, maybe finding a stolen car or lost child. The vital stuff will not go in," said a ranking BKA officer.

Agreed upon at the Maastricht summit in December 1991, Europol was still the subject of truculent and inconclusive debate in the autumn of 1993. Ministers had spent hours at the last summit of 1992, "dancing round the edge of hair-splitting semantics," said British Home Secretary Kenneth Clarke.[11] Much time was lost debating the merits of Siemens (German) versus Bull (French) to furnish Europol's computerized data system. EC ministers at the December 1992 summit could still not agree on where the headquarters should be (they chose Holland a year later) or which of the nine languages spoken in the EC should prevail in its communications or which country's representative should head it.

In any case, the persistence of twelve disparate juridical systems promised a contentious future. "Europol could not work because there does not yet exist a corpus of European criminal law permitting [it] to act across national frontiers," said a special commission of the European parliament.[12]

On the face of it, the United States resolved such internal problems two centuries ago when its independent states agreed on a Federal constitution. States' rights are still strong in America. A New York cop wouldn't dare chase a criminal across the Hudson River into New Jersey; many wouldn't believe how hard it is to get a wanted person extradited from Texas to Alabama. But America has Federal agencies empowered to cross state lines, and there lies its enormous advantage over the nascent union of Western Europe. Authorized to act nationwide, the FBI has been running a Uniform Crime Reporting System since the 1930s and a giant data base on organized crime since the early 1980s. It includes names, numbers, profiles, electronic surveillance. Over a hundred intelligence research specialists review and analyze the material, all selected by competitive testing, proven ability and sensitive background checks. Controls over the material and access to it are nearly foolproof.

Several other U.S. agencies have formidable data banks and operative powers across state lines: the DEA, Customs, Immigration, the Treasury, and Internal Revenue. Singly and jointly they have mustered massive forces to combat the mafias invading America. But for all that, they cannot contain the criminal power taking hold across the country.

Forever the prime target, America was the first to realize the futility of trying to cope on its own. It has been urging other nations for years to work together on drugs, money laundering, counterfeiting, fraud—to perceive modern organized crime as the planetary phenomenon it is.

"These guys have been having their own way with us for twenty years, and that's got to change," said Greg Passic. Speaking of the drug trade in particular, he said,

> Sure our own cocaine situation is getting better in the
> United States; cocaine use is way down among our

youth, and our seizures are way up. But seizures don't hurt the cartels—they have so much.

And Europe is far worse off. The drug cartels are expanding their markets and influence alarmingly over there. They're gaining strength every day. There's a tremendous movement into the East bloc also. The Europeans were seizing a few hundred kilos of coke at a time just a couple of years ago. Now Holland is seizing two and a half tons at a time, London a ton, Portugal multiple tons.

All the signs are there: Anyone who has trouble reading them should think again. We'll never have enough resources to intercept the stuff coming in—not here, not in Europe. We need to hit the big cartels at the top, take out the kingpins, take away their money, disrupt the organization, dismantle the leadership. For that we need partnership, coordination, exchange of information. The community of nations has to begin to give international police the tools and instruments to make the job doable. But Europe lacks a sense of urgency. Its *police* feel this strongly, but we doubt Europe's political will.[13]

The single exception until recently was Italy, working closely and productively with U.S. law enforcement agencies since the early 1980s. Several others are starting now to talk with their fellow sufferers and the sources of their torment. The DEA has training courses for narcotics agents in the ex-Soviet republics: the BKA, the FBI, and the Italian DIA (anti-Mafia superpolice) are starting to coordinate information with their counterpart in Moscow.

Nobody in law enforcement imagines that any country or continent or hemisphere can defend itself on its own anymore. Condemned to work together, however, sovereign states still stand on their prerogatives.

Their sole international interlocutor continues to be Interpol, which goes back to World War I. A private organization with no politics and no powers of its own, Interpol is a neutered body passing no information from one country to another without express permission and orders to that effect. For nearly a century it has served simply as a conduit for requests transmitted among member states, mostly to execute international arrest warrants for trans-border fugitives. Renovated and reinforced by sophisticated technology, however, Interpol has the capacity to do much more now. Apart from the most advanced and comprehensive international data bank in the world, it has 158 member states—almost the entire roster of the United Nations. All the countries infested by the big crime syndicates belong to it, including post-communist Russia, the rest of the ex–Soviet Union, and its former satellites in Eastern Europe. Here is an organization already in place, expandable, open to improvement, where professionals in law enforcement from every continent might see the interlocking criminal circuit in its entirety and explore every avenue pointing toward worldwide defense.

But Interpol is an independent entity, not subject to political direction—"not ministerially driven," observed its secretary-general, Raymond Kendall. Few member states are more than lukewarm to the idea of broadening its functions. Rather than build on it, the EC's twelve have chosen to build an entity of their own, costing more, taking longer, and reaching no further than their common outer frontier. The notion of a Europol operating across more than the western half of a single continent is not even spoken of—this as the eastern half is taken over by the biggest players in the international underworld.

Shouldn't it be the other way around? If ageless barriers can go down for trade, it should be possible to lower them for mutual protection. The great trading blocs in formation offer a chance the planet has never known.

A great many countries have pooled resources already to face a lesser enemy. An impressive network of paragovernmental and intergovernmental bodies, official and otherwise, has come into being to fight terrorism—rising above national politics and frontiers, pooling resources, and sharing deeply sensitive intelligence information. Fear of terrorism can do that. We have only to realize that the Mafia and its confederates are the ultimate terrorists of our time.

NOTES

Prologue

1. My visit to the FBI, Washington, D.C., September 1993.
2. See Chapter 1.
3. Associated Press dispatch in the *Washington Times*, April 29, 1993.
4. My visit to the FBI, Washington, D.C., September 1993.
5. Associated Press dispatch in the *Washington Times*, April 29, 1993.
6. Violante's statement on the Italian RAI news channel, GR 2, October 10, 1993.

Chapter 1: Happy Families on Treasure Island

1. Full-page story by Maria Antonietta Calabrò in *Corriere della Sera*, Mar. 4, 1993. Reportage by Emilio Piervincenzi in "Venerdì" of *La Repubblica*, Apr. 2, 1993. Associated Press dispatch from Oranjestad, Aruba, "Under the Sun-and-Fun: Mafia, Drugs and Money Laundering," 179229, May 1993.
2. The U.S. threat to kidnap the Cuntreras was essentially confirmed by Undersecretary of State Melvyn Levitsky, who said that "the United States had done its part to assure the delivery of the Cuntreras to Italian justice." ADN Kronos Agency, Sept. 15, 1992.

   The Supreme Court ruling was in the case of the *United States v. Alvarez-Machain*, decided June 15, 1992. The case involved the DEA's forcible kidnapping of a Mexican citizen, Alvarez-Machain, to be brought to Texas and arrested for the kidnapping and murder of a DEA agent and his pilot in Mexico. The ruling said that "a court may properly exercise jurisdiction even though the defendant's presence is procured by means of a forcible abduction." The U.S. extradition treaty with Mexico did not specifically prohibit abduction, the Court said. Its ruling was based on a Supreme Court decision in 1906, in *Ker v. Illinois.*

Italian arrest warrants were first issued for Pasquale and Paolo Cuntrera in 1984, following a lengthy investigation of the Sicilian Mafia's activities abroad by the Criminalpol in Milan and Rome. Formal requests for their extradition from Venezuela followed and were ignored.

3. Judge Falcone's statement to a seminar in Wiesbaden, Germany, sponsored by the Bundeskriminalamt in November 1990. Cited in *MicroMega,* June 25, 1992. See also Judge Falcone's speech in Rome a few days before his death, ADN Kronos, May 24, 1992.

4. Estimate given in the Stewart-Clark report to the Investigating Committee of the European Parliament, 1986, cited in *La Mafia dell' Eroina,* Luciano Violante.

5. In his lecture to the Bundeskriminalamt, Falcone offered a broader definition of the word *mafia* to include all these big crime syndicates. He spoke of the "operational welding" taking place among them and the "nonaggression pact" already stipulated by the fall of 1990. In a speech a few days before his death in 1992, Falcone underlined the danger of these syndicates joining forces, pointing specifically to the Sicilian-Colombian partnership formed in 1987. See also Note 18 for Chapter 2.

6. Estimate given in the Stewart-Clark report.

7. Rogatory testimony of Joseph Cuffaro before Judge Falcone in the U.S. Southern District, Jan. 30, 1990.

8. These were John and Joe Gambino, Rosario Naimo, Paolo Loduca, Lorenzo Mannino, and Domenico Mannino.

9. From *Octopus,* by Claire Sterling.

10. From *Octopus,* by Claire Sterling.

11. The demand for an exclusive franchise and the threat were confirmed to me by Judge Giusto Sciacchitano of Palermo.

12. The Pizza Connection Case, the first to expose the Sicilian Mafia's twenty-year-old heroin network in the United States, came before a Federal court in New York in 1986 after six years of investigation. Its thirty-odd defendants, all Sicilian, represented only one of several concentric heroin rings answering to the Mafia in Sicily, many of which are still in place. The name "Pizza Connection" derived from the fact that all the defendants operated in or through pizzerias in the New York area.

13. See Chapter 7 of *Octopus* by Claire Sterling.

14. Interview with Louis Freeh in New York. See *Octopus* by Claire Sterling.

15. DEA estimate beginning 1985. Interpol figures in report to French senate by Gérard Larcher on behalf of a special commission studying the lowering of EC frontiers, Jan. 15, 1992. See also *London Independent,* Mar. 31, 1992.

16. Interview with Greg Passic, Washington, D.C., Sept. 1993.
17. Summary of the Green Ice Operation in DEA press release Sept. 28, 1992.

    Interviews with Greg Passic, head of the DEA's money laundering division, December 1992 and September 1993.

    See also *La Repubblica* and *Corriere della Sera*, Sept. 29, 1992, and the weekly *Panorama*, Oct. 11, 1992.
18. The five Colombian cartels were Medellín, Cali, Pereira, Costa, and Valle del Norte.
19. The Cupola is the governing commission of the Sicilian Mafia.
20. Report to the French Chamber of Deputies by Francois D'Aubert, president of its Anti-Mafia Commission, Feb. 28, 1993. Report to French senate by Gérard Larcher, Jan. 15, 1993. The two-hundred-ton estimate by DEA director Robert Bonner, in the *Independent* of London, Mar. 31, 1992.
21. The description of the Italian part of this episode was related to me by Alessandro Pansa, Rome, Oct. 1992.
22. Information from Alessandro Pansa.
23. Greg Passic, head of DEA's money-laundering section, in *The European*, Oct. 1–4, 1992. He said, "The Colombians have chosen Italy as their warehouse to store cocaine for distribution throughout Europe."
24. Alessandro Pansa in *La Repubblica*, Sept. 29, 1992. He said of Operation Green Ice: "We've learned how the Corleones intend to monopolize the cocaine traffic in Europe and how the Colombian cartels trust them."
25. Judge Falcone, cited in a report by François D'Aubert, Anti-Mafia Commission of the French Chamber of Deputies, Jan. 23, 1993.
26. Alessandro Pansa, quoted in *La Repubblica*, Sept. 30, 1992.
27. Interviews with Greg Passic, head of the DEA's money-laundering section, Washington, D.C., Dec. 1992 and Sept. 1993.
28. Interview with Luciano Violante, president of the Anti-Mafia Commission of the Italian parliament, Apr. 1993.
29. Interview with Greg Passic, Washington, D.C., Sept. 1993.
30. The Cuntreras' investment in Russia, *Corriere della Sera*, Mar. 4, 1993. This was confirmed to the *Corriere's* reporter, Maria Antonietta Calabrò, by the Italian intelligence service SISDE.
31. *La Repubblica*, Feb. 13, 1993. See also the *International Herald-Tribune* of the same date.

Chapter 2: After the Wall

1. Testimony of Leonardo Messina before Italy's Parliamentary Anti-Mafia Commission, Dec. 11, 1992.
2. The boss in question was Giuseppe Madonia, boss of Gela in southern Sicily.
3. "If there was competition among these crime syndicates, we would be turning up a lot of dead bodies. But so far the evidence is that

they are looking for ways to work together," said Judge Giuseppe Ayala, former chief prosecutor in Palermo's first maxi-trial and presently a member of Italy's Parliament for the Republican Party. Stated in *The Washington Post*, Oct. 5, 1992.

I was told essentially the same thing by senior police officials in Moscow, Warsaw, Budapest, Prague, the BKA in Wiesbaden, the FBI, and various Italian authorities in the police and judiciary. These will be cited in subsequent chapters.

4. *The Washington Post*, Oct. 5, 1992.
5. Falcone's lecture to the German Bundeskriminalamt in Wiesbaden, Nov. 1990, cited just after his death in *MicroMega*, June 1992. Quoted more fully in Chapter 1.
6. The drug traffic figure of $500 billion and comparison to the arms trade is the estimate of GAFI, the G-7's Groupe Anti-Fraude International.
7. Report to the European Parliament, Oct. 15, 1991, cited in a report to the French parliament by François D'Aubert for its Anti-Mafia Commission, Feb. 1993.
8. *Manchester Guardian* cited in *Corriere della Sera*, Aug. 18, 1992.
9. The Holland figure comes from a report to the U.N. Rome conference, "International Crime Survey," cited in *La Stampa*, Jan. 5, 1993.
10. The EC Commission issued its White Paper on completion of the Single Market in June 1985. The Single Market Act was approved in 1987.
11. Interview with Charles Saphos, who was then tracking the global narcotics traffic, Washington, D.C., Sept. 1990. Saphos was subsequently appointed general counsel for Interpol U.S.
12. Report by Pier van Reenan, *European Affairs*, Summer 1989. The situation he described in 1989 persisted practically without change until late in 1992. Even then, most of the problems he referred to remained unchanged.
13. The Schengen agreement of June 14, 1985, originally covered five EC states, Germany, France, Belgium, Holland, and Luxembourg, and was designed to prepare the way for the EC Single Market through the gradual abolition of internal borders among these five. Although all the other EC states save Great Britain, Ireland, and Denmark adhered to the agreement later, they were unable to solve all the problems involved by the end of 1992, when the Single Market itself was to come into effect.
14. Council of Europe report by Co-operation Group to Combat Drug Abuse, the so-called Pompidou Group, Strasbourg, France, Apr. 9, 1991.
15. Josef Jaffe in Munich's *Suddeutsche Zeitung*.
16. FBI's 1990 program report, "Attacking Organized Crime: 1991 National Strategy."
17. Robert Friedman's excellent article in *Vanity Fair*, Jan. 1993.
18. In a lecture to Germany's Bundeskriminalamt in Wiesbaden, in November 1990, Falcone said, "Organizations like the Triads, the Yakuza, and the Russian clans growing exponentially are all en-

dowed, like the Mafia, with formal structures and great flexibility, capable of converting to every kind of illegal activity in an extraordinarily short time. All these organizations have a great deal of money, resort to violence, and try in every way to guarantee inaction by the police and judiciary as well as political connivance." Cited in *MicroMega*, June 25, 1992.

In a speech a few days before his death, Falcone said,

> One asks if the Mafia model is exportable and susceptible, not so much and not only of imitation in other countries but of generating relationships, almost a sort of international illicit joint venture. In my opinion, the Mafia's criminal model with particularly specific environmental characteristics would not be transformable to other realities. But . . . we must also judge whether Mafia criminality apart from [such] specifics . . . can be susceptible to imitation abroad. Put in these terms, the big organizations present characteristics that are not dissimilar to the Mafia's.

19. *Yakuza* by David E. Kaplan and Alex Dubro.
20. Libro Bianco su Racket e Criminalità, FIPE (Federazione Italiana Pubblici Esercizi), 1992. See also *International Herald Tribune*, June 28, 1991. Six thousand police were deployed when the seventeen hundred companies held their meetings.
21. *The Day Is Born in Darkness* by Mikhail Dyomin.
22. Description by Joe Serio. See Mikhail Dyomin, *The Day Is Born in Darkness*, p. 46: "Thieves have no dictators. They do, though, have their own form of ruling center, a kind of legislative committee composed of the worthy and the authoritative." The national policy meetings were and are called *skhodka*; the common kitty is called *obschak*.

Chapter 3: Crime Without Frontiers

1. Dinner with Chancellor Helmut Kohl at his residence in Bonn, May 8, 1990.
2. Interviews with Gennady Chebotarev, head of the Russian Interior Ministry's Sixth Department to combat organized crime, in 1992; with Alexander Gurov, his predecessor in that post and in the same post for the Soviet Union before its collapse; with the KGB officer watching the Russian Mafia abroad; with Anatoly Volobuev, formerly of the Sixth Department's research division, Moscow, Nov. 1991 and July 1992.

See Arkady Vaksberg's *The Soviet Mafia*, p. 359: "In the spring of 1990, the Soviet Interior Ministry got operational intelligence of a business meeting between Soviet and Western mafiosi for June in Warsaw, to discuss future cooperation during the Soviet switch to a market economy. One of the main items was a method for moving Soviet antiques to the West. The Ministry sent agents, and a journalist went along. They found nothing. The venue was changed after arrangements leaked. Later, a senior militia officer told me that the meeting was in East Berlin. Organizers had said Warsaw to throw authorities off the scent."

3. *The Day Is Born in Darkness* by Mikhail Dyomin.
4. Interview with the captain, Berlin, Oct. 29, 1992.
5. Interview with the deputy police chief, Warsaw, Sept. 1991.
6. Interview with Alexander Herzog, Warsaw, Sept. 3, 1991.
7. Interview with Jurgen Maurer of the BKA Organized Crime Section, Wiesbaden, Feb. 20, 1992.
8. Judge Pierluigi Vigna of Florence, investigating Eastern European arms traffic passing through Italy, *La Repubblica*, Feb. 14, 1993.
9. BKA (Bundeskriminalamt) figures for 1990. BKA's 1992 figure cited in *Welt am Sontag*, Oct. 18, 1992.
10. Interview with the captain of the German border guards, Berlin, Oct. 1992.
11. See *Octopus*, by Claire Sterling.
12. Ibid.
13. Ibid.
14. Ibid. The quotation is by the Sicilian Mafia's first major defector, Tommaso Buscetta.
15. Tribunale Civile e Penale di Palermo, Ufficio Istruzione Processi Penali, communication by Judge Gioacchino Natoli addressed to the Bundeskriminalamt in Wiesbaden, Nov. 24, 1989.
16. Ibid.
17. Ibid.
18. Riina's one-time driver, the *pentito* (defector) Baldassare Di Maggio, told authorities of Riina's German visits in January 1993. Nuvoletta's and Alfieri's residences in Germany were confirmed by Servizio Centrale Operativo of Italy's Criminalpol.
19. Interview with Alessandro Pansa of the Italian Criminalpol's Rome Servizio Centrale Operativo, May 11, 1990.
20. Interview with Hans-Ludwig Zachert, Apr. 24, 1991.
21. *Der Spiegel*, Aug. 4, 1992.
22. Falcone's statement to conference in Wiesbaden, Nov. 7–8, 1990.
23. Interview with Hans-Ludwig Zachert. Several details confirmed in *Corriere della Sera*, Apr. 11, 1991.
24. BKA in-house report on Italian organized crime, Wiesbaden, Apr. 2, 1992.
25. Interview with Alessandro Pansa.
26. BKA figures for 1990 and 1991. Cited in *Berliner Zeitung*, Jan. 16–17, 1993, and *Die Welt*, Jan. 25, 1993.
27. Briefing by BKA officers, Wiesbaden, Apr. 1991.
28. Interpol General Secretariat, Drugs Subdivision, "The Balkan Route: Increased Shipment of Southwest Asian Heroin to Europe, 1986–1990," Jan. 1991.
29. Briefing by BKA, Apr. 24, 1991.
30. Ibid. "Contro e Dentro: Criminalità Istituzioni Società," CENSIS (Fondazione Centro Studi Investimenti Sociali), report, Jan. 7, 1992.

31. Briefing by BKA. German press agency DPA July 26, 1991. The traffickers were indicted in Mainz.

32. *Der Spiegel*, Aug. 28, 1992.

33. BKA in-house study. I was told of the BND study during my interviews with BKA officials in Wiesbaden, Mar. 4, 1993.

34. *Corriere della Sera*, June 26, 1990. The Philip Holzmann case was among several brought to the attention of Italy's Parliamentary Anti-Mafia Commission.

35. Estimate of 80 percent by Frankfurt's state counsel Wolfgang Schaupensteiner, *Corriere della Sera*, Apr. 14, 1993.

36. Conference of Italian, French, Spanish, and German police chiefs in Rome, as reported in *L'Independente*, Nov. 21, 1992.

37. "Contro e Dentro," CENSIS report, Jan. 7, 1992.

38. Report by FIPE (Federazione Italiana Pubblici Esercizi), 1992.

39. Reported by Hans-Ludwig Zachert at the conference of police chiefs in Rome. The untranslatable word Buscetta used to describe German legislation was *garantista*.

40. Interview with Jurgen Maurer of BKA's Organized Crime Section, Wiesbaden, Feb. 20, 1992.

41. Interview with Jurgen Maurer.

42. FIPE report, 1992.

43. Parliamentary Anti-Mafia Commission Report to the U.N. Assembly, extraordinary session on world drug problem. Communicated to the prime minister on Mar. 20, 1990.

Chapter 4: The Sicilian Mafia Looks East

1. Leonardo Messina's testimony before Italy's Parliamentary Anti-Mafia Commission, Dec. 11, 1992.

2. Judge Giovanni Falcone was killed on May 23, 1992; Judge Paolo Borsellino the following July 19.

3. See *Octopus* by Claire Sterling for a fuller description of the Great Mafia War.

4. Testimony of Gaspare Mutolo to the Parliamentary Anti-Mafia Commission, Feb. 9, 1993. The mother, sister, and aunt of Francesco Mannino Mannoia, a major defector, were all shot dead on the same day in Palermo.

5. He was Pietro Vernengo, a world-famous drug trafficker, recaptured some months after his escape.

6. Leonardo Messina's testimony before the Parliamentary Anti-Mafia Commission, Dec. 11, 1992. Another high-ranking *pentito* (defector), Gaspare Mutolo, used the word "combined" instead of "adjusted" in his testimony before the commission.

7. Gaspare Mutolo's testimony before the Parliamentary Anti-Mafia Commission, Feb. 10, 1993. A heavy drug trafficker working with Saro Riccobono's Family, he turned over one thousand names of mafiosi and their friends and helpers when he decided to collaborate in the spring of 1992.

8. The verdict of the Corte di Cassazione was announced on Jan. 30, 1992.

9. Communication of the Italian senate, requesting permission to investigate Andreotti, from the *Procura della Repubblica* of Palermo, Mar. 27, 1993.

10. Testimony of a half a dozen *pentiti,* including Leonardo Messina and Gaspare Mutolo. Testimony of major defector Francesco Mannino Mannoia on the fact that Salvo Lima was a sworn-in Man of Honor.

11. For Sicilian figures, see *Octopus* by Claire Sterling. For these together with the southern mainland, see the weekly *Il Mondo,* cited in *La Repubblica,* Mar. 1, 1992.

12. See text of Antonino Calderone's testimony under interrogation by judges in Palermo. *Corriere della Sera, Mar.* 15, 1988.

13. Testimony of Leonardo Messina, Gaspare Mutolo, and Antonino Calderone before the Parliamentary Anti-Mafia Commission. See also *Octopus* by Claire Sterling on Stefano Bontate's preparations to join a covered lodge in 1977.

14. Combined testimony of Leonardo Messina, Gasparo Mutolo, and Antonino Calderone to the Parliamentary Anti-Mafia Commission, Dec. 1992 to Feb. 1993.

    In June 1993, a court in Trapani convicted the head of a covered Masonic lodge called Iside 2 for the crime of "secret association," the first such conviction ever in Italy. The lodge membership had included leading Christian Democrats, businessmen, and Mafia bosses, among whom was the notorious boss of Mazara del Vallo, Mariano Agate, first on the list of defendants in Palermo's historic maxi-trial. *Corriere della Sera,* June 6, 1993.

15. Licio Gelli's P2 became a national scandal in the early 1980s, when the stupefying list of its more prominent members was discovered. Though formally dissolved, it continues to make headlines as an alleged occult force behind Italy's ongoing problems of terrorism and massive corruption.

16. See *Octopus* by Claire Sterling, p. 201.

17. Draft report to the European Parliament by Patrick Cooney for the Committee of Enquiry into the Spread of Organized Crime Linked to Drug Trafficking in Member States of European Community, Oct. 28, 1991.

    See also *Il Giornale,* Nov. 25, 1989.

18. See *Octopus* by Claire Sterling for a fuller account of Corrado Carnevale's record.

19. Testimony of Gaspare Mutolo, former lieutenant of Mafia boss Saro Riccobono, to the Parliamentary Anti-Mafia Commission, Feb. 9, 1993.

20. Leonardo Messina's testimony to the Parliamentary Anti-Mafia Commission.

21. Report to Italy's Parliament by Interior Minister Nicola Mancino, March 1993.

22. Interview with head of financial police in Prague, Oct. 1992, on Mafia buying banks in Slovakia. A new Sicilian-American Mafia

bank in Sverdlovsk, in the Russian Urals, is described in Chapter 6.

Roberto Palazzolo, the Mafia's big money launderer in the Pizza Connection case, went on to become governor of the Bank of Sibekwe in Zimbabwe, near the South African border.

23. The French parliament's Anti-Mafia Commission report, by its president, François D'Aubert, citing Liliana Ferraro of Italy's Ministry of Justice. Speaking at a money-laundering conference sponsored by Italy's Parliamentary Anti-Mafia Commission, Colonel Cappelli of the DIA (anti-Mafia police) estimated Mafia legitimate investments inside Italy as 60 percent in the financial sector, 17 percent in real estate, 11 percent in commerce, 5 percent in industry, agro-industry, and gold mining. *La Stampa*, CENSIS (Fondazione Centro Studi Investimenti Sociali), May 15, 1993.

24. "Contro e Dentro: Criminalità Istituzioni Società" report, Jan. 7, 1992. Estimate of income for all organized crime inside Italy was twenty trillion lire, according to this study. Its income from the *pizzo* alone was thirty trillion lire, according to a report by the Confederazione di Esercizi Pubblici (bar and restaurant owners), "Estorti e Riciclati," released to the press on Apr. 24, 1991.

25. The estimated EC swindles came to 345 billion lire, just for grain. *La Stampa*, June 6, 1993.

26. Leonardo Messina's testimony before the Parliamentary Anti-Mafia Commission.

27. Testimony before the Parliamentary Anti-Mafia Commission by Domenico Sica, then high commissioner to combat the Mafia, *The New York Times*, July 23, 1989. Sica spoke of "total possession" of "parts" of Sicily, Calabria, and Naples. Many police and government authorities have enlarged the definition since then.

28. Draft of the commission's report to Parliament on relations between the Mafia and politics, Mar. 27, 1993.

29. Ruling by Judge Luigi Russo in Catania, *Corriere della Sera*, Apr. 5, 1991. Interview in *La Repubblica*, Apr. 6, 1991. The Chamber of Commerce proposal was reported in *The New York Times*, July 1, 1991.

30. Interview with Antonio Mauri, president of the Catania Association of Industrialists, *Corriere della Sera* and *La Repubblica*, Nov. 2, 1992.

31. Salvo Lima's role in Sicily's so-called Tangentopoli was defined in a report to the judiciary by the special Carabiniere anti-Mafia unit, ROS (Riparto Operativo Speciale). *Corriere della Sera*, May 28, 1993.

32. *La Repubblica*, Mar. 11, 1992.

33. *La Repubblica*, Mar. 4, 1992.

34. The car park in Via Salomone was in contact with various city officials, a high functionary of the Defense Ministry in Rome, and a big real estate operator heading a local Masonic lodge. Police phone intercepts revealed that the band running this center was planning to assassinate Judge Antonio Di Pietro, leading "Operation Clean Hands" in Milan. *Corriere della Sera*, Sept. 2, 1992. For a summary of the roundups, see *La Repubblica*, Feb. 5, 1993.

35. Interview with Sergio Pininfarina, president of Confindustria, *La Repubblica*, Nov. 9, 1990.

36. Parliamentary Anti-Mafia Commission report on Milan and the province of Lombardy, July 1990.
37. Interview with Interior Minister Antonio Gava, *La Repubblica*, July 6, 1989.
38. Francesco Saverio Borelli's address to a conference in Palermo, "Mafia, Che Fare?" organized by Sicily's Regional Assembly. *L'Independente*, Dec. 13, 1992.
39. "Libro Bianco su Racket e Criminalità," FIPE (Federazione Italiana Pubblici Esercizi), 1992. Guardia di Finanza report, *Corriere della Sera*, May 6, 1989.
40. Guardia di Finanza report, *Corriere della Sera*, May 6, 1989.
41. Interview with Piero Bassetti, president of Milan's Chamber of Commerce, *La Repubblica*, Nov. 9, 1990.
42. "Bozza di Relazione del Gruppo di Lavoro Incaricato di Svolgere Indagini Sulla Situazione di Milano," Italy's Parliamentary Anti-Mafia Commission, July 13, 1990.
43. "Operation Clean Hands" began with the arrest of a Milanese Socialist functionary named Mario Chiesa, caught taking a seven-million-lire payoff in Feb. 1992. The judges were Antonio Di Pietro, Gherardo Colombo, and Pier Camillo Davigo, under the quietly firm command of Milan's prosecutor-general, Francesco Saverio Borelli.
44. Summary by Barry James, *International Herald Tribune*, July 29, 1993.
45. Li-Mo was the office in Chiasso used by Giuseppe Lottusi in the Big John cocaine case cited in Chapter 1. The same agent, "Enzo," allegedly provided laundered dollars to the administrative secretaries of the Christian Democratic and Socialist parties, Citaristi and Balzamo. See *L'Espresso*, May 2, 1993.
46. Piero Bassetti, president of Milan's Chamber of Commerce, at a press conference on May 17, 1992. *Il Giornale Nuovo*, Milan, May 18, 1992.
47. Interview with Domenico Sica, former high prefect to combat the Mafia. Sica estimated the Italian state tobacco monopoly turnover at around eleven trillion lire a year, roughly $9 billion. The Camorra's contraband trade was equal to this amount or more, he told me.
48. The vice-president of the EC Commission, Martin Bangemann, said that "restrictions on imports among member states are forbidden" under Article 30 of the Treaty of Rome. He threatened an injunction against the Italian government unless the ban was lifted within twenty-four hours. *La Repubblica*, Dec. 19, 1991.
49. For tobacco profits and tax losses see the Italian Interior Ministry's report to parliament, May 1993.
50. See *Octopus* by Claire Sterling, Chapter 9.
51. Report to the French assembly by François D'Aubert, head of its special anti-Mafia Commission, Feb. 28, 1993.
52. Report to the French assembly by François D'Aubert, Feb. 28, 1993.
53. Report to the French assembly by François D'Aubert, Feb. 28, 1993.
54. *Corriere della Sera*, July 22 and Sept. 9, 1992.
55. Among Italian charges against him are the murders of Alfredo

Taborra and Giuseppe Barbera on June 27, 1977, in complicity with Camorra boss Lorenzo Nuvoletta.

56. Zaza's villa is located in Villeneuve Loubet, twenty kilometers from Nice.
57. Report to the French assembly by François D'Aubert, Feb. 28, 1993.
58. Zaza's latest arrest was part of a roundup that included thirty-five others in Italy and France, in "Operation Green Sea." *La Stampa*, May 13, 1993.
59. A map of Giuseppe Madonia's holdings was published in *La Repubblica*, Nov. 21, 1992.
60. Semi-annual report by the DIA, Italy's police superforce, *La Stampa*, July 3, 1993.
61. "Relazione sull'Attività delle Forze di Polizia e sullo Stato Dell'Ordine e della Sicurezza Pubblica Nel Territorio Nazionale" (Report on the Activity of the Police Forces and State of Public Order and Security on the National Territory), Interior Ministry, Rome, Mar. 1993. See also *Corriere della Sera*, May 21, 1993.
62. Report of Leonid Fituni, director of the Academy of Science's Center for Global and Strategic Studies, 1993.
63. Judge PierLuigi Vigna of Florence, investigating the two-way arms traffic between Italy and Eastern Europe. *La Repubblica*, Feb. 15, 1993.

Chapter 5: The Russian Mafia Looks West

1. Official estimate of the Russian Interior Ministry. Interview with I. Pavlovich, deputy chief of the Interior Ministry's Sixth Department to Combat Organized Crime, July 1, 1992. See also the report of the Suzdal Conference on International Organized Crime, Oct. 28 to Nov. 1, 1991.
2. *The Soviet Mafia* by Arkady Vaksberg.
3. *Moskovskiye Novosti*, in the BBC's *Current Digest of the Soviet Press*, vol. 40, no. 17. See also *The Soviet Mafia* by Arkady Vaksberg, p. 158. The mafia boss was Rashidin, who died during the investigation and was buried in a Lenin memorial that is supposed to be the tallest statue of Lenin in the world.
4. Geidar Aliev returned in triumph to become president of Azerbaijan in June 1993. *Corriere della Sera*, June 19, 1993. For Aliev's role, see *The Soviet Mafia* by Arkady Vaksberg.
5. *Moskovskiye Novosti*, Feb. 10, 1991.
6. From *The Soviet Mafia* by Arkady Vaksberg.
7. Tass correspondent Larisa Kislinksaia in a speech to the Woodrow Wilson Center, Washington, D.C., Nov. 14, 1989.
8. Boris Yeltsin in an address to an emergency conference of one thousand government officials, magistrates, and policemen on the need to fight corruption. Reported in *La Repubblica*, Feb. 13, 1993. See also the Reuters dispatch in the *International Herald Tribune*, Feb. 13, 1993, and the Associated Press dispatch from Moscow of the same date.

9. Interview with Nina Piskaryova, economist of the All-Union Research Institute, Moscow, Oct. 1991.

10. Prosecutor-General A. Y. Sukharev, reporting to the Second Congress of the U.S.S.R. People's Deputies, Dec. 1989, quoted in *Pravda* and *Izvestia*, in the BBC's *Current Digest of the Soviet Press*, vol. 42.

11. Alexander Gurov, head of the Soviet Interior Ministry's Sixth Department to Combat Organized Crime, cited in *La Nazione*, May 9, 1991. Confirmed to me by Gurov, Moscow, Oct. 1991.

12. *The Washington Post*, quoting Moscow Police Chief Murashev, Feb. 26, 1991.

13. Interview with Alexander Gurov, Nov. 1991. The latter part of Gurov's statement is also quoted in *La Nazione* of Florence, May 9, 1991.

14. The *Washington Post*, Feb. 26, 1991.

15. Interview with Tatjana Korjagina, then the Soviet Interior Ministry's top social economist, Moscow, Oct. 1991. The same estimates were given to me by Alexander Gurov, who headed the Interior Ministry's Sixth Department at the time.

The 1993 estimate by Gen. Mikhail Egorov of the Sixth Department, quoted in *La Stampa*, Dec. 24, 1993.

Boris Yeltsin's statement was given to a special conference on the problems of organized crime, attended by one thousand government functionaries, judges, and police officers, Associated Press dispatch, Feb. 13, 1993.

16. Cited by Tass in Russian for abroad, July 9, 1991. The estimate was confirmed to me by Tatjana Korjagina, July 1992.

17. On July 20, 1993, Russian Interior Minister Yerin gave the figure of 14,800 homicides in Russia in the first six months of 1993. *La Repubblica*, July 21, 1993.

Russia's yearly homicide rate was eighteen thousand in 1992, or around fifty a day, the official figure given by Attorney General Valentino Stepankov at a press conference in Moscow. *Corriere della Sera*, Feb. 12, 1993.

18. Stepankov announced that he would present a bill to parliament to this effect. Reported in *Corriere della Sera*, Feb. 12, 1993.

19. *La Stampa* from Moscow, July 17, 1993.

20. Report by Interpol's deputy chief in Moscow, Anatoly Terechov, to the John Jay College International Conference on Organized Crime, St. Petersburg, June 20 to July 3, 1992.

21. *Argumenty i Fakty*, no. 51–52, Dec. 1992.

22. From a secretly filmed video in the possession of Captain Aleksandr Sirotkin of Russia's Sixth Department to Combat Organized Crime, cited in *La Stampa*, June 3, 1993.

23. From a study by Joe Serio, presently a consultant on organized crime in Moscow.

24. A full description is provided in an admirable study by Joe Serio.

25. Interviews with Alexander Gurov, Nov. 1991 and July 1992, when he had become head of the Russian KGB's public relations office; with Gennady Chebotarev, Gurov's deputy in the Soviet Sixth De-

partment, who became deputy head of the Russian Republic's Sixth Department in 1992; with Anatoly Volobuev, formerly of the Sixth Department and later contributor to *Vizimayeva Novosti*; with Joe Serio of Chicago's Institute on International Organized Crime; with Tatjana Korjagina; and with Evgen Mizlovsky, head of Russia's independent Anti-Mafia Commission, founded in 1992.

26. Estimate by Anatoly Volobuev, confirmed to me by the Sixth Department.

27. Interview with I. Pavlovich in Moscow, July 1, 1992. The Sixth Department captain is Alexandr Sirotkin, cited in *La Stampa*, June 3, 1993.

28. Alexander Gurov on Soviet TV, Jan. 24, 1991.

29. Interview with Tatjana Korjagina, Nov. 1991.

30. Interview with Tatjana Korjagina, Nov. 1991. See also the Tass section of *Krim-Press* as cited below; London's *Independent on Sunday*, Feb. 9, 1992; *Corriere della Sera*, Jan. 31, 1992.

31. Tass section of *Krim-Press*, Jan. 31, 1992. The fact of the meeting was confirmed to me by Gennady Chebotarev, Russia's Sixth Department, in Moscow, July 1992.

32. Interview with Tatjana Korjagina, Nov. 1991. Ninety-two billion rubles were worth around $100 million in early 1992.

33. Cited in London's *Independent on Sunday*, Feb. 9, 1992.

34. Tass section of *Krim-Press*.

35. Cited in *La Repubblica*, Jan. 13, 1993.

36. *Moscow Business Week*, June 4, 1992.

37. Anatoly Verdenin, quoted in *The European*, Jan. 1992.

38. The news story appeared in *La Repubblica*, Nov. 27, 1991. It was confirmed in part, with blistering comments, by the director of the Russian Commodities and Raw Materials Exchange, Konstantin Borovoi, in the *Moscow Times*, May 19, 1992.
    Interview with Tatjana Korjagina, Moscow, July 1992.

39. The charge was made by Konstantin Borovoi.

40. Interview with Boris Uvarov, chief investigator for big crimes in the Russian prosecutor-general's office, Moscow, July 1, 1992.

41. United Press International dispatch from Moscow, Oct. 14, 1990.

42. A "galloping" crime rate is reported in the territories named in *Sovetskaya Rossiya*, June 11, 1991.

43. Tass, Jan. 16, 1991. The Italian documentary was shown on Speciale TG I, RAI TV, Aug. 10, 1991.

44. Tass, Dec. 26, 1990. *La Repubblica*, Feb. 6 and Feb. 11, 1992. *The European*, Oct. 18, 1991. *Corriere della Sera*, Jan. 9, 1992. Interview with General Nino Sotgiu, head of Italy's Anti-Narcotics Squad after his visit to Moscow.

45. *Corriere della Sera*, from Moscow, Jan. 17, 1992.

46. See Chapter 3, my interview with Alexander Herzog, former prosecutor-general of Poland, Oct. 1991.

47. The financial weekly *Commersant*, Dec. 4, 1991, reported in *The New York Times*, Dec. 6, 1991. For more recent and fuller detail, see Joe Serio's study of the Russian mafia.

48. Interview with Boris Uvarov, July 1, 1992.
49. Interviews with Gennady Chebotarev and Anatoly Volobuev, Moscow, June 28 and July 2, 1992. Interviews with the BKA in Wiesbaden and the police of Prague and Warsaw.
50. *Chicago Tribune*, Oct. 14, 1991.
51. My briefing at BKA headquarters, Wiesbaden, April 1991.
52. *Moskovskie Novosti*, cited in *La Repubblica*, Aug. 15, 1991.
53. Interview with Colonel Alexander Sergeev, head of the anti-narcotics unit of the Soviet Interior Ministry, Nov. 1991.
    See also the U.N. International Narcotics Control Board 1991 report.
54. Interview with Colonel Alexander Sergeev, Nov. 1991.
55. *Chicago Tribune*, Oct. 15, 1991.
56. Report by Vladimir Burlaka, anti-narcotics chief of St. Petersburg, to the International Conference on Organized Crime, June 20 to July 3, 1992. The latest 1992 estimates from anti-narcotics authorities of London are quoted in *Corriere della Sera*, Sept. 6, 1992. On Chernobyl, *Commersant*, Apr. 6, 1992, cites the investigation of opium cultivation by the International Association Against Proliferation and Use of Drugs in Moscow. Confirmed by Observatoire Geopolitque des Drogues.
57. Associated Press release 112109, May 1993.
58. Report on the Schengen Agreement to the French senate by the commission president, Paul Masson, Dec. 11, 1991.
59. Report by anti-narcotics authorities in London, cited in *Corriere della Sera*, Sept. 6, 1992.
60. Interview with Colonel Alexander Sergeev. Interview with Vitaly Karpetz, director of the Research Institute of the Soviet prosecutor-general's office, Nov. 1991 and July 1992. See also the report of the International Narcotics Control Board, 1991.
61. Alexander Gurov's TV interview, Jan. 24, 1991.
62. Interview with Colonel Alexander Sergeev, Nov. 1991.
63. The one-and-a-half million figure from Sergeev was cited by the Associated Press on Feb. 16, 1993. Sergeev had given me a similar figure in Moscow the previous July.
    For higher estimates, see interviews with I. A. Mamedov and Gela Georgiyeovich Lezhava, cited in dispatches from Foreign Broadcast Information Service and Tass, as reported by Graham Turbiville, Jr., in "Counter-Narcotics, International Dimensions of a Soviet Internal Security Problem," Soviet Army Studies Office, Fort Leavenworth, Kansas.
    Report by St. Petersburg's anti-narcotics chief, Vladimir Burlaka, to the 1992 conference in St. Petersburg.
64. Interview with Colonel Alexander Sergeev, Nov. 1991.
65. Interview with Interpol's deputy chief, Andrzej Koweszko, Warsaw, Oct. 1992. See also ADN Kronos Agency, Rome, citing an interview with Koweszko in the British newspaper *The Guardian*, Aug. 29, 1992.

66. *The European*, July 30, 1992. An Interpol flyer on the sandal shipment was sent to all member countries.
67. Interview with Vitaly Karpetz, Moscow, Nov. 1991 and July 1992 (when he held the same post in the Russian Republic as previously in the U.S.S.R.). See also *Corriere della Sera*, Apr. 25, 1991.
68. *Intersec*, vol. 2, no. 4, Sept. 1992.
69. The American was Ukrainian-born Alexander Dokijchuk, with a joint venture called D&K-Sov Group. Interview with Boris Uvarov, Moscow, July 1992. That summer the black market ruble exchange rate was around 145 rubles to the dollar. See Chapter 10.
70. Interview with Gennady Chebotarev, Chief of Russia's Sixth Department, Moscow, July 1992.
71. The sum was specified by the Russian Interior Ministry on June 15, 1992. See *Commersant*, June 23, 1992. The whole story was confirmed to me in interviews with Boris Uvarov and Gennady Chebotarev, Moscow, July 1992.

    The top black market exchange rate in July 1992 was 145 rubles to the dollar.
72. Interview with Gennady Chebotarev. See also *Commersant*, June 2, 1992.
73. At a press conference, July 7, 1992, V. Soltaganov, head of the Interior Ministry's Main Department to Combat Economic Crime, gave the figure of 150 billion to 200 billion rubles for the first half of 1992. The full year's figure was published in *Argumenty i Fakty*, No. 51–52, Dec. 1992.

    The figure of $1 billion foreign capital investment was in *Izvestiya*, Dec. 30, 1992.
74. Boris Yeltsin's address to a special conference on crime and corruption, Moscow, Feb. 12, 1993. Reuters dispatch from Moscow, *International Herald Tribune*, Feb. 13, 1993. See also *La Repubblica*, Feb. 13, 1993, and Associated Press dispatch, Feb. 13, 1993.
75. Boris Yeltsin's address to a special conference on crime and corruption, Moscow, Feb. 12, 1993.
76. Interview with Nina Piskaryova, Moscow, Oct. 1991.
77. *Moscow Times*, May 19, 1992.
78. Cited in the *Los Angeles Times*, republished in the *International Herald-Tribune*, May 27, 1991.
79. Moscow Innovation Commercial Bank Annual Report, January 1, 1990.
80. *Izvestiya*, June 5 and July 9, 1992; *Komsomolskaya Pravda*, Feb. 9, 1991; *Stern*, Sept. 1991.
81. Tarasov has himself confirmed this oil deal with Marc Rich in an interview with *Izvestiya*, July 9, 1992. See Chapter 10.
82. Tarasov's statement on selling in the West for $176 a ton, and on the $11 million remaining in Monaco was made to *Izvestiya*, July 9, 1991.

    The Russian TV program *Vesti* said on Sept. 17, 1991, that Tarasov owes the Russian government $48 million. According to Vadim Bewlyk, who wrote the original story on this operation for *Izvestiya*,

Tarasov's successor at Istok, Leonid Tretyak, made a formal request on Sept. 17, 1991, to the Russian Interior Ministry's Sixth Department to Combat Organized Crime for an audit of Tarasov's financial operations and "a legal evaluation of the activities of Istok's officials." (*Izvestiya*, July 9, 1992.)

83. *Izvestiya*, July 9, 1992.
84. Interview with Anatoly Terichov, Moscow, July 1992. Terichov's report to St. Petersburg International Conference on Organized Crime, June 20 to July 3, 1992. See also the interview with Constantin Rodionov, chief of Interpol Moscow until 1992, in *Corriere della Sera*, Aug. 15, 1991.
85. Boris Yeltsin's address to the conference on crime and corruption. Feb. 13, 1993.
86. Interview with Boris Uvarov, Moscow, July 1992.

Chapter 6: In Europe

1. Interview with BKA's organized crime division, Wiesbaden, Feb. 1993.
2. Himbank's full name is Commercial Bank of the Chemical Industry of Russia. Its address in Moscow is 20 Mjanickaja St. Its address in Rochester is 111 Alexander Street. See Chapter 9.
3. Report on "Operation Europa 1," a year-long investigation by Judges Nicola Gratteri and Andrea Canciani in Locri, Calabria. *La Repubblica*, Nov. 5, 1993.
4. Two Chechen, the Utseyev brothers, were murdered in 1993. They had been sent to Britain by General Dzahkar Dudaeyev, president of the Chechen Republic. *Corriere della Sera*, Mar. 8, 1993.
5. ADN Kronos report from Warsaw, Aug. 29, 1992. The essentials of the report were confirmed to me in Warsaw the following October by Interpol chief Andrzej Koweszko.
6. *Le Monde*, Jan. 27, 1993.
7. Interview with Jurgen Maurer and Wolfram Bieling, BKA Wiesbaden, Feb. 1993. According to BKA official figures, German authorities investigated 641 organized crime cases in 1992, 46 percent of which involved gangs of just one nationality. The rest were multinational gangs, some with up to one hundred members.
8. Sources in the Russian MVD (Interior Ministry) to Joseph Serio, consultant on the mafia and president of Eurasian Business Services in Moscow. Vladimir Lupskii and Boris Lysenko, "Russkaya Mafia v FRG Dyeistvuyet Slovno u Sebya Doma," *Izvestiya*, May 27, 1993.
9. Interview with Jurgen Maurer, Wiesbaden, Feb. 1993.
10. Interview with Wolfram Bieling, BKA, Wiesbaden, Feb. 1993.
11. The murdered pair were Ruslan and Nasabek Utseyev, who claimed to be semi-official representatives of General Dzahkar Dudaeyev's rump Chechen Republic. British police thought they controlled the London market in East European art objects stolen from museums.

Interview with Scotland Yard's Organized Crime Section. See also *Corriere della Sera*, Mar. 8, 1993.

12. Interviews with Maurer and Bieling, Wiesbaden, Feb. 1993.
13. ADN Kronos report, Berlin, Aug. 11, 1991; *Der Spiegel*, Aug. 17, 1993.
14. The border crossing is twenty-eight kilometers south of Kolbasowo, near Stettin. Confirmed by the BKA.
15. When I checked my list of companies with Kroll Associates in London, investigating currency frauds for the Russian government in 1992, they got a couple of KGB hits. The list was provided in a report to the Polish parliament, the Sejm, Aug. 17, 1991, by two deputies from the Committee on Economic Relations with Foreign Countries.
16. The monetary union was agreed upon in July 1990.
17. United Press International dispatch, Oct. 8, 1990.
18. Interview with Maurer, Wiesbaden, Feb. 1993. See also *Frankfurter Allgemeine*, Feb. 6, 1993.
19. Interview with Jurgen Maurer, Wiesbaden, Feb. 1993. They checked the figure with ZERV at my request. The *proven* figure came to 8 billion deutsche marks. The 20 billion figure was an informed estimate. The figure on all other damage by organized crime was 3.6 billion deutsche marks in 1991, according to the BKA.
20. The BKA figures given to me in Wiesbaden, Mar. 4, 1993 were as follows: Of all organized crime cases in 1991, the criminals involved were 5,482. Of these, German nationals were 49.8 percent.
21. *La Stampa* of Turin, citing BKA's president, Hans-Ludwig Zachert, and the head of Germany's police union, Hermann Lutz, Jan. 23, 1993. See also *Die Welt*, Jan. 25, 1993; *Berliner Zeitung*, Jan. 17, 1993; and *Dusseldorf Handelsblatt*, Mar. 29, 1993.
22. *Die Welt*, Jan. 21, 1992, reported 655 arrests in a major Kurdish drug bust.
23. German Interior Minister Rudolf Seiters in *Hamburg Bild*, Feb. 12, 1993.
24. *L'Independente*, May 28, 1992, and the *Rheinische Post*, Sept. 23, 1992.
25. Umberto Vecchione, Naples police chief and head of Italian Criminalpol for the south, provided the figure of camorristi in eastern Germany. Cited in *Bild Am Sonntag*, Aug. 2, 1992.
26. ZFD television program *Frontal*, June 8, 1993.
27. Half-yearly report to the Italian parliament by Interior Minister Nicola Mancino, May 1993.
28. Interview with Jurgen Maurer, Wiesbaden, Mar. 3, 1993. The estimate of $120 billion in drug money alone circulating worldwide yearly was made by GAFI (Groupe d'Action Financière Internationale) in Apr. 1990.
29. *Le Monde*, Jan. 27, 1993.
30. *Yakuza* by David E. Kaplan and Alex Dubro.
31. *The European*, Apr. 9, 1993.
32. The President's Commission on Organized Crime Hearings on Asian Organized Crime, Oct. 23–25, 1984. See Chapter 7.
33. *Yakuza* by Kaplan and Dubro.

34. Patrick Cooney's report for the Committee of Enquiry into the Spread of Organized Crime Linked to Drugs Trafficking in the Member States of the European Community, Oct. 28, 1991.
35. The two Japanese police officers were Hidenori Yoshida, ministerial counsellor for the anti-Mafia department, and Uchida Yunichi, deputy director of the criminal police. *Corriere della Sera*, Mar. 1992.
36. Interview with an intelligence source, Australian embassy, Rome, Feb. 6, 1992.
37. *La Stampa*, Mar. 17, 1993, and *La Repubblica* of the same date.
38. Investigation by Roberto Cavaciocchi, deputy police chief of Milan, reported at length in *Il Mondo*, Mar. 1–8, 1993. Criminalpol report on Triad penetration of Italy, Mar. 1993.
39. Interview with Alessandro Pansa of Criminalpol, Rome, Mar. 25, 1993.
40. Interview with François D'Aubert, head of the French Parliamentary Anti-Mafia Commission, Paris, Feb. 28, 1993.
41. The sum was 1.5 billion francs, roughly $300 million, washed by various sources including the Chinese community and the Colombian Medellín cartel. A wave of arrests ended this operation in May 1991. François D'Aubert's Commission report. Also, a report to French Interior Ministry's Institut des Hautes Etudes, Apr. 8, 1993.
42. Interview with Paul Nesbitt. U.N. Conference on Organized Crime in Suzdal, Russia, Oct. 1991.
43. *Corriere della Sera* from Hong Kong, Mar. 18, 1992.
44. *The Chinese Mafia* by Fenton Bresler, p. 207.
45. See *Octopus* by Claire Sterling, p. 289, citing the proceedings of Palermo's maxi-trial.
46. Interpol report to Dutch authorities. Interview with Roelof Gerrard, senior Dutch police officer, St. Petersburg, June 1992.
47. Speech by Mayor Gabor Demszky in Budapest, reported in *The Uncaptive Mind*, Apr. 1992. Interview with head of Polish Interpol, Andrzej Koweszko, Warsaw, Oct. 1992.
48. This information from Russian intelligence was confirmed to me by the BKA and the FBI, Mar. 1993.
49. Kenneth R. Timmerman, editor of the confidential newsletter *Mednews*, in *The Wall Street Journal*, June 14, 1992. See Chapter 12.
50. Report to Parliament on Public Security ("Relazione sull'Attività delle Forze di Polizia e sullo stato dell'Ordine e della Sicurezza Pubblica nel Territorio Nazionale") for the year 1992 by Italy's Interior Ministry, Mar. 1993.
51. Interview with Alessandro Pansa of SCO (Servizio Centrale Operativo), Rome, Mar. 24, 1993. SCO's findings in Russia and Eastern Europe covered 1991–92.
52. Interview with Andrzej Koweszko, Warsaw, Oct. 29, 1992.
53. Interview with Miroslav Oprovil, Oct. 29, 1992.
54. *The European*, Dec. 20, 1992.
55. *Corriere della Sera*, Aug. 7, 1991.
56. The Charleroi ring was briefly described in a BKA report to Italian Interpol in 1989.

57. L'Evénément du Jeudi, Aug. 20–26, 1992. See also *L'Europe des Parrains* by Fabrizio Calvi. The young reporter was Stéphane Steigner.
58. *Corriere della Sera*, Sept. 9, 1992.
59. François D'Aubert Commission report.
60. The joint company was Semacor.
61. The figure in the Commission report is 80 percent to 85 percent.
62. François D'Aubert Commission report. The incinerator is in Saint-Aulbas (Ain).

Chapter 7: In America

1. Phone intercept, quoted by Pennsylvania Crime Commission in "A Decade of Change," 1990.
2. The FBI's National Strategy Report of 1991 lists La Cosa Nostra strongholds as the East Coast from Philadelphia to Boston; west to Buffalo and other Great Lakes cities; Miami, Tampa, and Atlanta in the Southeast; New Orleans and Houston in the South and Southwest; Kansas City, Denver, Phoenix, and Las Vegas in the Midwest; and on to California on the West Coast.
3. FBI National Strategy Report of 1991. Jim Moody, chief of the Bureau's Organized Crime Section, confirmed to me that the situation described was substantially unchanged in December 1992, as he did again in September 1993. See also Pennsylvania Crime Commission 1990 Report: "Organized Crime in Pennsylvania: A Decade of Change."
4. FBI National Strategy Report of 1991.
5. Interview with Jim Moody, Washington, D.C., Dec. 1992.
6. The reporter was Daniel Klaidman; the date, Sept. 8, 1992.
7. The 1991 estimate in FBI's "1991 National Strategy." The 1992 estimate, "FBI Packet on Organized Crime 1992," which indicates Camorra presence at two hundred to three hundred, and 'Ndrangheta's at over one hundred. The latest estimate in my interview with Jim Moody, Dec. 1992.
8. *Octopus* by Claire Sterling, p. 309. FBI intercept.
9. Sammy Gravano's testimony at John Gotti's trial, Feb. 1993.
10. *Octopus* by Claire Sterling.
11. *Octopus* by Claire Sterling, Chapter 12. John Gambino also organized the fake kidnapping of Sindona in 1979, bringing him to Palermo for an accounting with top Mafia bosses.
12. *Octopus* by Claire Sterling, Chapter Four.
13. "Overview of Patriarca La Cosa Nostra Induction Ceremony, Boston, Massachusetts, October 29, 1989." FBI, Washington, D.C.
14. *Crime, Inc.: The Story of Organized Crime* by Martin Short.
15. These charges came under two crucial American laws: the "drug kingpin" RICO statute, acronym for Racketeer Influenced and Corrupt Organizations; and the Continuing Criminal Enterprise Act of 1970, directed against organized drug trafficking. Nicodemo Scarfo was convicted in Nov. 1988.

16. Pennsylvania Crime Commission 1991 Report.
17. *Octopus* by Claire Sterling.
18. Joseph D. Pistone and Richard Woodley, *Donnie Brasco* (New York: NAL Dutton, 1989).
19. Pennsylvania Crime Commission 1991 Report.
20. Robert Mueller's testimony to the Committee on Governmental Affairs, Nov. 6, 1991.
21. *Octopus* by Claire Sterling, p. 310.
22. FBI 1991 Strategy Report.
23. President's Commission on Organized Crime, hearings on Organized Crime of Asian Origin, Oct. 23–25, 1984.
24. President's Commission on Organized Crime hearings, Oct. 23–25, 1984.
25. President's Commission on Organized Crime hearings, Oct. 23–25, 1984.
    Pennsylvania Crime Commission Report 1991.
26. *Yakuza* by David E. Kaplan and Alex Dubro.
27. The Sun Yee On dominates the Chinatowns of San Francisco, Los Angeles, Portland, Boston, Philadelphia, and New York. The 14K works the same cities. The Wo Hop To controls Asian organized crime in the San Francisco Bay area. The United Bamboo Gang does Denver, Phoenix, Chicago, and Atlantic City as well as New York and the West Coast. Report by U.S. Senate Permanent Subcommittee on Investigations, Dec. 1992.
28. U.S. Senate Permanent Subcommittee on Investigations hearings Oct. 3, 1992. Testimony of Michael T. Lempres, Immigration and Naturalization Service.
29. Testimony of Assistant Attorney General Robert Mueller to Senate Permanent Subcommittee on Investigations.
30. Senate Subcommittee on Investigations Report on Asian Organized Crime.
31. The 1993 figure cited in *Time*, Feb. 1, 1993. In his testimony before the Senate Subcommittee on Investigations, Immigration and Naturalization Service Commissioner Michael T. Lempres said that fifty-seven thousand Chinese nationals, "the vast majority smuggled," were issued employment authorization documents in the sixteen months ending in Jan. 1991. An additional thirteen thousand overstayed their visas in that period.
32. *Time*, Feb. 1, 1993.
33. *Time*, Feb. 1, 1993.
34. Senate Permanent Subcommittee on Investigations.
35. *La Stampa*, Mar. 7, 1991.
36. President's Commission on Organized Crime, Asian Organized Crime Hearings.
37. *Los Angeles Times*, Feb. 12, 1992. Also Senate Subcommittee on Investigations Report.
38. The company with alleged Yakuza connections, Cosmo World, sold out in 1992 when its request to sell club memberships in lieu

of payment was turned down. Senate Subcommitee on Investigations.

39. Report of Senate Subcommittee. One Japanese national named Ken Mizuno owned an estimated $400 million worth of hotels and golf courses, recently seized by the courts.

40. According to the Kyoto News Service, Susumu Ishii set up a company called Hokusho Sangyo in 1985 to handle his speculative stock dealings and West Tsusho as its "overseas investment arm." *The Washington Post*, June 11, 1991. See *San Francisco Chronicle*, July 10, 1991, and *Los Angeles Times*, Feb. 12, 1992.

41. President's Commission on Organized Crime, Asian Hearings. Senate Subcommittee on Investigations.
    Yakuza by David E. Kaplan and Alex Dubro.

42. *Yakuza* by David E. Kaplan and Alex Dubro.

43. *Yakuza* by David E. Kaplan and Alex Dubro.

44. *Yakuza* by David E. Kaplan and Alex Dubro.

45. Robert Friedman in *Vanity Fair*, Jan. 1993.

46. The five hundred figure was an FBI estimate in an article by Daniel Burstein in *New York Magazine*, Nov. 24, 1986.

47. Article by Nathan Adams in *Readers' Digest*, Aug. 1992. "Russian Mafia in Brighton Beach," *New York Times*, Feb. 14, 1983, cited in *The Soviet Way of Crime* by Lydia S. Rosner, South Hadley, Mass.: Bergin & Garvey, 1986.

48. *The New York Times*, June 4, 1989.

49. Interview with Alex Grant, Dec. 1992.

50. *The New York Times*, June 4, 1989.

51. Robert Friedman in *Vanity Fair*, Jan. 1993.

52. Robert Friedman in *Vanity Fair*, Jan. 1993.

53. *Washington Times*, Sept. 29, 1991; *USA Today*, July 10, 1991.

54. Robert Friedman in *Vanity Fair*, Jan. 1993.

55. Robert Friedman in *Vanity Fair*, Jan. 1993.

Chapter 8: The Buildup

1. "Large suspicious transactions involving rubles" were reported by Belgian, German, and Dutch police." *London Sunday Times*, Feb. 19, 1991.

    A trainload of rubles was seen passing through Poland late in 1990. Interview with Alexandra Zawlocka, financial reporter for *Tygodnik Solidarnosc* in Warsaw.

    A TIR truck packed with rubles was tracked across Western Europe by Italian and Belgian intelligence agents in the same months. "The TIR was protected by KGB men. From Avignon to Marseilles to Turin, we seized two million rubles, another two million, and another 300,000, but the TIR got away," the Italian agent in charge told me.

    On May 29, 1990, Italy's Guardia di Finanza taped discussion of a deal actually made with, and in the office of, a director of the Banco Lariano in the northern city of Como. One of the Italians present bought $5 million worth of rubles in cash from another, to be delivered through the bank.

2. Report by Leonid L. Fituni, president of the Russian Academy of Science's Center for Global and Strategic Studies. In Wilbad Kreuth, 1993.

3. *Philadelphia Inquirer*, Feb. 16, 1991.

4. *L'Europe des Parrains* by Fabrizio Calvi. See also *La Repubblica*, Oct. 10, 1990.

5. Interview with undercover agent Fausto Cattaneo, who bought the rubles, Bellinzona, Sept. 23–24, 1991.

6. *Journal de Genève*, January 13, January 17, and February 28, 1991.
   Interview with Judge Jean-Pierre Trembley by that newspaper's Silvie Arsever. *Sunday Times* of London, February 17, 1991.

7. *Sunday Times* of London, February 17, 1991.

8. Interview with Domenico Sica, presently prefect of Bologna, Jan. 13, 1992.

9. Order of arrest for twenty-four Sicilian, German, Austrian, and Turkish defendants, signed by Judge Agostino Gristina, Mar. 16, 1992.

10. Interview with Judge Carmelo Carrara, Apr. 21, 1992. The purchase was confirmed in the Italian Interior Ministry's annual report for 1992, published May 1993.

11. Mariano Troia's son Antonio was a member of the hit team selected by Totò Riina to assassinate Judge Giovanni Falcone.

12. Interview with Judge Roberto Sapio, Rimini, June 1993.

13. Interview with Alessandro Pansa, Rome, Sept. 1991.

14. All details of the case as written above are from the arrest order (Ordinanza di custodia cautelare) by Judge Agostino Gristina, Mar. 16, 1992.

15. From the arrest order by Judge Agostino Gristina, Mar. 16, 1992.

16. The black market rate was 120 lire or ten cents per ruble in the description of the Bahl case provided by Achille Serra, head of Criminalpol's Nucleo Centrale Anticrimine (Central Anticrime Nucleus), cited in *La Repubblica*, Mar. 19, 1992. By December 1990, however, the sliding ruble was down to six or seven cents. For a fuller description of the ruble's free-fall, see Chapter 9.

17. Interview with Judge Carmelo Carrara, Palermo, Apr. 21, 1992, and with Judge Roberto Sapio on Roberto Coppola's interrogation, Rimini, June 1993.
   Interview with Judge Carmelo Carrara in Palermo, April 1992. The Marsala-Jumblatt transaction passed through the Union des Banques Suisses in Lugano and another bank in Lichtenstein, Judge Carrara told me.

18. Phone intercept, Nov. 29, 1990.

19. Copies of all credentials listed are in my possession. See Russian photocopies in the picture section. Boris Yeltsin and Andrei Kozyrov signed theirs on Oct. 16, 1990. According to *Komsomolskaya*

Pravda, the government had given the appointment in error before his background was checked, and in January 1991 Russia informed Italy the appointment had been revoked.

20. *Manchester Guardian* report from Moscow correspondents Dan Atkinson and Mark Milner was cited in *Pravda,* Sept. 24, 1991. Viktor Geraschenko was quoted in *Izvestiya* and *Trud,* cited by *Corriere della Sera* and *La Repubblica,* Nov. 17, 1991. His statement was confirmed in full by Aleksandr Orlov, head of the Control Commission of the Supreme Soviet, in the same day's Moscow press.

The estimated reserves of two thousand to three thousand tons were cited by Lawrence Malkin in the *International Herald Tribune,* Oct. 17, 1991; also *The Washington Post* was cited in the *International Herald Tribune,* Sept. 30, 1991.

The remaining 240 tons in the Central Bank was reported by Grigori Yavlinsky to G-7, *Herald Tribune,* Sept. 30, 1991.

Izvestiya of Nov. 5, 1991, reported five tons of gold and platinum exported illegally from the U.S.S.R. in the previous six weeks.

Chapter 9: The Deal

1. Holman Jenkins, Jr., in the *Washington Times'* "Insight," June 17, 1991.
2. Alexander Pochinok's statement, read into the parliamentary record, proposed that "the legislature should not cast doubt on the motives which guided the government members nor on their probity." *Izvestiya,* Feb. 18, 1991.
3. Chief investigator Vladimir Kalinichenko still knew nothing of this ruble traffic when I first met him in October 1991, nor did I.
4. All the documented material cited in this book is stored in a bank vault and will be made available for any legitimate inspection.
5. The Commission of Inquiry issued a preliminary report on Feb. 15, 1991, and a final one on Mar. 1.
6. Preliminary Commission of Inquiry report, Feb. 15, 1991.
7. The Protocol of Intent was signed Aug. 31, 1990. The black market ruble stood at around ten to the dollar at the time.
8. Interview with Chief Investigator Kalinichenko in the Soviet prosecutor-general's office, Moscow, Nov. 1991.
9. The Commission of Inquiry quotes only part of this letter. The full text, read in closed session, was reported by Yuri Nikolayev in *Sovetskaya Rossiya,* Feb. 21, 1991. Nikolayev's reporting on this case was consistently accurate, I was told by Chief Investigator Vladimir Kalinichenko.
10. Russian Commission of Inquiry report.
11. Interview with Vladimir Kalinichenko, Moscow, July 1992.
12. Article 154 of the Russian Republic's criminal code states: "Speculation in currency or securities on a large scale is punishable by deprivation of freedom for five to fifteen years with confiscation of property, with or without additional exile for a term of two to five

years, *or by death with* confiscation of property. The abolition of the death sentence was reported by Reuters, Dec. 5, 1991.

13. Gennady Filshin's letter of guarantee was sent to Colin Gibbins on Jan. 11, 1991.
14. Gennady Filshin quoted in *Izvestiya*, Jan. 26, 1991.
15. Cited in the London *Times*, Feb. 17, 1991.
16. Interview with an agent who cannot be identified, pursuing the case for British customs, London, Jan. 1992. The British warrant for Gibbins's arrest was issued in July 1984.
17. Interview with Alexander Gurov, Moscow, July 1992.
18. Telephone interview with David Frye in Johannesburg.
19. Interview with the same British customs agent.
20. *The Independent on Sunday*, July 1991.
21. Final report of the Commission of Inquiry, Mar. 15, 1991.
22. Preliminary report of the Commission of Inquiry, Feb. 15, 1991.
23. Commission of Inquiry's final report, Mar. 1, 1991.
24. Gennady Filshin's interview in *Izvestiya*, Jan. 26, 1991.
25. *The Independent*, Nov. 6, 1991.
26. Boris Yeltsin's statement on Gennady Filshin was cited in *Izvestiya*, Feb. 22, 1991. Filshin is presently the Russian government's trade representative in Vienna. Former Prime Minister Silaev is the Russian government's representative to the EC in Brussels.
27. Tass, Feb. 22, 1991.
28. *Sunday Times* of London, Feb. 17, 1991.
29. *Corriere della Sera*, Jan. 20, 1992.
30. As no federal case has been opened against Leo Emil Wanta in the United States, the FBI spokesman prefers not to be named.
31. The Austrian arrest warrant for Leo Wanta was issued on July 29, 1991, and is still outstanding.
32. The gas masks were offered on Feb. 7, 1991. The same gas masks were on offer at the time by KGB Colonel Alexander Kuzin, running a huge arms traffic out of Vienna. See Chapter 12.
33. Phone interview with U.S. Attorney Keith Corbett of Detroit, Dec. 1992.
34. Phone interview with Keith Corbett, Dec. 1992.
35. Michael Preisfreund's account number is in Vaduz.
36. Interview with Boris Uvarov, July 1992.
37. Moscow Radio World Service reported on Nov. 5, 1991, that Russia's prosecutor-general and forty investigators had begun to look into a sum of 5.5 billion rubles exported by old-guard communist leaders the previous year. This was just one of a great many cases.
38. Leo Emil Wanta's fax to Michael Preisfreund's Consulting Liberty Group, July 2, 1990.
39. A heavily documented report on the KGB's project was published by *Literaturnaya Gazeta* on June 24, 1992. It provides the dates and numbers of coded cables, the names of top KGB officials involved, and the name of a French national, Jean-Pierre Tercu, allegedly recruited to help in the undertaking. Known as Jacques, Tercu is said in the article to have used the same Knights of Malta ploy as

"Monsignore" Roberto Coppola to work a $5 billion scam on the Ukrainian government.

In 1993, scandalous revelations about old Communist Party money going abroad from 1990 on revolved around the ambiguous figure of Boris Bershteyn and his Seabeco Group, accused of arranging ruble–dollar transfers amounting to billions of dollars, and of bribing many top Russian government officials, including Vice-Premier Alexander Rutskoi. Bershteyn, presently residing in Canada, is a wealthy businessman and financier with multibillion-dollar dealings in the ex-Soviet republics. The full story of his secret deals with the old communist regime was just coming to light when this book was completed.

40. Mr. X's faxed letter to me, Apr. 12, 1993.
41. There is no evidence that any of the numerous banks that Wanta had accounts with had any knowledge of his schemes.
42. Tremonti's letter is dated July 9, 1990. See photo section. The other transactions are dated as follows: Hutschenraiter, June 27–28, 1990; Impex Vienna, July 4, 1990, confirmed by buyer July 3; Unitrade, July 9, 1990; Budapest bank, July 13, 1990; Van Moerre, Santerre, July 25, 1990; Faisal Finance, Oct. 7, 1990; Volksbank, Wachtberg-Villip confirming letter, Oct. 8, 1990; Sofidad, Sept. 26, Oct. 5, Oct. 26, and Dec. 8, 1990; Leo Emil Wanta's Metishe Bank offer, Sept. 16, 1990; Noweka through Regio Bank, Oct. 8, 1990; AB Invest for client Gamma Kelberg, Nov. 28, 1990; for Kerakos of Le Laren, the Netherlands, Nov. 28, 1990; Corep-Gestion, Oct. 25, 1990; Starl, Sept. 24, 25, 1990.
43. Central Bank estimate reported by Reuters from Moscow, Dec. 24, 1990. Leonid L. Fituni, president of the Russian Academy of Science's Center for Strategic and Global Studies, made this report to a conference in Germany in 1993.
44. Interview with Gennady Chebotarev, Moscow, July 1992.
45. Holman Jenkins, Jr., in the *Washington Times* "Insight," June 17, 1990.
46. Mr. X memo of conversation with Leo Emil Wanta, Feb. 19, 1991.
47. Telephone interview with David Frye in Johannesburg.
48. Commission of Inquiry report.
49. Article by Holman Jenkins, Jr., *Washington Times* "Insight," June 17, 1991. For a fuller account of such deals, see Chapter 10.
50. Leo Emil Wanta opened his Russian bank account for the joint venture on Dec. 20, 1991. See Chapter 10.
51. Interview with Vladimir Kalinichenko, July 1992. See Chapter 10.
52. The Geneva arrests were made July 20, 1993. The Vicenza arrests were made Aug. 25, 1993. Cesium-133 is stable but highly explosive when treated. See Chapter 11.
53. On June 30, 1993, federal investigators shut down Himbank's Rochester branch, seized documents, and began a criminal investigation of the branch.
54. The Italian investigators looking at Leo Emil Wanta are agents of the SIOS (Servizio Italiano Operazioni Speciali), who do not want to be

named. Seizure of the $25 million in Himbank's CDs was confirmed
to me by the carabinieri of Vicenza and by Judge Pecori, in charge of
the case, Aug. 25, 1993. Upon learning of this seizure, the FBI got
into the act.

55. Leonid Fituni's report in 1993.
56. Leo Emil Wanta's fax of Jan. 16, 1991: "We, New Republic/USA Financial Group Ltd., G.m.b.H., with full legal and corporate respon-
sibility, offer the following under the terms and conditions set forth,
as AU Bullion 999.5/1000 fineness or better with accepted international hallmarks." His banking coordinates listed are Algemene
Spaar-En Lufrentekas, Brussels, bank manager Farouk Khan.
57. Leo Emil Wanta's fax on "availability, closing location, and discount
offering" of gold, Jan. 16, 1991. A thick wad of similar faxes followed.
58. The query from Moscow was on June 11, 1991. Interview with Interpol, Washington, D.C., Dec. 1992.
59. *Kuranty,* cited in *Corriere della Sera,* Sept. 15, 1992.
60. Report by Leonid L. Fituni.
61. *Kuranty* article. Judge Jean-Louis Crochet's opinion is cited by Leonid Fituni in his German report.

Chapter 10: The Payoff

1. Valery Grishin's statement in the *Corriere della Sera* from Moscow,
Nov. 16, 1991. Similar statement by Boris Yeltsin's economic adviser
Yegor Gaider, *Los Angeles Times,* Nov. 16, 1991. See also *Washington
Post,* Nov. 16, 1991. The licensed export figures by V. Isayev, section
manager of the Oriental Studies Institute, Russian Academy of Sci-
ences, in *Argumenty i Fakty,* no. 29–30, Aug. 1992.
2. Moscow financial daily, *Commersant,* Mar. 16, 1992, lists domestic
market price at $26 a ton at the going exchange rate for rubles.
3. *Financial Times,* May 13, 1992. The deputy minister was Leonid Za-
palsky. He was within a month of leaving the Ministry when he
issued the licenses.
4. Presentation of the U.S.S.R. delegation, written by Gennady Chebotarev, to the Twentieth European Regional Conference of Interpol, London, April 3–5, 1991.
5. Interview with Gennady Chebotarev, Moscow, July 1992.
6. VEK reports from Russia's Sixth Department, Dec. 18–25, 1992.
7. Article by Vladimir Kuznetsov in *Rossiyskaya Gazeta,* July 2, 1992.
8. Associated Press dispatch from Moscow citing Russia's top defense
daily *Krasnaya Zvezda,* Oct. 24, 1992.
9. Mikhail Gurtivoy's interview in *Trud,* Oct. 2, 1992.
10. *Izvestiya* in *Current Digest of the Soviet Press,* vol. 43, no. 22, up to Oct.
16, 1991.
11. Moscow VEK, Nov. 27 to Dec. 4, 1992. The department chief was
Alexander Gurov, transferred from the Interior Ministry's Sixth Department to this new post in the Security Ministry.

12. *Moscow Times*, May 19, 1992.
13. Interview with I. Pavlovich in Russia's Sixth Department, Moscow, July 1992.
14. "Draft Decree of the Russian President on the Liberalization of Foreign Economic Activity in the Russian Federation," *Commersant*, Nov. 16, 1991.
15. *Il Sole–24 Ore*, Milanese financial daily, May 3, 1991. Also the head of St. Petersburg customs in St. Petersburg, Andrei Belonaiov, at John Jay College's international conference on organized crime. "Foreign investors with over 15 percent holdings in a plant need not be licensed for export—so exporters name these plants in customs declarations," he said.
16. Central Bank estimate reported by Reuters from Moscow, July 1992. Leonid L. Fituni, president of the Russian Academy of Science's Center for Strategic and Global Studies, made this report to a conference in Germany in 1993.
17. Report by Leonid L. Fituni.
18. Report by Leonid L. Fituni.
19. Interview with Vladimir Kalinichenko, July 1992.
20. Mr. X. told me that Wanta and Dokiychuk often worked together.
21. Interview with Vladimir Kalinichenko, Moscow, July 1992. See also *Moscow Times*, Apr. 20, 1992.
22. Interview with I. Pavlovich, the Sixth Department's deputy chief, Moscow, July 1, 1992.
23. Interview with Vladimir Kalinichenko.
24. Nineteenth report by the House of Representatives' Committee on Government Operations, May 27, 1992.
25. *Izvestiya*, Aug. 15, 1992: "TV Star Marc Rich and His 'Producers.' "
26. *Izvestiya*, June 5, 1992. Also, interview with Vladimir Kalinichenko, Moscow, July 1992.
27. *Rossiyskaya Gazeta*, Aug. 21, 1992, article by Professor Igor Kaszakov of the Marketing Department, Foreign Trade Academy. *The Wall Street Journal*, Europe, May 13, 1993.
28. Ignatov is quoted at length in *Izvestiya*, Aug. 15, 1992, in a long article on Marc Rich. The TV film commissioned and paid for by Rich was done in a program called "Reporter." Same *Izvestiya* article.
    See also *Bilan*, Sept. 1992.
29. *Forbes*, quoted in *Izvestiya*, July 31, 1991.
30. *The Wall Street Journal*, Europe, May 13, 1993.
31. *The Wall Street Journal*, Europe, May 13, 1993.
32. *The Wall Street Journal*, Europe, May 13, 1993.
33. *Izvestiya*, June 5, 1992. The permits were allotted in part to "Marc Rich & Co." and in part to his joint venture "Rosrich" as follows: 230,000 tons of diesel fuel to "Marc Rich" and 1.3 million tons to "Rosrich"; 716,000 tons of heating oil to "Marc Rich" and 1.9 million tons of heating oil to "Rosrich." Total, 4,146,000 tons.
    A continuing exemption on export duties for food suppliers is confirmed by Dr. Igor Kazakov, the Marketing Department of Rus-

sia's Foreign Trade Academy, in "We Say Homeland, Meaning Raw Materials," *Rossiyskaya Gazeta*, Aug. 21, 1992.

34. Report by Leonid L. Fituni.
35. Alexander Rutskoi's address to the emergency conference on crime and corruption attended by a thousand judges, police officers, and government officials. Also addressed by President Yeltsin in tones of great alarm. Moscow, Feb. 12, 1993. Associated Press dispatch from Moscow, Feb. 13, 1993. Also reported in *La Repubblica* of the same date.
36. Interview with Judge Romano Dolce of Como, coordinating this investigation with Russian authorities. See also *Corriere della Sera* and *La Repubblica*, Dec. 17, 1992, and *Corriere della Sera*, Jan. 23, 1993. For more details on the arms traffic, see Chapter 12.
37. Interview with Judge Toro, investigating magistrate for the theft of CDs amounting to a quarter of a billion dollars (294 billion lire), from Rome's Banco di Santo Spirito in Nov. 1990; Rome, July 2, 1993.
38. *The European*, Mar. 18–21, 1993.
39. *The European*, Mar. 18–21, 1993.
40. Dispatch from Moscow by Fiammetta Cucurnia, *La Repubblica*, July 12, 1993. Prosecutor Nikolas Makarov made the announcement to the Russian parliament in the last week of June. On July 23, Russia's prosecutor-general, Valentin Stepankov, formally asked parliament to lift the immunity of Vice-Premier Vladimir Shumeiko and Information Chief Mikhail Poltoranin. The Russian parliament, loathing both as the hated Boris Yeltsin's lieutenants, was happy to oblige.
41. *La Repubblica*, Feb. 13, 1993. See also *International Herald Tribune* of the same date.

Chapter 11: The Spinoff

1. *Corriere della Sera*, Feb. 2, 1993.
2. The Middle East estimate was made by Safeword Foundation, present at the fair.
3. *Corriere della Sera*, July 25, 1993.
4. Leonid Fituni's report to the Hanns Seidel Foundation in Germany, 1993.
5. Kenneth R. Timmerman, editor of the confidential newsletter *Mednews*, in *The Wall Street Journal*, June 14, 1992.
6. Kenneth R. Timmerman in *The Wall Street Journal*, June 14, 1992.
7. *La Stampa* from London, May 29, 1993.
8. *Commersant*, Oct. 21, 1991.
9. This last was the most credited version offered to investigating magistrate Romano Dolce in Como, he told me.
10. Interview with Czech Deputy Interior Minister Petrushka Sostrova, Sept. 1991.
11. Alexander Rutskoi's address to the Russian parliament, Apr. 16, 1993, in *La Stampa* the following day.

12. Article by A. Craig Copetas in *Moscow Times Review*, Jan. 16–17, 1993.
13. The expert did not want to be named. The Institute, ENEA, is among the most authoritative in Europe.
14. The analyst in Washington is Richard Levine. The British customs agent, who does not want to be named, had several good laughs whenever I called to report yet another red mercury sighting.
15. Interview with Judge Romano Dolce. See also *Corriere della Sera*, Nov. 13, 1991.
16. Text of Jorgen Quist Nielsen's interrogation by Judge Romano Dolce, Oct. 30, 1991.
17. Two-day-long interviews with Judge Romano Dolce and his prize investigator Antonio Erdas in Como.
18. Texts of Dezider Ostrogonac's interrogation by Judge Romano Dolce, Jan. 21, Jan. 29, and Feb. 14, 1992.
    Others named were General Abramov and KGB Officers Kudeziev and Ilurin.
19. Leonid Fituni's report to the Hanns Seidel Foundation, 1993.
20. Judicial Police of Como Report to the police command in Lugano, Switzerland, April 24, 1992. Interview with Judge Romano Dolce. "Boris" is named by several Kuzin intermediaries now known to Italian undercover agents. Who "the friends" are is not specified.
21. Prospectus dated Aug. 7, 1991. No substantial change has been noted since.
22. Extract of the Register in Udine's Chamber of Commerce, June 10, 1992.
23. The phrase "daughter-company" is used by the BKA agents tracking similar chains of Russian mafia front companies.
24. Interview with Judge Romano Dolce and Antonio Erdas.
25. I have photocopies of Marco Affatigato's transactions in rubles and red mercury.
26. See Chapter 9.
27. Interview with Judge Romano Dolce and his tenacious investigator Antonio Erdas. Dezider Ostrogonac's testimony and other interrogations in the Como documents.
28. Judicial police of Como report to the police command in Lugano, Switzerland, Apr. 24, 1992.
29. Dezider Ostrogonac interrogation by Judge Romano Dolce.
30. Interviews with Jan Dubrowski of Lidove Noviny; Deputy Interior Minister Petrushka Suslova, and U.S. Public Affairs Officer Tom Hull, Sept. 2–9, 1991.
31. Testimony of Rensselaer W. Lee III before the Subcommittee on International Security, Committee on Foreign Affairs, U.S. House of Representatives, Nov. 4, 1993.
32. Interview with an agent of Italy's SIOS who cannot be named.
33. *Commersant*, Mar. 23, 1992.
34. Leonid Fituni report.
35. Vienna TV documentary, Jan. 23, 1992. The trafficker was Yugoslav-born Marian Sokolovic.

36. Associated Press dispatch from Berlin, Oct. 13, 1992; *Bild Am Sonntag*, Oct. 11, 1992; *The European*, Oct. 22, 1992.
37. Three grams of cesium were impounded in Geneva on July 16, 1993. Ten grams were impounded in Vicenza on Aug. 25, 1993.
38. *Hamburg DPA*, Oct. 16, 1992. See also *Corriere della Sera*, Oct. 17, 1992.
39. *Corriere della Sera*, Apr. 5, 1993.
40. Judge Pierluigi Vigna in an address to a national arms exhibition, "Exa '93," in Brescia, *La Repubblica*, Feb. 15, 1993.

Chapter 12: Getting the Money

1. Gaspare Mutolo's testimony, Feb. 9, 1993.
2. Italy seized 3.5 trillion lire, roughly $3 billion, in money and assets from Italian organized crime between Aug. 1992 and Aug. 1993. Italian Interior Minister Nicola Mancino, cited in all Italian papers, Aug. 17, 1993.
3. "Global Drug Trafficking" by Alison Jamieson, Research Institute for the Study of Conflict and Terrorism, Sept. 1990.
4. Interview with the DEA's Greg Passic in Washington, D.C., in Sept. 1993, when he said the DEA was seizing an average of $200 million a year of Colombian cocaine money.
5. Report to the French senate by Gérard Larcher for the Senate's Commission of Information on the Schengen Accord, Jan. 15, 1993.
6. U.N. Crime Congress 1990, U.S. Senate Subcommittee on Terrorism, Narcotics and International Operations hearings, Sept. 27 and Oct. 4, 1989.
7. Interview with Alessandro Pansa, Rome, Sept. 1992.
8. *The European*, Jan. 7–10, 1993.
9. Interview with experts of BKA's organized crime section on American Express Moneygrams, Feb. 1993.
10. International Narcotics Control Board Strategy Report, U.S. State Department, Mar. 1990.
11. The Swiss law, passed in November 1989, does not make all laundering a crime but does "establish liability for money laundering where it impedes investigation into some other act that is a crime under Swiss law." See "International Trends in the Criminalization of Money Laundering" by William Hannay and John Hedges, *International Trade*, 1991.
12. *Corriere della Sera* report on Italian Interior Minister Nicola Mancino's visit to Vienna to discuss the problem, Feb. 11, 1993.
13. *Corriere della Sera*, Sept. 27, 1992.
14. *Le Figaro*, January 16–17, 1993.
15. Gérard Larcher report to the French senate, Jan. 15, 1993.
16. *International Herald Tribune*, Jan. 23–24, 1993.
17. Paris daily *Libération*, June 7, 1991. For confirmation of Monaco's continuing role as a fiscal paradise, see the Report to the French Assembly by François D'Aubert's Anti-Mafia Commission, Feb. 1993.

18. Hungary was the first ex-communist state actually to copy Austria's inflexible bank secrecy laws.
19. Gérard Larcher report to the French senate, Jan. 15, 1993.
20. *Business Week*, Sept. 23, 1991.
21. Belize ad in *Commersant*, inserted by a newly born joint venture called MIROS whose founders and charter capital were unknown, Mar. 16, 1992.
22. "Drug Trafficking After 1992" by Alison Jamieson. See also International Narcotics Control Board Strategy Report, Mar. 1990.
23. See *Octopus* by Claire Sterling for a lengthy documented account of the Michele Sindona fake kidnapping.
24. The reigning prince was Stefano Bontate, murdered by the Corleones in 1981. The confidant was future defector Francesco Mannino Mannoia.
25. *Le Mani della Mafia*, by Maria Antonietta Calabrò, an outstanding book for a comprehensive and documented report on the Roberto Calvi affair.
26. Michele Sindona's life sentence in Italy was for commissioning the murder of Giorgio Ambrosoli, who had been appointed to investigate his fraudulent operations in the Banco Ambrosiano before turning it over to Roberto Calvi and skipping the country. He died in Mar. 1986.
27. Calvi died on June 17, 1982.
28. *La Repubblica*, July 28–29, 1991.
29. Francesco Di Carlo, ranking member of the Altofonte clan, which was actually created by the Corleones, was working directly with the Cuntrera brothers in London. He was arrested there in June 1985 in the act of shipping fifty-nine kilos of heroin to the United States via Canada. A British court sentenced him to twenty-five years in prison.
30. Revelation by Umberto Ortolani, Gelli's financial right arm, who said that he and Gelli were approached directly by Roberto Calvi for the Mafia contract. *L'Independente*, Feb. 25, 1993.
31. Francesco Mannino-Mannoia's testimony is summed up in the Italian Parliamentary Anti-Mafia Commission report, "Relations between the Mafia and Politics," Mar. 12, 1992. See also *La Repubblica*, July 29, 1991, and Apr. 28, 1992.
32. *Le Mani della Mafia* by Maria Antonietta Calabrò.
33. *Le Mani della Mafia* by Maria Antonietta Calabrò.
34. *Le Mani della Mafia* by Maria Antonietta Calabrò.
35. "Drug Trafficking After 1992" by Alison Jamieson.
36. The exact figure is $249 billion. Hearings by the U.S. Senate Subcommittee on Terrorism, Narcotics and International Operations, Sept. 27 to Oct. 4, 1989.
37. Hearings of Subcommittee on Terrorism, Narcotics and International Operations of the U.S. Senate Committee on Foreign Relations, Sept. 27 to Oct. 4, 1989.
38. The EC's proposed directive on money laundering in 1990 specified that tax evasion would not be considered a "serious crime" in leg-

islation outlawing the laundering of money deriving from serious crimes.

Among the countries whose laws distinguish between criminal money and undeclared capital are Germany, France, Great Britain, Holland, Luxembourg, Switzerland, Spain, and Belgium. Italy was preparing to abolish this distinction in 1993.

39. Report on Confiscation Law and Asset Tracing in the United Kingdom by Tim Wren, National Criminal Intelligence Service, London, May 1992.
40. Alison Jamieson, "Drug Trafficking After 1992: A Special Report," Research Institute for the Study of Conflict and Terrorism, London, April 1992. The estimate of UK suspicious disclosures rose to around four thousand by 1993, according to sources in the British Embassy in Rome.
41. Tim Wren, quoted in *Valeurs Actuelles,* Dec. 7, 1992.
42. The British case in "Drug Trafficking After 1992" by Alison Jamieson for the Research Institute for the Study of Conflict and Terrorism. The Italian figure released by Italy's CNEL (Consiglio Nazionale dell'Economia e Lavoro"), cited in *Corriere della Sera,* Mar. 2, 1993.
43. Interior minister Nicola Mancino's report to the Italian parliament.
44. *Hamburg Welt Am Sonntag,* May 2, 1993.
45. Interview with Roelof Gerrand at John Jay College's International Conference on Organized Crime, St. Petersburg, June 28 to July 3, 1992.
46. Interview with Eva Klovacova, consultant for the Czech Ministry of Privatization, Prague, Sept. 8, 1991.
47. Senate Subcommittee hearings, Sept. 27 to Oct. 4, 1989.

Chapter 13: Trust Thy Neighbor (If You Can)

1. The ASEAN states are Indonesia, Philippines, Malaysia, Thailand, Singapore, and Brunei.
2. Final report to the French Senate by Paul Masson on behalf of the Commission to Study the Schengen Agreement, June 23, 1993.
3. French Senate Commission of Inquiry on the Application of the Schengen Agreement, "Note on the Drug Problems in the Netherlands," p. 52. Rapport d'Information Déposé par M. Paul Masson, président, et établi par Gérard Larch, sénateur, tome II, document 9, "Documents de Reference." This volume is attached to Senator Masson's Final Report, June 23, 1993.
4. *ANP* (Amsterdam Press) news bulletin, Aug. 20, 1992.
5. *Agence France-Presse,* June 8, 1992.
6. Report to the French senate by the Commission's president, Paul Masson, tome III, Nov. 27, 1991.
7. Eighth Annual Policing Executive Conference, Madrid, Apr. 1991.
8. Eighth Annual Policing Executive Conference, Madrid, Apr. 1991.
9. Interview with Barry Price at Scotland Yard. The European Drugs Intelligence Unit was approved by EC ministers at the Lisbon sum-

mit in 1992. It still cannot get off the ground, largely because of arguments over what information should go into its data bank.

10. Declaration of the EC Commission on the proposed directive of the EC Council of Ministers "concerning the protection of persons relative to the handling of personal data," Sept. 24, 1990. Exceptions to the right of access are specified "in certain cases, counterbalanced then by an indirect right of access." Report to French senate by the Masson Commission, Dec. 11, 1991.

11. *International Herald Tribune*, Dec. 2, 1992.

12. The Patrick Cooney Report to the European parliament.

13. Interview with the DEA's Greg Passic. These views were underlined in my interview with Robert Nieves, heading the DEA's new Operation Kingpin, Washington, D.C., Sept. 1993.

BIBLIOGRAPHY

Anderson, Malcolm. *Policing the World*. Oxford: The Clarendon Press, 1989.

Andrew, Christopher, and Andrew Gordievsky. *KBG*. London: Hodder & Stoughton, 1990.

Arlacchi, Pino. *Gli Uomini del Disonore*. Milan: Arnoldo Mondadori Editore, 1992.

Auchlin, Pascal, and Frank Garbely. *Contre-Enquete*. Lausanne: Editions Favre, 1990.

Booth, Martin. *The Triads*. London: Grafton Books, 1990.

Bresler, Fenton. *The Chinese Mafia*. New York: Stein & Day, 1981.

Calabrò, Maria Antonietta. *Le Mani della Mafia*. Rome: Edizioni Associate, 1991.

Calvi, Fabrizio. *L'Europe des Parrains*. Paris: Bernard Grasset, 1993.

Chalidze, Valery. *Criminal Russia*. New York: Random House, 1977.

Clutterbuck, Richard. *Terrorism, Drugs, and Crime in Europe After 1992*. New York: Routledge, Chapman & Hall, 1990.

Copetas, A. Craig. *Bear Hunting with the Politburo*. New York: Simon & Schuster, 1991.

di Gennaro, Giuseppe. *La Guerra della Droga*. Milan: Arnoldo Mondadori Editore, 1991.

Dyomin, Mikhail. *The Day Is Born in Darkness*. New York: Alfred Knopf, 1976.

Ehrenfeld, Rachel. *NarcoTerrorism*. New York: Basic Books, 1990.

Francis, Diane. *Contrepreneurs*. Cincinnati, OH: Scorpio Publishing Ltd., 1988.

Gurwin, Larry. *The Calvi Affair*. London: Macmillan, 1983.

Kaplan, David E., and Alex Dubro. *Yakuza*. Reading, MA: Addison-Wesley Publishing Co., 1986.

Labrousse, Alain. *La Drogue, l'Argent et les Armes*. Paris: Arthème Fayard, 1991.

Ministero dell'Interno. *L'Attività Antidroga Della Polizia Giudiziaria*. Rome: Utet, 1991.

Naylor, Robin T. *Denaro che Scotta*. Milan: Edizioni di Communità, 1987.

O'Brien, Joseph F., and Andris Kurins. *Boss of Bosses*. New York: Simon & Schuster, 1991.

Orlando, Leoluca. *Palermo*. Milan: Arnoldo Mondadori Editore, 1990.

Palermo, Carlo. *Armi e Droga*. Rome: Editori Riuniti, 1988.

———. *L'Attentato*. Trento: Editrice Publiprint, 1993.

Rosner, Lydia S. *The Soviet Way of Crime*. South Hadley, Mass.: Bergin & Garvey, 1986.

Russo, Enzo. *Il Quattordicesimo Zero*. Milan: Arnoldo Mondadori Editore, 1990.

Short, Martin. *Crime, Inc.: The Story of Organized Crime*. London: Methuen, 1984.

———. *Inside the Brotherhood*. London: Grafton Books, 1989.

Sobchiak, Anatoli. *Leningrado, San Pietroburgo*. Milan: Arnoldo Mondadori Editore, 1991.

Sterling, Claire. *Octopus*. New York: W. W. Norton, 1990.

———. *The Time of the Assassins*. New York: Holt Rinehart, 1983.

Terrill, Richard J. *World Criminal Justice Systems: A Survey*. Cincinnati, OH: Anderson Publishing Co., 1992.

Tosches, Nick. *Power on Earth*. New York: Arbor House, 1986.

Vaksberg, Arkady. *The Soviet Mafia*. New York: St. Martin's Press, 1992.

Violante, Luciano. *La Mafia dell' Eroina*. Rome: Editori Riuniti, 1987.

Wistrich, Ernest. *After 1992: The United States of Europe*. London: Routledge, 1989.

Ziegler, Jean. *La Suisse Lave Plus Blanc*. Paris: Seuil, 1990.

INDEX